CW01650025

…lbum
9

The Arado Ar 234

Sections

Airframe Album No.9
The Arado Ar 234
A Detailed Guide to the Luftwaffe's jet bomber
by Richard A. Franks

First published in 2016 by
Valiant Wings Publishing Ltd
8 West Grove, Bedford, MK40 4BT, UK
+44 (0)1234 273434
valiant-wings@btconnect.com
www.valiant-wings.co.uk
valiantwingspublishing

ISBN: 978-0-9935345-0-8

Note

There are many different ways of writing aircraft designations, however for consistency in this title we have used one style, e.g. Ar 234 V1, Ar 234B-2 etc.

Cover

The cover artwork depicts an Arado 234 of the *Versuchsverband* OKL above a wintery landscape during a reconnaissance flight as part of the preparations for the Ardennes offensive in late 1944. This artwork was specially commissioned for this title.
© Seweryn Fleischer 2016

In Memory

This title has to be dedicated to one of the few British pilots to have flown the Ar 234, and one of the greatest pilots of our time, Captain Eric M. 'Winkle' Brown CBE, DSC, AFC, Hon. FRAeS, RN, who sadly died on the 21st February 2016 at the age of 97. In his astonishing career he flew no fewer than 487 different aircraft types, more than anyone else in history, undertook 2,407 landings and 2,271 take-offs from a carrier deck (a world record) and survived 11 aircraft crashes. His memorable accounts of test flying many ex-Luftwaffe types have enriched the lives of all of us with an interest in this field, and we will sadly never see his like again.

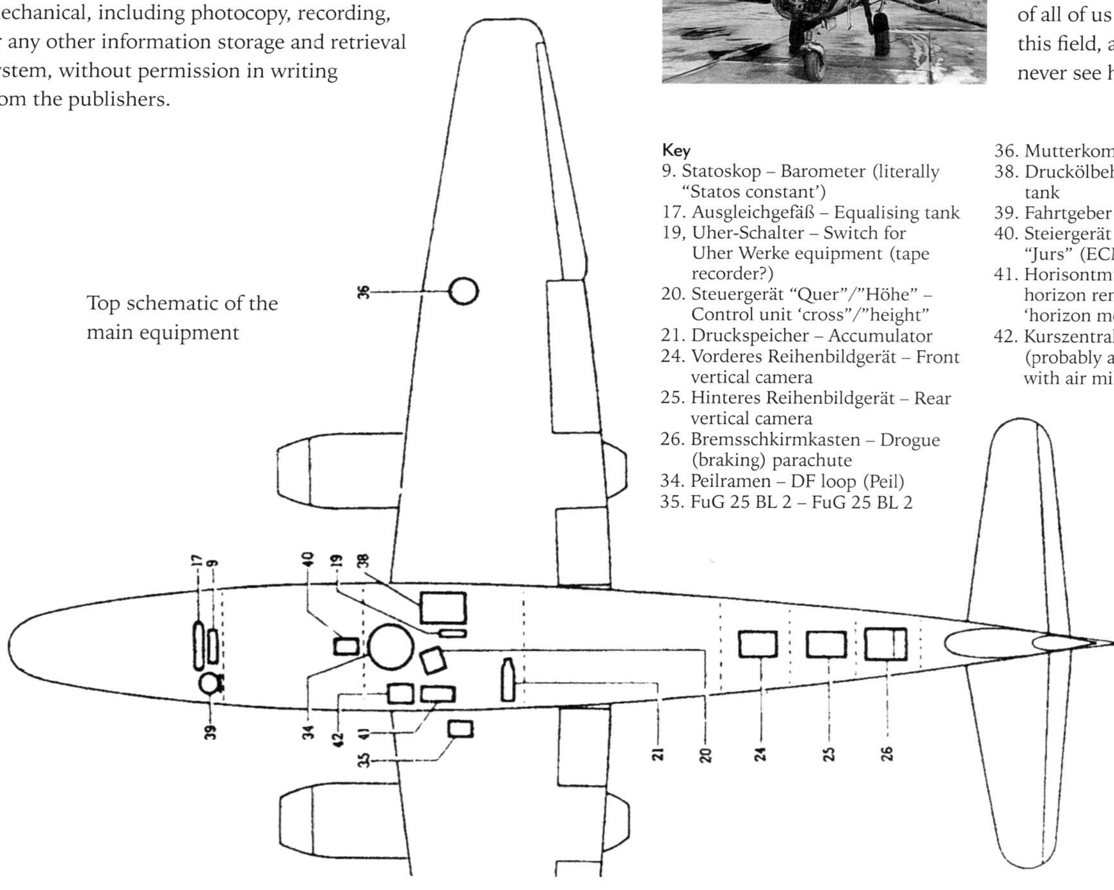

Top schematic of the main equipment

Key
9. Statoskop – Barometer (literally "Statos constant')
17. Ausgleichgefäß – Equalising tank
19, Uher-Schalter – Switch for Uher Werke equipment (tape recorder?)
20. Steuergerät "Quer"/"Höhe" – Control unit 'cross"/"height"
21. Druckspeicher – Accumulator
24. Vorderes Reihenbildgerät – Front vertical camera
25. Hinteres Reihenbildgerät – Rear vertical camera
26. Bremsschkirmkasten – Drogue (braking) parachute
34. Peilramen – DF loop (Peil)
35. FuG 25 BL 2 – FuG 25 BL 2
36. Mutterkompaß – Master compass
38. Druckölbehälter – Pressure oil tank
39. Fahrtgeber – Motion controller
40. Steiergerät "Jurs" – Control unit "Jurs" (ECM)
41. Horisontmutter – Artificial horizon remote unit (literally 'horizon mother')
42. Kurszentrale – Course centre (probably a control unit to do with air mileage)

AufklärungsGruppe (AufklGr) ...... Reconnaissance Group
BK ...... *Bordkanone* (aircraft cannon)
BMW ...... Bayerische Motorenwerke GmbH
ETC ...... *Elektrische Trägervorrichtung für cylinder bomben* (Electrically operated carriers for cylindrical bombs)
Funkgerät (FuG) ...... Radio or radar equipment
Generalluftzeugmeister ...... Director-General of Luftwaffe Equipment
HWK ...... Hellmuth Walterwerke KG (Keil, Beerberg, Hirschberg & Bosau)
Jumo ...... Junkers Motorenwerke
kg. ...... Kilogram (= 2.20462lb)
km/h ...... Kilometres per hour (= 0.621mph)
KW ...... Kilowatt (= 1.341hp)
Lt ...... Litre (= 0.22 Imperial Gallons)
m ...... Metre (3ft 3 3/8in)
MG ...... *Machinengewehr* (machine-gun up to 20mm calibre)
MK. ...... *Machinenkanone* (cannon over 20mm calibre)
NI VVS ...... Russian Air Force Test Centre
Oberst ...... Colonel
OKL ...... *Oberkommando de Luftwaffe* (Luftwaffe High Command)
PS ...... *Pferdestarkes* (Metric Horsepower)
RLM ...... *Reichsluftfahrtministerium* (Reich Air Ministry)
rpm ...... Revolutions per minute
Rüstsatz ...... Field conversion pack
SC ...... *Splitterbombe, cylindrisch* (standard, high explosive fragmentation bomb)
SD ...... *Splitterbombe, dickwändig* (thick-walled, high explosive fragmentation bomb)
SG ...... *Sondergerät* (special device)
Staffel ...... Squadron
Stammkenzeichen ...... Primary identification (code letters)
Technisches Amt ...... Technical Office
Versuchs or *Versuchsmuster* ...... Research or test aircraft (V-series)
Werknummer (W/Nr.) ...... Works (construction) number

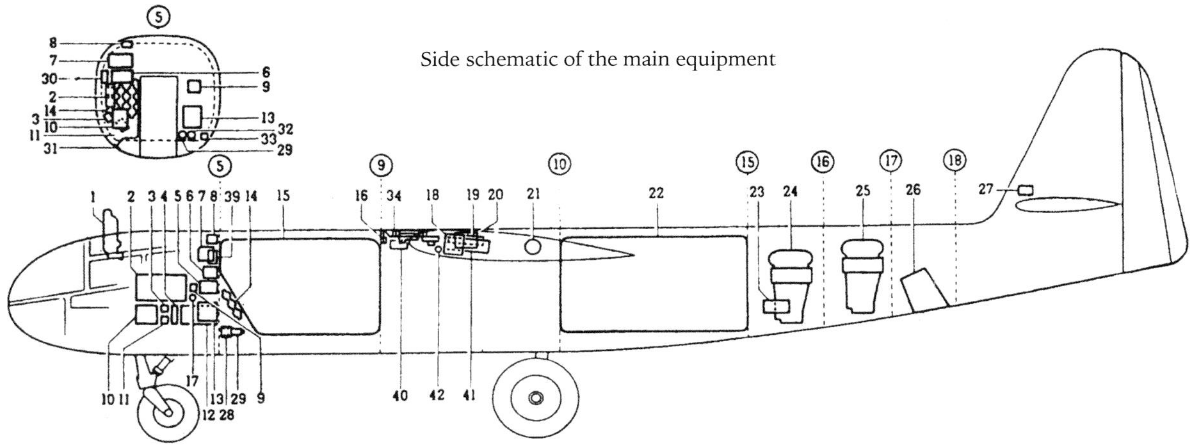
Side schematic of the main equipment

Key
1. Rücklickperiskop – Periscope
2. Schalttafel – Switchboard
3. Bediengerät – Control panel
4. Leuchtpatronenkasten – Flare cartridge box
5. Umformer U 17 – Converter U 17
6. Verstärker – Amplifier
7. Umformer U 11 – Converted U 11
8. Widerstandskasten – Resistance boxes
9. Statoskop – Barometer (literally “Statos constant’)
10. Zielflugempfänger EZ6 – Homing receiver EZ6
11. Anschlußdose – Junction box
12. Geräteblock Fu G 16 – Equipment block Fu G 16
13. Sammler – Connectors
14. Sauerstoffflaschen – Oxygen cylinders
15. Vorderer Kraftstoffbehälter – Front fuel tank
16. Ventilbatterie – Valve battery
17. Ausgleichgefäß – Equalising tank
18. Dämpfungsregler – Adjustable attenuator, radio signal
19. Uher-Schalter – Switch for Uher Werke equipment (tape recorder?)
20. Steuergerät “Quer”/”Höhe” – Control unit “cross”/”height”
21. Druckspeicher – Accumulator
22. Hinterer Kraftstoffbehälter – Rear fuel tank
23. Leonard-Umformer – Converters ‘Leonard’
24. Vorderes Reihenbildgerät – Front vertical camera
25. Hinteres Reihenbildgerät – Rear vertical camera
26. Bremsschkirmkasten – Drogue (braking) parachute
27. Antennenanpassungsgerät – Antenna matching unit
28. Widerstandkasten – Resistance boxes
29. Umformer für PDS – Converted for PDS
30. Membranlunge – Oxygen regulator (literally ‘membrane lung’)
31. Außenbordanschluß für Sauerstoff – Outside connection for oxygen
32. Umformer für Wendehorizont – Converter for artificial horizon
33. Wilderstandkasten – Survival equipment storage box
34. Peilramen – DF loop (Peil)
35. FuG 25 BL 2 – FuG 25 BL 2
36. Mutterkompaß – Master compass
37. Entfällt – Deleted
38. Druckölbehälter – Pressure oil tank
39. Fahrtgeber – Motion controller
40. Steiergerät “Jurs” – Control unit “Jurs” (ECM)
41. Horisontmutter – Artificial horizon remote unit (literally ‘horizon mother’)
42. Kurszentrale – Course centre (probably a control unit to do with air mileage)

Preface

This shot from the front of the V1 on roll-out shows the original narrow, tapering profile of the fuselage that was a result of the simple skid landing gear

The Ar 234 started life as the E.370 project, which was initially the work of Emil Eckstein prior to his departure from Arado in January 1941, whereupon the project (which was a private venture for Arado) was backed by Company Director Dipl. Ing. Walter Blume and the Board of Directors. Under the leadership of Blume and Ing. Hans Rebeski and Wenzel, along with the help of Dipl. Ing. R. Kosin for the aerodynamic elements, the E.370 was submitted to meet the RLM's requirement for a high speed reconnaissance aircraft powered by two of the new turbojet engines then under development by Junkers and BMW. Eckstein's original design consisted of a semi-monocoque fuselage, shoulder-mounted upswept wing, cruciform tailplane and an engine slung under each wing. Initially Eckstein also favoured the use of a conventional retractable tricycle undercarriage, to avoid the problems associated with jet blast striking the ground behind an aircraft with the conventional trailwheel undercarriage layout. This was an innovative design and it was not favoured by those who took over the project, so they proposed two alternative undercarriage systems. The first had nine small wheels below the fuselage, similar to that used on a larger scale by the Ar 232, with retractable hydraulically damped skids under each engine nacelle. The second was to use a specially designed trolley that was jettisoned on take-off; the aircraft landed on the skids fitted under the fuselage and engine nacelles. The first system, although shortening the landing run was considered to be too complex, so the second system was adopted.

On the 24th October 1941 the *Technisches Amt* of the RLM decided in favour of the E.370 project and the type was given the RLM designation of 8-234. It was decided, after a meeting with leading Luftwaffe reconnaissance experts including *Oberst* Theo Rowehl, to develop the 8-234 into a detailed Luftwaffe specification. However, when the *Generalluftzeugmeister* Ernst Udet committed suicide less than a month later, it looked as if the 8-234 had little future. On the 4th February 1942 *Generalfeldmarschall* Ernard Milch, the new *Generalluftzeugmeister*, visited the

This rear port view of the V1 on its trolley clearly shows the soft demarcation of the camouflage along the fuselage

With the V1 viewed from the port side you can see the soft demarcation running along both fuselage and engine nacelles

Arado facility and was impressed by what he saw. As a result a contract was obtained to go ahead with structural development of the 8-234 and to build a wooden mock-up. A little over two months later official authorisation was given to build six prototypes of the new Ar 234, with work being overseen by Ing. Wenzel during the spring and summer of 1942. On the 28th December 1942 the order for six prototypes was increased to twenty, designated the V1 through to the V20. The order came with a request to investigate the fitment of conventional retracting undercarriage, so that a bomber version might be developed with the capacity to carry a large bomb under the fuselage. As a result of this request, much of Eckstein's original calculations and drawings had to be retrieved. The thin aerofoil section selected for the wing meant that the undercarriage had to be fitted within the fuselage, plus the fuel tanks within the fuselage had to be redistributed to deal with the narrow-track layout that would result. On the 9th February 1943 the RLM agreed that Arado should build two experimental fast-bombers

Few images of the V2 exist, as it only flew 3 times before being destroyed; this shot, although of poor quality, shows it on take-off

with conventional retractable undercarriage. During that month the sixth and sixteenth Junkers Jumo 004A-0 engines were sent to Arado to be installed in the Ar 234 V1. Work on the next four skid-equipped prototypes continued but early engine runs with the V1 proved that the 004A-0s were not providing the projected 1,850lb static thrust. Arado made an approach to the RLM, prior to the V1's first flight, to ask if four BMW 003 engines could

The V3 taxiing out during the winter of 1943/44

The V4 comes in to land after an early test flight

be considered as an alternative. Although producing less power than the 004, the 003 was 530lb lighter, so it was a viable alternative even when Junkers projected better thrust-to-weight ratio for the production 004B-1 version.

The V1 (W/Nr.130001) took to the air for the first time on the 30th July 1943, with Flugkapitän Selle at the controls for a trouble-free fourteen-minute flight. The second flight on the 10th August saw Selle airborne for no less than 54 minutes and a top speed of 404mph was achieved. The third flight ended in a forced belly-landing, when Selle mishandled the engine controls. The second prototype, the V2 (W/Nr.1300002) only lasted a few weeks after its first flight, when it was totally destroyed in an unexplained accident on the 1st October 1943. This was followed by the next three prototypes (V3 to V5, W/Nr.130003 to 005) at roughly monthly intervals thereafter, and the V5 was the first to receive the B-series 004 engines, which were 220lb lighter that the A-series. On the 26th November 1943 the V3 was sent, dismantled, by road to Insterburg in East Prussia for static display to Adolf Hitler, leading Nazi party officials and high-ranking officers of all the armed forces. Hitler was impressed by all the jet and rocket aircraft he saw and issued instructions that Arado was to have a free hand in obtaining the manpower and materials to produce 200 Ar 234Bs by the end of 1944. Even ground-crew from disbanded bomber units were to be diverted to help on the assembly lines.

Flugkapitän Janssen climbs aboard the V5 prior to another test flight

The V6 (W/Nr.130006) was the first to be fitted with four BMW 003A-0 engines, fitted in individual nacelles below each wing. This layout was not a success, but it proved that a four-engine version was possible and laid the way for the C-series, which would use engines in 'paired' nacelles.

By January 1944 the situation for Nazi Germany was such that drastic cutbacks were imposed on aircraft production by Hitler, under advice from Albert Speer. Arado

Spinning up one of the engines in the V6 prior to ignition with the help of a truck engine mounted on a special trolley

The V6 after its crash-landing on the 1st June 1944

were affected by the ending of Heinkel He 177 production, which they had undertaken under licence, but top priority was given to development of the Ar 234E and F variants. The Ar 234F was a scaled-up development of the Ar 234D, which had been a planned two-seat, multi-role type based on the Ar 234C series. It weighed in at 15 tons and was to be powered by either four HeS 011 engines or two Jumo 012s. The Ar 234D project was also to be further developed as the P-series (P-1 to P-5), night fighter but all these plans came to naught, though, as the Allied bombing of Germany led to a drastic rethink in aircraft production, with exotic jet types now having to take a back seat to increased production of piston-engine fighters to attack the Allied bomber streams. Once He 177 production jigs were removed from Arado's site, production of the Fw 190, already undertaken by them at their Warnemünde plant, was increased. A new production site planned for the Ar 234 at Neubrandenburg was also slated and the site used for production of the Fw 190G. Production of the B-1 and B-2 production variants was now only undertaken at Alt-Lönnewitz, some 100 miles south of Berlin, where the hangars of this ex-Luftwaffe base were converted for aircraft production. The administration of Arado as a whole also moved to Landeshut in Silesia, while another ex-Luftwaffe base at Küpper was also earmarked for Ar 234 production.

The first prototype with retractable undercarriage, the V9 (W/Nr.130009, PH+SQ), took to the air on the 12th March 1944 and in early June 1944 the first pre-production B-0 (W/Nr.140101) was delivered to the test facility at Rechlin. Most of the twenty pre-production B-0s were used for testing at Rechlin, as well as Tarnewitz (weapons trials), Gotenhafen (air-to-sea weapons development), Werneuchen (radio and radar), Udetfeld (bomb development) or Karlshagen (missile testing).

With the successful flight of the V8 with 'paired' BMW 003s instead of the individual units of the V6, this proved that the installation gave better airflow and thus handling. It proved that such an engine installation was a better option, so that the envisaged Ar 234C series that would have resulted could operate faster and higher than the B-series. By June 1944 no fewer than 3,500 Ar 234C-3s were on order, with the first three due to be delivered by March 1945. The first real prototype for the series was the V19, which first flew on the 30th September 1944. The airframe was basically a B-1 with four BMW 003A-1 engines in coupled nacelles. The type also featured a larger nosewheel and is reported to have had experimental air brakes fitted, although clarification of whether these were wing- or fuselage-mounted is not available from surviving documents. The V19 was followed by the V20, which was identical other than the fitment of a full pressurised cockpit. The production C-1 and C-2 were to be four-engine versions of the B-1 and B-2, but with additional features of the V20, plus the C-1 was also to have two rearward-firing MG 151/20 cannon in the aft (lower) fuselage. Only a small number of pre-production C-0 and production C-1 airframes were ever completed, though, because all were cancelled in favour of the C-3. The C-3 series was capable of both reconnaissance and bombing and five prototypes (V21 to V25) were built. The most noticeable change was the bulge in the cockpit canopy, adopted to improve visibility, but the type had in addition to the two rearwards-firing guns, two others fitted, one either side of the nose firing forwards. Bombs of various sizes could be carried via the ETC 504 racks installed in the recess under the mid-fuselage and one under each engine nacelle. Many projected versions of the C-series were envisaged such as

The V8 comes in to land after a test flight

The V9 was the first airframe to receive retractable undercarriage, so it also featured the revised (non-tapering) cross-section to the fuselage

The V13 was the first to have four engines installed, but it only flew a couple of times before being badly damaged and consigned to a training school

the C-3/N night fighter armed with two MK 108 30mm cannon, FuG 218 *Neptun V* radar and FuG 350Zc *Naxos* homing device. The C-4 was to be a pure reconnaissance version, with provision for two cameras and armed with four MG 151/20 cannon (two rearwards and two forward-firing). The C-5 version actually had a prototype, the V28, and it was a two-seat multi-role aircraft with pilot and bomb-aimer sitting side-by-side. The V29 acted as the prototype for the proposed C-6 two-seat reconnaissance version. The D-series had two prototypes being built when the war ended, the V31 as the D-1 reconnaissance version and the V40 for the D-2 bomber. The projected E series was a destroyer version based on the D, whilst the F series was a scaled-up version that would have used four HeS 011 or Jumo 012 engines, but none of these got any further than the drawing board.

A proposed development based on the projected C-7 lead to the P-series of night fighters. The P-1 would have been powered by four BMW 003A-1 engines and had a crew of two, seated side-by-side in a pressurised cockpit with a FuG 245 radar scanner installed in a bulge in the nose. Armament would have comprised two MG 151/20 and two MK 108 30mm cannon. The P-2 was similar to the P-1 but featured heavy armour and a redesigned cockpit made from 13mm armour plate. The P-3 was similar to the P-2 but would have used the HeS 011A engine, whilst the P-4 had the Jumo 004D. The P-5 was a three-seat night fighter powered by the HeS 011 and armed with one MG 151/20 in the port side of the nose and four MK 108 30mm cannon in a ventral pack.

Only two photos are known to exist of the V15, this one shows the nose section during construction

The very last Ar 234 variant was the R-series, which was a reconnaissance aircraft powered by a single Walter rocket motor. It would have been mounted on the back of a Heinkel He 177, which then climbed to altitude and released the Ar 234R.

Numerous other variants based on the Ar 234 were proposed, none of which got any further than the drawing board, plus the type was envisaged as a Mistel composite, however these are all well outside the confines of this title.

The V17 was fitted with two BMW 003 engines, as can be seen here, which had a narrow yet deeper engine cowling and a revised exhaust set-up in comparison with the Jumo 004

As the prototype for the C-3, the V19 was fitted with four 003 engines in coupled nacelles

Operational Use

Reconnaissance

When the Allied forced landed in continental Europe on the 6th June 1944, it became obvious that the Nazi forces needed accurate and up-to-date reconnaissance over the Allied beachheads. Allied air superiority over the area meant that conventional piston-engine types stood little chance, so a jet powered aircraft was the only option and the Ar 234B fitted the bill. 1./*Versuchsverband des Oberkommandos der Luftwaffe* (Luftwaffe High Command's Experimental Flying Unit) at Oranienburg, just north of Berlin, was selected to take photos over the beachheads. On the 7th July, a month after D-Day, the V5 and V7 took off from Alt-Lönnewitz and set course for Oranienburg, where they would be modified to take aerial cameras. Once these modification were completed on the 20th July, the aircraft along with pilots, groundcrew and Arado technical staff were based at Juvincourt, near Rheims, northern France. The first mission took place on the 2nd August (photographying Allied airfields around St. Pierre and the artificial harbour at Asnelles-sur-Mer) and was the first aerial reconnaissance mission by a jet. Both aircraft performed well, achieving altitudes of 37,730ft and the hand-built engines also had good serviceability. The skid landing gear meant that they had to use a grass strip instead of the concrete runway, as the latter was badly marked as a result of bombing. The V5 undertook twenty-two hours of flight, whilst the V7 did twenty-four. On returning from one sortie, pilot Eric Sommers noted French resistance in the woods near the airfield, taking pictures and soon afterwards the RAF bombed the airfield. Neither Ar 234 was damaged, but they both departed Juvincourt on the 28th August (some state the 27th) and moved to Chievres, then on the 31st August to Volkel and finally, on the 5th September, to Rheine. Here the unit gained an additional Staffel, operating two Ar 234B-0s, and by 1st November twenty-four sorties had been flown. The production engines in these B-0s were more prone to problems than the hand-built engines in the V-series, with cracks in the impeller, turbine wheels and vane rings. This eventually led to brand new engines being overhauled before operations, with a subsequent overhaul at 10 hours and an expected life of just 25 hours. In September 1944 *Sonderkommando Götz* was formed from part of 1./*Versuchsverband des Oberkommandos der Luftwaffe* operating four Ar 234B-1s, while 1./*Versuchsverband des Oberkommandos der Luftwaffe* tested the four-engine V6 and V8 airframes. This was followed in November 1944 by the creation of two further test units, *Sonderkommandos Hecht* and *Sperling*. By January 1945 however all three of the test units were disbanded and replaced by 1.(F)/100 and 1.(F)/123 at Rheine and 1.(F)/33 in Denmark. These units continued to undertake operations, with the last flight over the UK being made by 1.(F)/33, and with both 1.(F)/33 and 1.(F)/100 continuing operations right up until the end of the war. *Sonderkommando Sommer* was formed at Udine, near Trieste to allow reconnaissance missions in Northern Italy after complaints from German forces in the region about the lack of adequate reconnaissance information. The unit operated three Ar 234B-1s and undertook flights up to 12,000m (37,372ft) over the Ancona and Leghorn regions.

Bomber

The adoption of the B-series as a bomber was also under way and on the 8th June *Oberst* Walter Stomp was given command of *Kampfgeschwader* 76. Post-war accounts get a little confused from here, as some state that the third *Gruppe* of that unit was chosen to bring the Ar 234B into combat, receiving B-0 W/Nr.140114 on the 24th August, whilst others state that IV.(Erg)/KG 76 was transferred to Alt-Lönnewitz in October 1944 to undertaken this element? At Alt-Lönnewitz the retraining of ex-Do 217, He 111 and Ju 88 pilots to fly the Ar 234 was increased. A fuselage was used as a static classroom to familiarise pilots with the controls, followed by training on engine start-up procedures by Arado staff and finally many hours of theoretical training. The quantum leap that the Ar 234 represented over a piston-engine bomber inevitably led to accidents, many fatal, when crew misjudged the speed of the type, or handled the engines roughly. IV.(Erg)/KG 76 was redesignated III./EKG 1 on the 27th

The V20 after being destroyed in an air raid at Wesendorf on the 4th April 1945

The V21 was another C-3 prototype with the distinctive revised nose and coupled 003 engine nacelles

This is probably the V23 or V24, both of which were intended to be converted (to night-fighter and ground-attack roles) by the war's end, but it never happened and they were captured by the Allies

January 1945 and it used two Me 262B-1a for conversion training. Stab./KG 76 commanded by *Oberst*lt Robert Kowalewski was the first element to become operational with the bomber version, followed by 6./KG76, the latter undertaking its first operation during the Ardennes offensive from the 16th December 1944 to the 25th January 1945. The first and third *Gruppe* started the training programme in January 1945, with III./KG 76 becoming operational in February. During mid-February Stab.III, and 6./KG 76 were engaged in operations against the Allied advance at Kleve and it was on the 24th that an aircraft of III./KG 76 (F1+MT, W/Nr.140173) was shot down by USAAF P-47s near Segelsdorf. The crashed aircraft was subsequently captured, dismantled and sent to the UK for evaluation, being the first intact Ar 234 to fall into Allied hands. KG 76 also undertook bombing runs against the Ludendorff bridge over the Rheine during the 7th to 17th March, supported by Me 262A-2a bombers from I. and II./KG 51. By the end of March lack of fuel had almost stopped all operations, I./KG 76 was based at Leck, 6./KG 76 was at Scheppern and III./KG was at Marx/Oldenburg. The whole of KG 76 was transferred to the control of Luftflotte Reich on the 10th April and on the 12th III./KG 76 received five new aircraft. The situation for Nazi Germany by this point was such that it is doubtful that many more operations were undertaken before the war in Europe came to an end on the 8th May.

Night Fighter

Kommando Bonow was an experimental unit formed in late March 1945 to use the Ar 234B-2 in the night fighter role. The unit was commanded by Major Kurt Bonow and operated two converted B-2s fitted with a ventral gun pack. The unit had only limited operational use before the war ended, though, and no confirmed kills were achieved by the type as far as surviving records show.

This is the twelfth production B-2, W/Nr.140112 which later served with Kommando *Sperling* as T9+GH

Rüstsatz sets:

b – Photographic set comprising two Rb 50/30 or Rb 75/30 cameras, or alternatively one Rb 75/30 and one Rb 20/30
i – Lofte 7K tachometric bombsight
p – Patin PDS12 autopilot
r – Auxiliary 300 litre drop tanks

Note that the designations for the last three were rarely ever added to the type (e.g. B-2i, B-2p etc.), although they were probably listed on each individual aircraft's records.

Projects & Prototypes

A large number of variants of the basic Ar 234 design were envisaged, many of which have already been covered in the previous section, but there were also a great number of developments planned. None of these ever reached fruition, however, and remain very much 'What If?', so what follows is a brief list of all those we could find:

- Ar 234B-2 with 2x MG 151/20 in a gondola above the mid-fuslage, firing forward
- Ar 234B-2 with a dorsal gondola housing two fixed MG 151/20 cannon above the mid-fuslage, firing aft
- Ar 234 Jäger, same as B-2 but with a side-by-side cockpit, solid nose and revised canopy, armed with MG 151/20 cannon in a gondola under each engine nacelle and four (some state three) MG 151 cannon in a ventral gondola under the mid-fuselage, facing forward
- Ar 234C-3/R2 fitted with two fixed MG 151 cannon in a gondola under the mid- fuselage, firing aft
- Ar 234C-3/R3 fitted with MG 151 cannon in a gondola under the mid-fuselage, firing forward
- Ar 234C-3 fitted with a MK 214A cannon in a gondola under the mid-fuselage, firing forward
- Ar 234C-3/W fitted with six R 100BS rockets under the nacelles and fuselage
- Ar 234C-3 fitted with nine 14WBS missiles under the nacelles and fuselage
- Ar 234C-3 with three rotary WGr.42 (four per unit) launchers; one each under the fuselage and each engine nacelle
- Ar 234C-3 modified to carry a Fritz X guided bomb under the fuselage
- Ar 234C-3 fitted with three pods containing 30x R4M rockets or 20x Panzerblitz, one each under the fuselage and each engine nacelle
- Ar 234C-3 *Höhenjäger* fitted with a ventral gondola containing two MG 151 cannon and armoured glass fitted within the nose cone
- Ar 234C-3 *Heeresflugzeug* with AB munitions containers under the fuselage and each engine nacelle, armoured glass within the nose cone and no sight above the cockpit
- Ar 234C-3 as a control unit mounted above an E.377 bomb as a Mistel composite, which used a trolley for take-off but the C-3 retained its retractable undercarriage for landing
- Ar 234C-5/T1 modified to carry a BT1400 bomb under the fuselage

W/Nr.140151 as T9+KH with Kommando *Sperling*, where it was flown by Walter Muffey and had nose art of a jet-propelled sparrow on the nose

Ar 234B W/Nr.140342, F1+AS of 8./KG76 at Magdeburg in December 1944 being towed by a Kettkraftrad

What was left of W/Nr.140439 was used as a decoy after removal of the engines and fitment of fake units

- Ar 234C-5/T2 modified to carry B&V L11 gliding torpedo under fuselage
- Ar 234C-5/F1 modified to carry the Hs 293 gliding bomb under the fuselage
- Ar 234C-5 fitted with a radar dish on a pylon above the mid-fuselage
- Ar 234C fitted with two Daimler-Benz DB 021 turboprop engines in place of the jets
- Ar 234C with a Fieseler Fi 103 mounted on a take-off trolley below, but retaining the single 20mm MG 151/20 cannon in the lower port side of the cockpit
- Ar 234C *Huckepack* with a Fieseler Fi 103 mounted on a trapeze on the upper rear fuselage
- Ar 234C *Deichselschlepp* modified to use a Fieseler Fi 103 (SG 5041 V1) towed via a rigid shaft mounted to the rear fuselage/base of tail. This installation was actually tested on the Ar 234 S8
- Ar 234C with a winged fuel tank towed via a rigid shaft mounted to the rear fuselage/base of tail
- Ar 234C-3 with revised ventral bay to accept the E.381 parasite fighter
- Ar 395.02 based on Ar 234 with HeS 011 engine, a single-seat cockpit under a bubble canopy, solid nose and armament comprising a mix of MK 108, MK 112 and MK 412 cannon and/or rocket projectiles
- TEW 16/43-23, heavily-armed fighter version based on the Ar 234, shoulder-mounted swept-back wing and tail, Jumo 012 or HeS 011 engines, tricycle undercarriage with spherical nose wheel and armament of 1x MG 151/15 plus aditional and 1x MK 108 cannon.

Lt Ziese is seen here getting into W/Nr.140153 whilst operating with Kommando *Sperling* in 1944

Few images of in-service C-series airframes exist, this well-known one shows W/Nr.250001 as found derelict at Prague-Rusin at the end of the war

This is W/Nr.140581, 8H+HH of 1(F)/AufklGr 123 captured at Stavanger, being ground run there by the RAF. Although not readily apparent in the original image you can see the fin flash applied over the painted-out swastika on the tail, so it probably also had the other markings painted out and RAF roundels applied above and below the wings and each side of the fuselage. Sadly the AirMin number for this machine is unknown, as it is one within the batch 227 to 229 that have not had what number applies to which aircraft unravelled yet

Captured & Evaluated

United Kingdom

The first intact Ar 234 to fall into Allied hands was W/Nr.140173, which was shot down by P-47s of the 366th Fighter Group near Selgersdorf on the 22nd February 1945. The aircraft was not heavily damaged and it was shipped to the RAE at Farnborough on the 21st March 1945. The airframe was re-assembled and subjected to detailed examination, but it was never flown by the RAE. Many photos depict this aircraft, devoid of its engines, on the far side of the Farnborough site; its ultimate fate is unknown, but it was probably scrapped in 1946.

- W/Nr.140491 previously operated by *Einsatzkommando* 1.(F)/5 and captured at Stavanger, this aircraft was probably dismantled and passed to the Norwegians.
- W/Nr.140596 previously operated by II./KG 76, this aircraft was surrendered to the RAF at Stavanger on the 10th May 1945, having been flown from Denmark on the 5th. It was repainted in RAF markings and flown from Stavanger to Grove, then on to Schleswig on the 24th September 1945 along with W/Nr.140581. The aircraft, once again with W/Nr.140581, took off en route to Farnborough on the 3rd October, but neither made their destination due to fog. W/Nr.140581 landed at Nordholz and eventually flew on to Farnborough later that month, but W/Nr.140596 force-landed at at Groningen/Eelde airfield in northern Holland and was thus unable to continue on to Farnborough. The damaged airframe was thus handed to No.417 Repair and Salvage Unit, with whom it was later scrapped. Note that various documents and post-war published sources state the remains were handed over to the Dutch forces; no other records remain to support this or its subsequent use.
- W/Nr.140107, this airframe was sent via land transport from Schleswig in the week ending the 6th October 1945. It is most likely that it was intended for weapons trials at Orfordness. No other records exist of its fate, but it is most likely that it ended up as a target on the ranges and was subsequently destroyed
- AirMin 24, W/Nr.140466 was surrendered at Grove (coded 8H+HH of AufklGr 33) and was ferried to Farnborough via Schleswig on the 27th August 1945 by Sqn Ldr J.C.S. Turner. On landing at Farnborough, though, the port undercarriage unit collapsed due to misalignment of the undercarriage locks and the aircraft was written off in the ensuing crash. The aircraft was SOC on the 15th November 1945, but the dismantled airframe had the rear fuselage, complete with extended

Although a poor shot, this shows W/Nr.140113 as F1+AA captured at Schleswig and later to become AirMin 54 and VH530. Of interest is the fact that the last two of the Werke Nr '13' have been applied in white on the tip of the vertical fin and that the engine cowlings seem to have the lightened RLM 76 overspray, whilst the rest of the airframe does not? This latter colour may in fact be winter (white) distemper, but it is still strange to be only on the cowlings unless these have come from another aircraft. The aircraft is lop-sided because the starboard main wheel tyre is flat *(via Internet)*

The first example to reach the UK crashed in Italy and was reassembled at Farnborough for examination; it never had the engines reinstalled, as they went to Power Jets Ltd for evaluation. This shot shows W/Nr.140173 back up on its wheels out the back at Farnborough. Note the overspray of lightened RLM 76 on the fuselage sides, the fact that this partially covers the 'F1' and 'M' elements of the code and how faint the 'T' seems to be. The swastika on the tail is also oversprayed and there is a yellow 'M' at the top of the vertical fin; we don't believe this was repeated on the port side, but can't find an image to confirm this *(©Air Ministry/RAE)*

Although often quoted as being W/Nr.140476, the camouflage on this machine denotes it could well be AirMin 226, W/Nr.140356 used by II./JG76 and captured at Stavanger. The application of the white seems to be more patchy and it also looks to extend to the upper surfaces, which is why we say it is white (distemper) and not lightened RLM 76. The Luftwaffe markings have all been crudely painted out, this could be in RAF colours or whatever was to hand at the time (ex-Luftwaffe paint stock?), and RAF roundels and fin flashes have been applied. No 'AirMin' number has been applied to the rear fuselage, but this is not uncommon and if this is 140356, then it never had it applied but did later have a patch extending from the fuselage roundel applied that held a prototype 'P' marking; this is confirmed for the port side only

A useful shot of W/Nr.140466, ex-8H+HH at Grove complete with full RAF markings comprising Type C roundel and fin flash and the full 'Air Ministry 24' on the rear fuselage, the latter is pretty unique as this was usually abbreviated to 'AirMin' or even 'AM' and some captured machines never had the Air Ministry numbers applied

W/nr.140476 at Farnborough in late 1946 as Air Ministry 26 and in full RAF markings. This machine never flew with the RAE and was only on display after return from storage, it soon went back and was scrapped. Oh, for it and the He 219 and Fw 200 behind to still survive today in the UK!

This is also probably W/Nr.140581, although it could be either 140141 or 140493, and it is seen here just after capture still in Luftwaffe markings and with RAF pilots using it as a photo backdrop *(via Internet)*

braking parachute on display in one of the hangars during the German Aircraft Exhibition there earlier that month. All parts of this airframe were probably disposed of as scrap in the immediate post-war period.

- Air Min 25, W/Nr.140608, captured at Grove marked as T9+GL of *Kommando Bonow*. Official records state the W/Nr. as 140008, but that was never allocated to an Ar 234, plus the codes as 'T1' but that unit was disbanded in early 1945 and never operated the Ar 234. Ferried from Grove to Schleswig and on to Farnborough on the 25th June 1945, then on to No.6 MU RAF Brize Norton on the 30th June. Allocated serial number VK880 on the 26th July, and erroneously listed as being at Farnborough on the 12th October 1945, however it was still at No.6 MU by the census of the 21st March 1946 and was SOC there on the 1st October 1948 and sold as scrap.
- AirMin 26 W/Nr.140476, captured at Grove marked as 8H+DH of 1.(F)/AufklGr 33. Ferried from Grove to Farnborough via Schleswig on the 25th June 1945. Flown into storage at No.6 MU RAF Brize Norton on the 3rd July. Allocated serial number VK877 on the 26th July and returned to RAF Farnborough on the 7th October for use in the static display during the German Aircraft Exhibition there. Presumed to have been subsequently scrapped at Farnborough.
- AirMin 54, W/Nr.140113 was surrendered at Schleswig (coded F1+AA of KG 76, flown by the unit CO, Obslt Robert Kowalewski) and ferried to Tangmere on the 5th June 1945 by Oblt Kolm of 8./KG 76. It was displayed at Tangmere as part of a collection of British and German types for the CFE then flown on to Farnborough on the 12th June. On the 19th June the RAF serial VH530 was allocated to it and it is presumed to have undertaken flight-testing at Farnborough before being flown to No.6 MU, RAF Brize Norton on the 7th September 1945. It remained in storage there until the 1st October 1948 where it was SOC and presumed to have been scrapped, either on site or via a private scrap merchant.
- AirMin 226, W/Nr.140356, flown from Grove to Stavanger on the 5th May 1945 then surrendered to the RAF on the 10th May. Ferried from Stavanger to Grove on the 23rd September by Lt Cdr E.M. Brown, then on to Schleswig on the 25th September. It flew from Schleswig to Melsbroek on the 6th October, and then on to Farnborough. The aircraft undertook flights from Farnborough on the 17th and 19th October, as well as taking part in the flying display within the German Aircraft Exhibition on the 2nd November. Two more flights were undertaken on the 8th and 16th November, for a total of 3 hours 15 minutes in Allied hands. The fate of this airframe is unknown, but it was most likely scrapped in the immediate post-war period.
- AirMin 227 to 229, this batch of numbers all relate to Ar 234s, but the exact allocation of each to what W/Nr. remains unknown, so we will list each by their W/Nr. only.
- W/Nr.140141. This was a machine from 1.(F)/AufklGr 123, which was flown from Grove to Stavanger on the 5th May 1945, then surrendered to the RAF on the 10th May. It was ferried from Stavanger to Grove on the 24th September and on to Schleswig on the 25th. It went to Farnborough via RAF Manston, arriving there on the 8th October. It is unlikely it ever undertook any test flying whilst at Farnborough, as it moved to No.6 MU RAF Brize Norton on the 15th October 1945 and was sold as scrap there on the 6th October 1948.
- W/Nr.140493, operated by *Einsatzkommando* 1.(F)/5 at Stavanger (probably 9V+CH), where it was captured and then ferried to Schleswig on the 9th July 1945. It then continued to Gilze-Rijen on the 13th July and on to Farnborough via Melsbroek and RAF Manston on the 14th July. It undertook twelve flights from Farnbor-

I don't believe the identity of this machine is as yet known, but the 'F' on the nose may well identify it as an AufklGr machine, so it could once again be in the AirMin 227 to 229 group. It is not W/Nr.140581, as it has the paint off the intakes and that machine did not, but it too is being ground run at Stavanger by the RAF and it has the Luftwaffe markings overpainted with RAF ones *(©RAF Museum)*

Very few images survive of the single complete example captured and tested by Russia, this shot from the Internet shows that machine W/Nr.140355, which was captured at Damgarten and tested by the NII-VVS in Russia still, it would seem, in full Luftwaffe markings. It is not known if these were later replaced with full Russian AF markings or not? *(via Internet)*

ough in the 28th July to 27th October period, totalling 9 hours and 25 minutes, before being sent to No.6 MU RAF Brize Norton on the 27th November 1945. It was sold for scrap there not long afterwards.

- W/Nr.140581, 8H+CH from 1(F)/AufklGr 123 flown from Grove to Stavanger on the 5th May 1945 and captured by the RAF on the 10th May. Ferried from Stavanger to Schleswig on the 24th September 1945. Took off from Schleswig for Farnborough on the 3rd October, but flight aborted en route due to fog and subsequently landed at Nordholz. Ferried from Nordholz via Melsbroek to Farnborough on the 27th October. It is unlikely it did any flight testing with the RAE as it was transferred to No.6 MU RAF Brize Norton on the 8th November 1945 and subsequently sold for scrap.

France

Two Ar 234Bs were transported to France in the immediate post-war era, both probably originating from the three aircraft surrendered at Schleswig.

Russia

One Ar 234B is known to have been captured at Damgarten and examined by NI VVS representative A. Kubyshkin. The airframe was taken to Rechlin (then in Russian hands) where it was tested, although details of what testing was undertaken are still unknown, as is the ultimate fate of this aircraft.

USA

The following list of 'USA' numbers relates to those aircraft captured by the RAF in Denmark and Northern Germany that were earmarked for the USA. The list of these aircraft was forwarded to Col. Harold E. Watson and if no such complete aircraft type existed already with his team's work elsewhere in Germany, the aircraft was handed over to the USAAF.

USAAF

- USA 5, W/Nr.140489, captured at Grove
- USA 6, W/Nr. unknown, captured at Grove
- USA 7, W/Nr. unknown, captured at Grove

Note: It seems certain that either USA 6 or USA 7 was the second Ar 234B allocated to the US Navy and subsequently tested at Patuxent River (W/Nr.140467 or 140486)

- USA 40, W/Nr.140311, surrendered to RAF at Stavanger, having been flown there by II./KG 76 on the 5th May. Handed over to Col. Watson where it later became FE1011 *(see elsewhere)*
- USA 50, W/Nr.140312, surrendered to RAF at Stavanger, having been flown there by II./KG 76 on the 5th May. Handed over to Col. Watson where it later became FE1010 *(see elsewhere)*

Watson's Whizzers

Selection of aircraft for evaluation in the USA was undertaken by a team led by Col. Harold E. Watson, hence the

This is either W/Nr.140128 or 140434 as 'Jane 1' at NAS Patuxent River post-war where it was used for ground-running the engines, as it was never returned to airworthiness. Note that this aircraft, along with 'Snafu 1' were repainted in Europe before being shipped to the USA and are thus Olive Drab over Neutral Grey. It also originally had the top of the vertical fin painted Insignia Yellow, but this seems to have been removed by this stage *(©US Navy)*

The other machine ground-run by the US Navy at Patuxent River was this machine, 'Snafu 1', which had previously been '303' with Watson's Whizzers *(©US Navy)*

This is how 'Jane 1' looked at Patuxent River by the late 1950s. derelict at the end of the runway. Either it or 'Snafu 1' ended up with the wings cut off and used as hardcore for the runway extension there in the 1960s. The tail end of it used to stick out of Patuxent Bay, but no-one in the US Navy high command would ever allow its recovery, due to the 'embarrassment' it would cause! *(via Internet)*

W/Nr.140312 at Wright Field in October 1945, with the Luftwaffe markings reapplied (albeit with the wrong colour, style and size of swastika). The vertical line on the side of the nose is not a marking, it is where the fabric tape over the transit join has not been reapplied, thus leaving a line of unpainted metal exposed *(©via J.M.G.Gradidge)*

The world's only surviving Ar 234, W/Nr.140312 is seen here when it arrived in the USA still marked as 'USA 50'

Here is W/Nr.140312 at a later stage in its career, not marked as T2-1010 and in an odd mix of green and brown camouflage applied by the USAF. Once again Luftwaffe markings have been reapplied, but they are all the wrong style and size

name 'Watson's Whizzers'. All aircraft were refurbished by the 54th ADS and then flown (via Grove and Melun) to the French coast (Cherbourg) to be loaded aboard a carrier (HMS Reaper) and shipped to the USA. All Watson's Whizzers used a three-digit number, and those allocated to Ar 234s are listed below:

- 202, W/Nr.140168, named 'Jane I', shipped to the USA on HMS Reaper, allocated to the US Navy. Given BuNo.121445 and sent to NAS Patuxent River *(see details elsewhere)*
- 303, W/Nr. unknown, named 'Snafu I', shipped to the USA on HMS Reaper, allocated to the US Navy. Given BuNo.121446 and sent to NAS Patuxent River *(see details elsewhere)*

A nice posed shot of test pilot Capt Bob Cardenas by W/Nr.140312 at Freeman Field in the post-war era. Cardenas was later to test the Me 262 and go on to such things as piloting the B-29 mothership in Chuck Yeager's flight in the X-1 *(©USAF)*

- 404, W/Nr.140311, ex-USA 40, shipped to the USA on HMS Reaper, to the USAAF and allocated evaluation code FE-1011 *(see details elsewhere)*
- 505, W/Nr.140312, ex-USA 50, shipped to the USA on HMS Reaper, to the USAAF and allocated evaluation code FE-1010 *(see details elsewhere)*

US Navy

Those aircraft allocated to the US Navy for evaluation were given BuAer [Bureau or Aeronautics] (BuNo.) numbers, those applying to the Ar 234 are as follows:

- BuNo.121445, ex-Watson's Whizzers '202', shipped to the USA on HMS Reaper. Flown from Newark to NAS Patuxent River by Lt Najeeb Halaby and allocated to the Flight Test Division. Not test flown due to a lack of spare tyres and subsequently struck off charge on the 31st December 1946. Presumed scrapped on-site.
- BuNo.121446, ex-Watson's Whizzers '303', shipped to the USA on HMS Reaper. Flown from Newark to NAS Patuxent River and allocated to the Tactical Test Division. Not test flown due to a lack of spares, but used to test engines for noise and heat hazards. Struck off charge on the 31st December 1946 and scrapped on-site

Foreign Aircraft Evaluation Centre

This was part of the Air Technical Service Command and was based at Wright Field, Ohio and Freeman Field, Seymour, Indiana, the latter having been handed over by the 1st Air Force on the 15th June 1945 to assist with the testing of the huge amount of captured equipment that Wright Field, Ohio could not handle in the immediate post-war era. All aircraft tested by the command were initially allocated an 'FE' number, although later this was changed to 'T2'.

W/Nr.140312 at Park Ridge, Illinois in storage in the 1960s. The airframe still carries the USAF-applied green and brown camouflage, plus various stencil notes and warnings applied by the USAF during testing *(©J.M.G. Gradidge)*

- FE-1010 W/Nr.140312, captured by the RAF at Stavanger and taken on by Watson's Whizzers as ex-USA 50, shipped to the USA on HMS Reaper arriving on the 28th July 1945. The aircraft was reassembled and flown to Freeman Field, where it was allocated the serial FE-1010. In July 1946 the aircraft received new engines, plus American radio and oxygen equipment and it was delivered to the Accelerated Service Test Maintenance Squadron of the Flight Test Division at Wright Field. The aircraft undertook more than 20 hours flying at Wright Field and the report on these tests was produced in February 1947. Shortly after test flying ended the aircraft was flown to Orchard Place Airport (today O'Hare International Airport), Park Ridge, Illinois for museum storage. It was transferred to the ownership of the Smithsonian Institute on the 1st May 1948 and during the early 1950s it moved to the Smithsonian's Paul E. Garber Restoration Facility at Silver Hill, Maryland. The airframe underwent a complete restoration between 1984 and February 1989 marked as F1+GS, although these markings were not found on the airframe during restoration: recent research shows this aircraft was most likely F1+DR. The aircraft was initially displayed within the National Air & Space Museum in downtown Washington DC but in 2005 is became one of the first aircraft to be moved into the new Steven F. Udvar-Hazy Center near Dulles International Airport, Chantilly, VA as the only surviving Ar 234 in the world
- FE-1011 W/Nr. 140311, captured by the RAF at Stavanger and allocated the code 'USA 40' before being handed over to Col. Watson. Shipped to the USA on HMS Reaper and allocated to the USAAF where it was given the evaluation code FE-1011. The airframe probably moved through Wright Field, but was recorded at Freeman Field by May 1946, having donated various parts to the restoration to airworthiness of FE-1010. By the 15th August 1946 it was 'recommended for salvage' and is therefore thought to have been scrapped there not long afterwards, although the Freeman Field Research Group have accounts of an Ar 234 having its wings cut off and being buried alongside one of the runways at Freeman Field, so this seems likely to be the manner in which 140311 was 'scrapped'. No trace of the airframe has thus far been discovered in the excavations at Freeman Field.

There are rumours that both Norway and Denmark received captured Ar 234s for evaluation and when you consider Stavanger is in the former and Grove in the latter, it is no surprise, as the RAF collected captured machines in both locations. This image shows a group of Danish offers inspecting a captured Ar 234B at Grove in the summer of 1945, with a Fw 189 alongside. It is not known if the Danish Air Force ever evaluated the type, or gained any to examine or use in training schools. As yet that aspect of the Ar 234 in the post-war era remains unrecorded

Specification

Engines	• V1 & V4: Two Junkers Jumo 004A-0 axial-flow turbojets rated at 840kg at 9,000rpm • B-2: two Junkers Jumo 004B-1, -2 or -3 axial-flow turbojets rated at 900kg static trust, 730kg at 440km/h at sea level and 590kg at 440km/h at 2,500m • C-3 & C-4: Four BMW 003A-1, turbojets rated at 800kg
Span	• V1 & V4: 14.20m • B-2, C-3 & C-4: 14.41m
Length	• V1: 12.58m • V4: 12.56m • B-2: 12.62m • C-3: 12.84m
Height	• V1 (without trolley, top of fin to extended skid): 3.75m • V4 (top of fin to extended skid): 3.81m • B-2: 4.29m • C-3: 4.15m
Weight	• V4 (airframe & engines): 4,250kg • V1 & V4 (basic): 4,750 • B-2 Empty (equipped): 5,200kg • B-2 Loaded (without bombs): 8,410kg • B-2 Take-off (maximum): 9,800kg • C-3 Empty: 6,530kg • C-3 Loaded: 11,050kg
Performance	• V4 Maximum speed: 760km/h • B-2 Maximum speed: 742km/h at 6,000m and 8,410kg • C-3 Maximum speed: 873km/h at 6,000m
Ceiling	• B-2: 10,000m • C-3: 11,000m
Range	• V4: 1,500km • B-2: 670km at sea level; 770km at 6,000m • C-3: 770km at 6,000m (some state 795km at 6,000m, others 1,215km!)
Armament	• V1 & V4: None • B-2: Two fixed, rearwards firing MG 151/20 cannon with 200 rpg [never installed] • B-2/N: Two fixed, forward-firing MG 151/20 cannon in a ventral pod • C-3 & C-4: Two fixed, forward firing MG 151/20 cannon with 250 rpg and two fixed, rearwards firing MG 151/20 cannon with 250 rpg
Ordnance	• B-2: Three 500kg SC500 or SC500 bombs, or one 1,000kg SC or SD1000 and two 250kg SC or SD250 bombs, or one 1,400kg PT1400 bomb, or three AB250 or AB500 anti-personnel bomb containers*
Camera	• V4 – None • B-2 & C-4: Two Rb 75/30, RB 50/30 or Rb 20/30 mounted vertically in the aft fuselage • C-3 – None • C-4 – Two Rb 75/30, RB 50/30 or Rb 20/30 mounted vertically in the aft fuselage
Radio etc.	• B-2/N: Fug 218 *Neptun V* (radar) • C-3: FuG 16, FuG 25 (IFF), FuG 102 (altimeter), FuG 136 (Nachtfee, ground-to-air), FuG 142 (Emergency navigational aid – never deployed operationally) and FuG 217 Neptun (radar)

** There are numerous ordnance combinations quoted for the B-2 in published works, but we have only listed those here that are in official documents for the type*

Note: Please note that as the Arado Ar 234 was built and tested using Metric measurements we have refrained from offering Imperial conversions in the above data

Arado Ar 234 V1, W/Nr.130001, TG+KB

Flown by Flugkapitän Selle at Brandenburg. RLM 70 Schwarzgrün and RLM 71 Dunkelgrün upper surfaces with RLM 65 Lichtblau undersides. Codes in black, repeated below the wings. White national markings above top surfaces and black/white crosses below wings

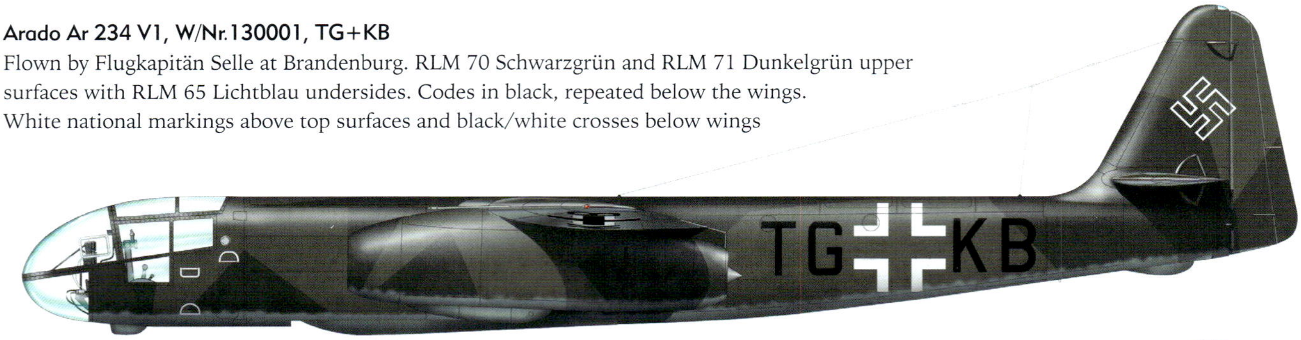

Arado Ar 234 V7, W/Nr.130007, T9+MH

Flown by Oblt. Erich Sommer, Juvncourt, 2nd August 1944. RLM 70/71 upper surfaces with RLM 65 undersides. Codes in black and white

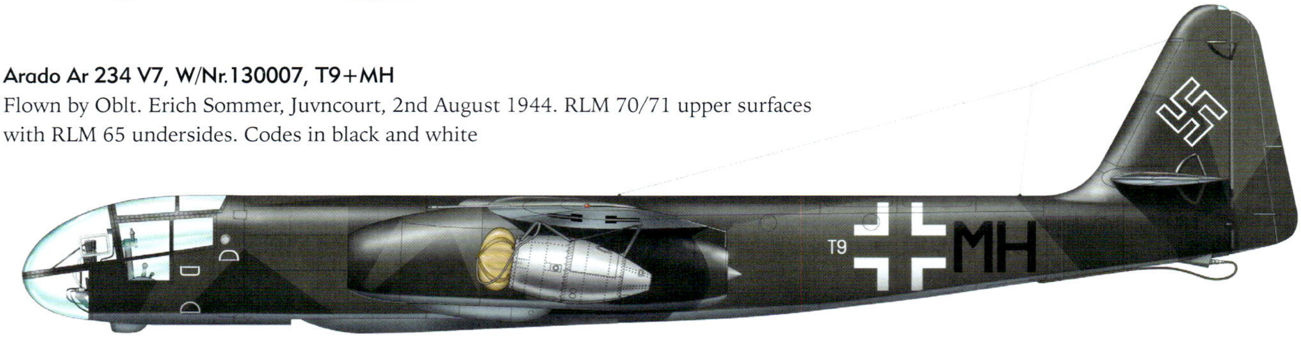

Arado Ar 234 S10, W/Nr.140110, E2+20

Used at Rechlin for tests with Hs 293 missiles between October and December 1944. RLM 70/71 upper surfaces with RLM 65 undersides. Yellow RLM 04 undersides to engine cowlings; black codes and white markings on fuselage, fin and above wings

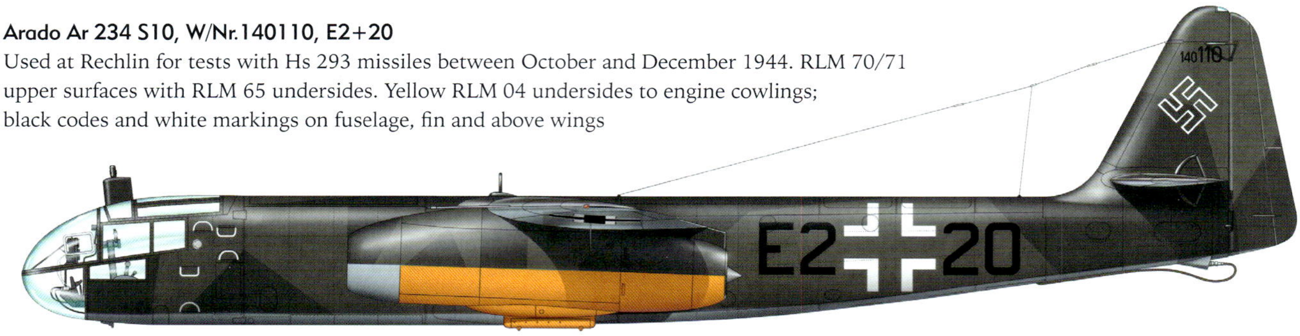

Arado Ar 234 V15, W/Nr.130025, T9+HL

Flown by Flugkapitän Johann Janssen, 3./Versuchsverband OKL. RLM 70/71 upper surfaces with RLM 65 undersides. Codes in white and black. Light grey (or unpainted) engine air intakes

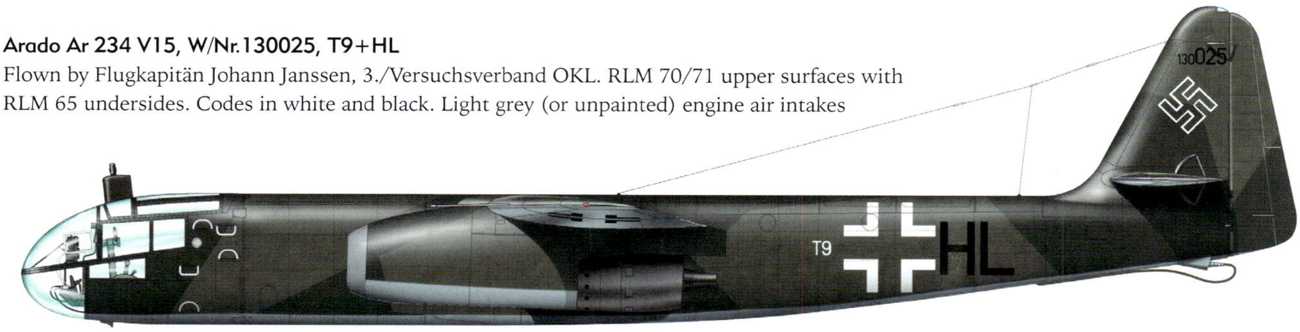

Arado Ar 234B-2b, W/Nr.140151, T9+KH

Flown by Oblt. Werner Muffey, Kommando Sperling, November 1944. RLM 81 Braunviolett and RLM 82 Lichtgrün upper surfaces with RLM 76 Lichtgrau undersides. White national markings on fuselage, fin and upper surfaces of wings. Code is white (T9) and black (KH)

Arado Ar 234B-2, F1+AD
Flown by Maj Hans-Georg Bätcher, commander of III./KG 76, early 1945. RLM 81/82 upper surfaces with RLM 76 undersides. Hellblau RLM 24 trim to engine air intakes and 'A' of fuselage code, the latter repeated just aft of the canopy glazing. Black rear section of engine cowlings

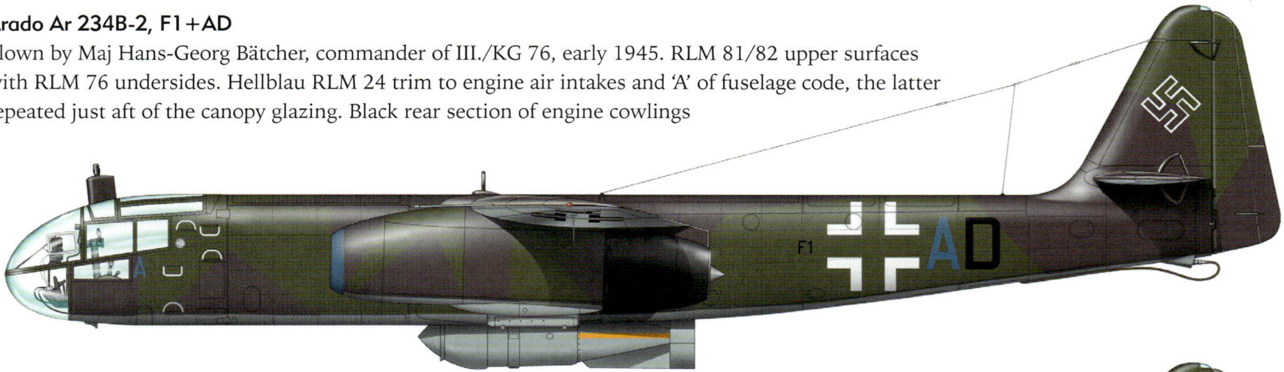

Arado Ar 234B-2b, W/Nr.140341, 9V+AH, of 1./FAG 5
Flown by Lt Hellmut Hetz. RLM 81/82 upper surfaces with RLM 76 undersides. White 'A' of code

Arado Ar 234B-2, W/Nr.140342, F1+AS, of 8./KG 76
Flown by Friedrich Bruchlos during the attack against the bridge at Remagen in March 1945. RLM 81/82 upper surfaces with RLM 76 undersides. Red (RLM 23) trim to engine intake and 'A' of code. White markings on fuselage; fin and upper surfaces of wings

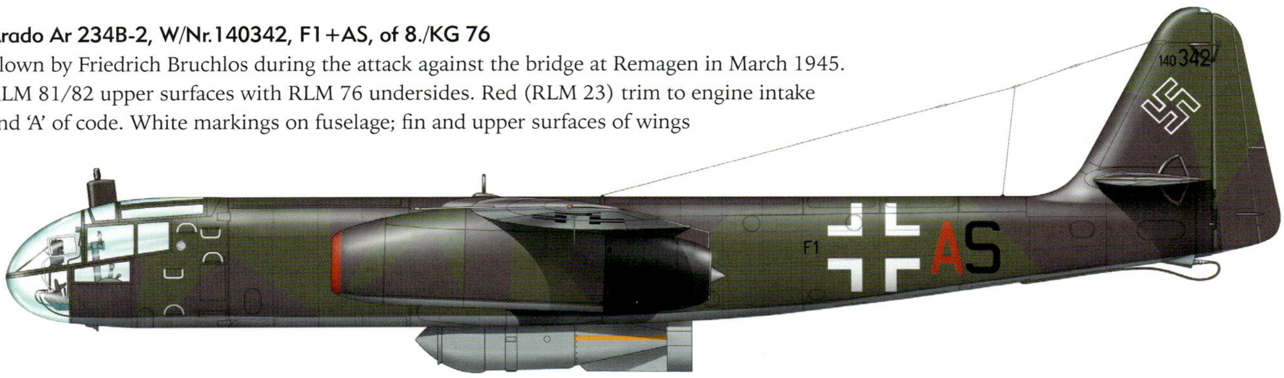

Arado Ar 234B-2, W/Nr.140325, F1+CS, KG 76, 1945
RLM 81/82 upper surfaces with RLM 76 undersides. Black codes with red (RLM 23) 'C' and engine air intakes. Black rear of engine cowling

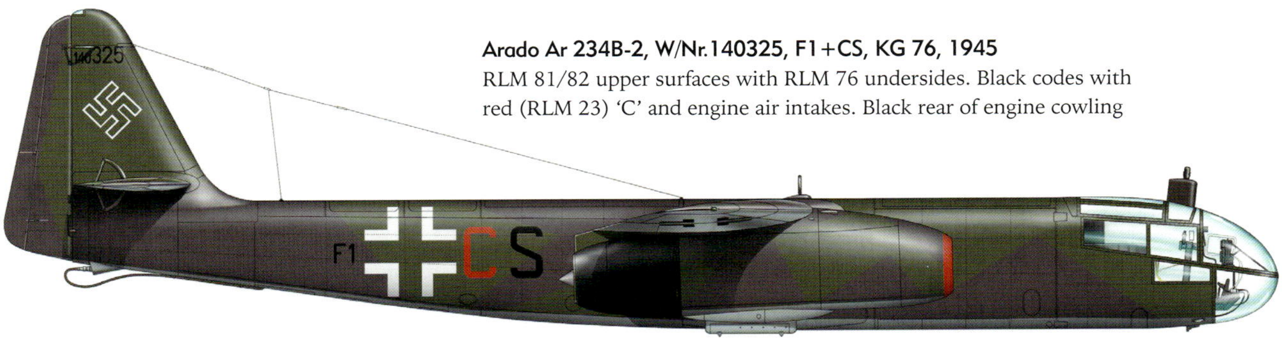

Arado Ar 234B-2, W/Nr.140173, F1+MT, of 9./KG 76
Flown by Hptm Josef Regler. RLM 81/82 upper surfaces with RLM 76 undersides. RLM 76 sprayed high on the sides of the cowlings, and in blotches on the other two top colours. Yellow (RLM 04) code letter 'M', repeated high on top of fin

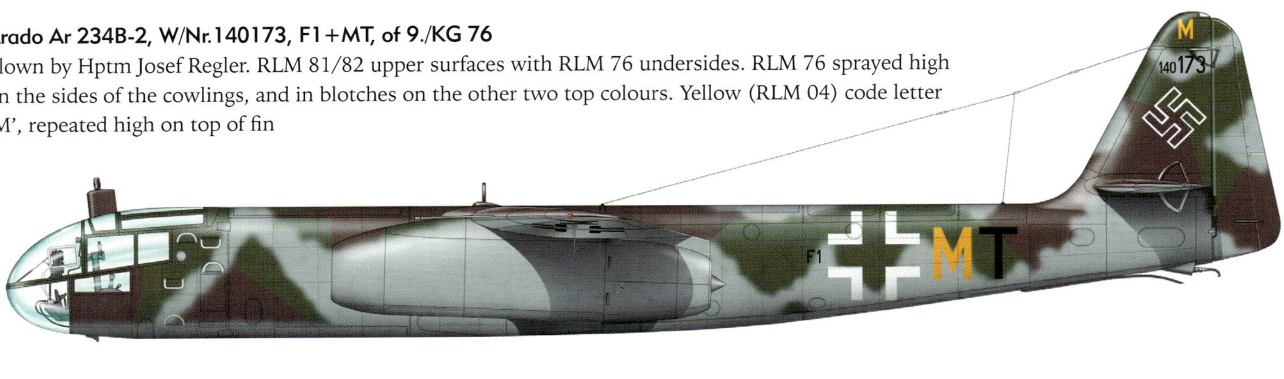

Arado Ar 234B-2b, W/Nr.140149, 4U+DH, of 1.(F)/123
Flown by Hptm Hans Felde (Staffelkapitän), shot down on 11th February 1945. Originally in RLM 81/82 upper surfaces with RLM 76 undersides. Top areas painted over either in a diluted white distemper or (as some sources claim) one of the lighter greys. Code '4U' and 'D' are in white; 'H' in black

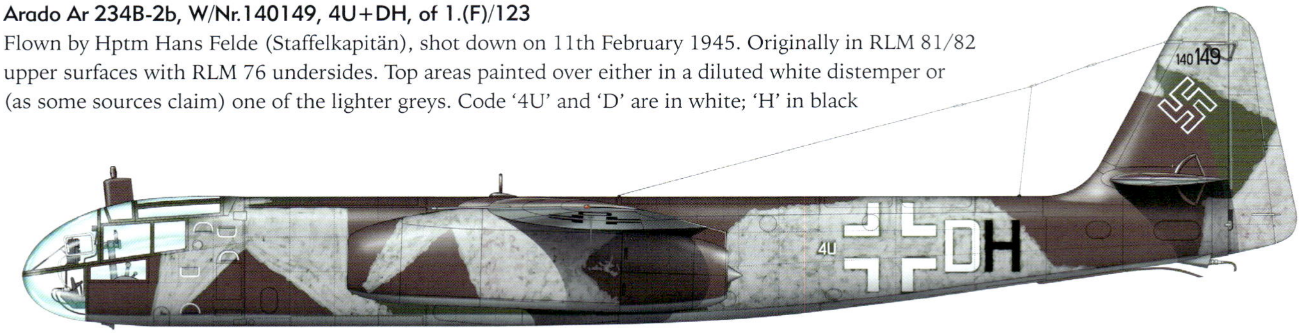

Arado Ar 234B-2b, W/Nr.140344, T9+EH
Flown by Oblt Erich K. Sommer. RLM 81/82 upper surfaces with RLM 76 undersides. White markings on fuselage, fin and upper wing surfaces; black under wings. Code 'T9' is white; 'EH' is white and black. Aircraft fitted with Magirus-bombe gun pack

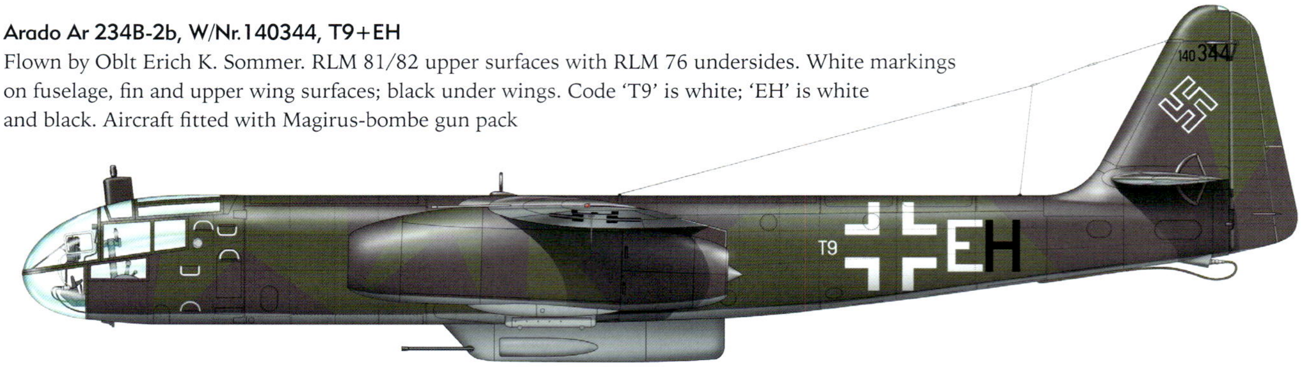

Arado Ar 234B-2, W/Nr.140160, F1+BT
Flown by Hptm Dieter Lukesch, commander of Einsatzstaffel III./KG 76, late 1944. RLM 81/82 upper surfaces with RLM 76 undersides. Yellow (RLM 04) trim to air intake, rudder and 'B' of code

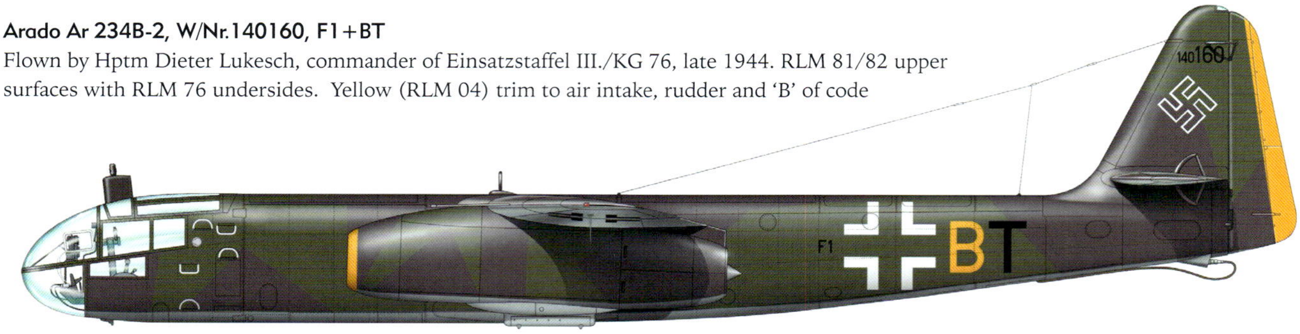

Arado Ar 234, W/Nr.140131, F1+AA, KG 76, March 1945
RLM 81/82 upper surfaces with RLM 76 undersides. Red (RLM 23) rudder trim, engine air intakes and 'A' of code

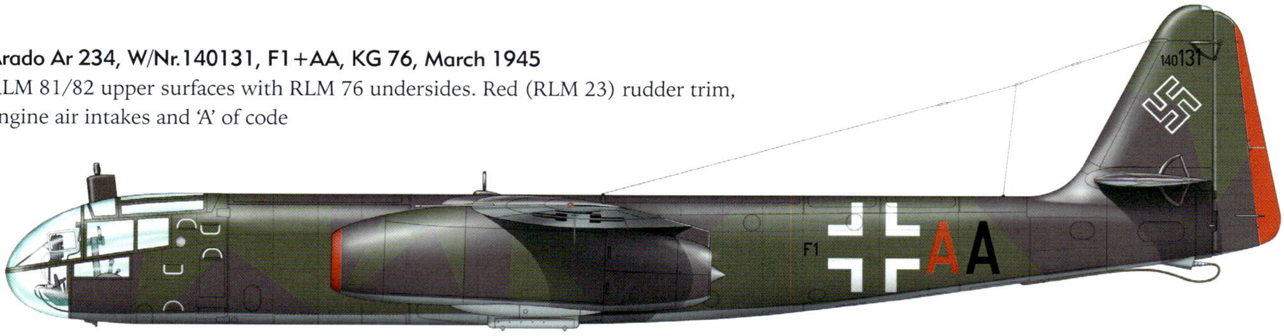

Arado Ar 234B-2, W/Nr.140489, 1.(F)/33, Wittmundhafen, early April 1945
RLM 81/82 upper surfaces with RLM 76 undersides. All lettering in black

Arado Ar 234B-2b, W/Nr.140466, 1./FAG 33, 1945
RLM 81/82 upper surfaces with RLM 76 undersides. All lettering in black

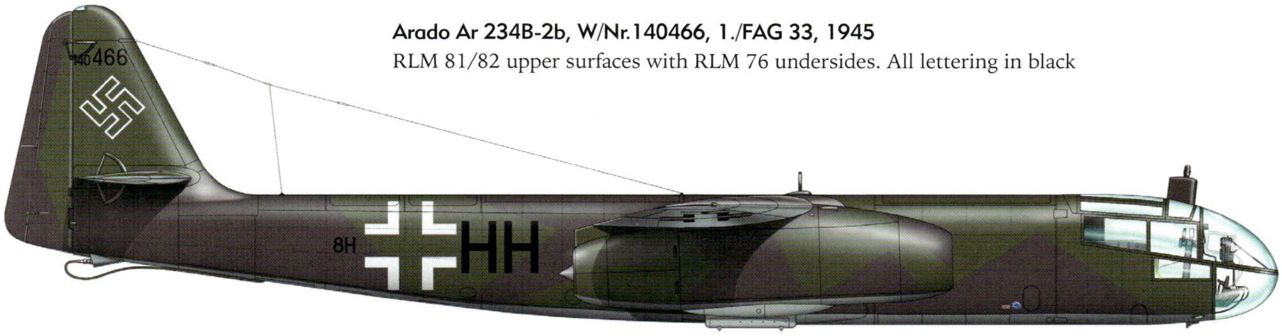

Arado AR 234B-2/N, WNr.140145, SM+FE
Flown by Hptms Bisping and Vogel, Kommando, Bonow, 1945. RLM 81/82 upper surfaces with RLM 76 undersides. All codes in black. Aircraft fitted with Magirus-bombe gun pack. Crashed at Oranienburg on 13 February 1945 killing the pilot and radio operator HptmVogl

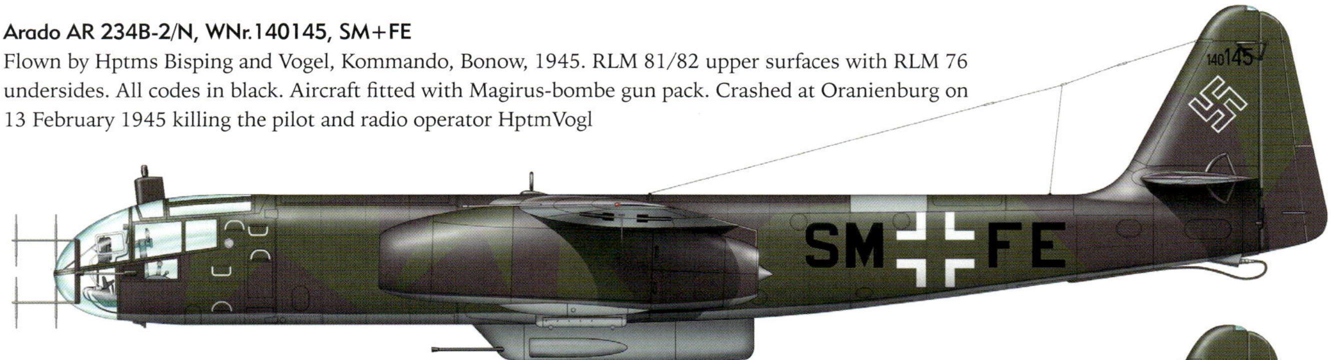

Arado Ar 234C-3, W/Nr.250008, III/KG 76, 1945
RLM 81/82 upper surfaces with RLM 76 undersides

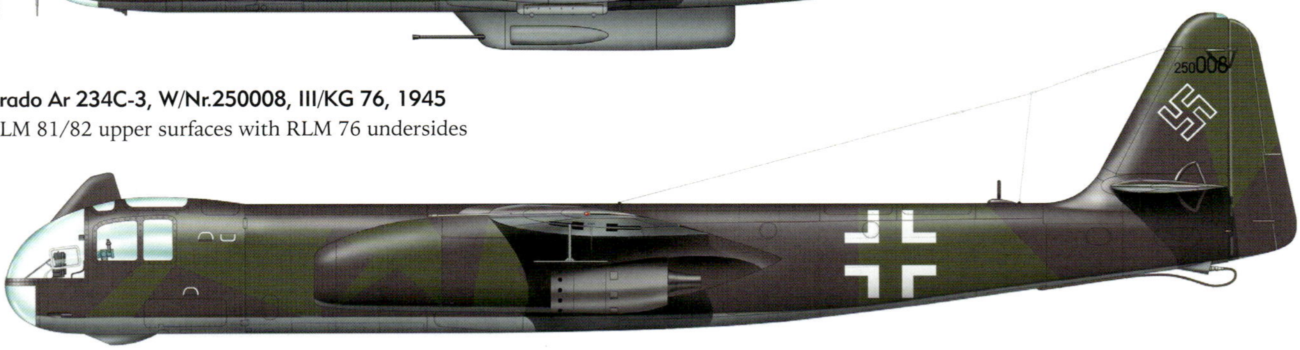

Arado Ar 234B-2, W/Nr.140476, VK877 (ex-8H+HH)
Royal Aircraft Establishment Farnborough, where it arrived on 25th June 1945. RLM 81/82 upper surfaces with RLM 76 undersides. All German markings painted over (probably in Dark Green) and non-standard British markings applied

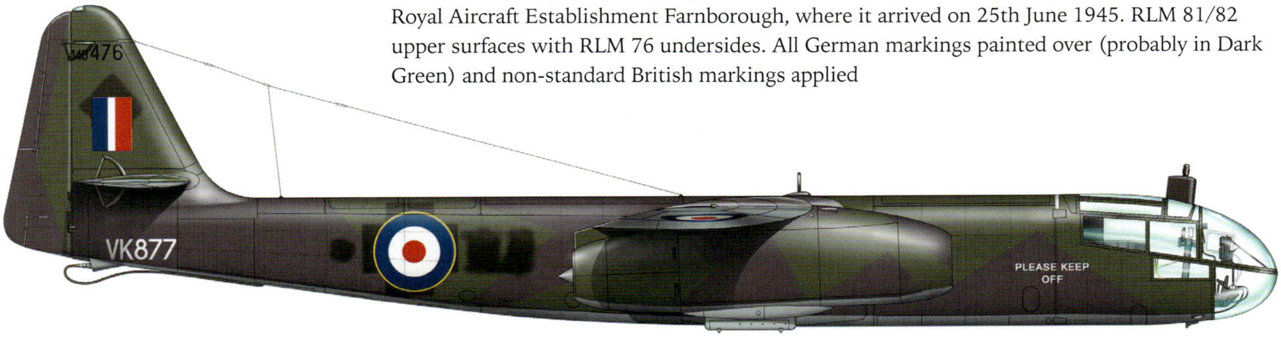

Arado Ar 234B-2, '303' and 'Snafu 1' (ex-W/Nr.140148)
Melun (France) before transfer for testing by the US Navy at Patuxent River. Olive Drab upper surfaces and Neutral Gray undersides. US markings on both sides of fuselage, above port wing and under starboard wing; fin/rudder tip in Insignia Yellow, as is the number '303' and the aircraft's name on the nose. Disney's cartoon was applied to a number of Ar 234s tested in the USA

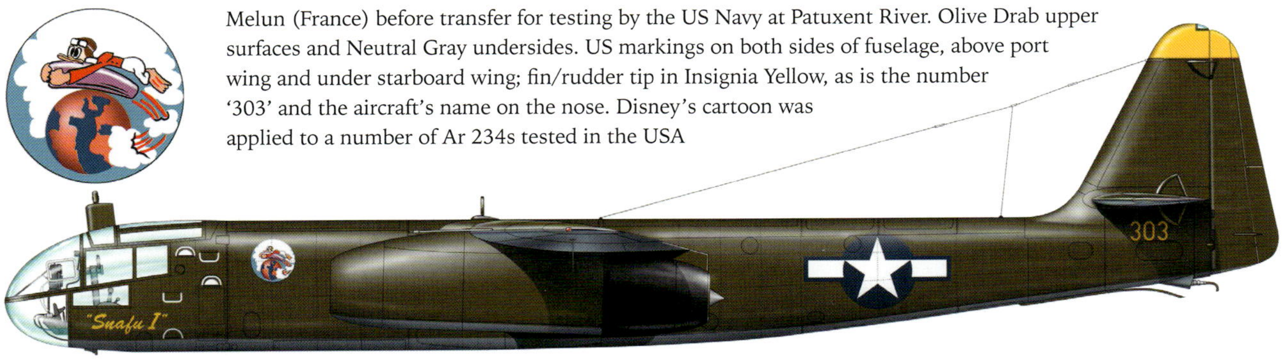

Technical Description

What follows is an extensive selection of images and diagrams that will help you understand the physical nature of the Arado Ar 234.

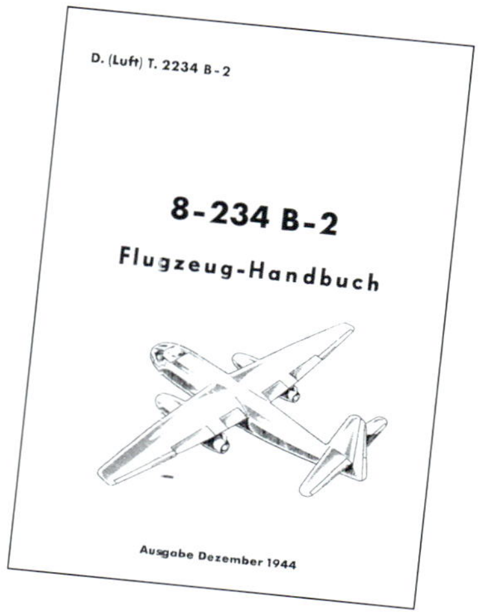

Now alongside an R-4 helicopter and their Fw 190F, W/Nr.140312 the world's only surviving complete Ar 234 is today available for all to see in the superb Steven F. Udvar-Hazy Center near Dulles International Airport in the USA *(©Scott Willey)*

This close-up of the cockpit area probably shows the V2, as it is a prototype due to the lack of the main panel crossing between the side consoles and the little up-stands at the front of each side console containing flight instruments. It also has the twin grab handles on the canopy frame and the large access panel that only applies to the skid-equipped V-series airframes

below: This photograph, of German origin certainly does not show one of the early machines, nor does it show a production machine either. It is therefore most likely the V9 going by how well photographed it was, or one of the S-series pre-production machines. Note the partial instrument panel and those instruments missing (removed or not yet installed) in the small panel at the front of the port side console

Now let's get inside the B-2 with NASM, here you are looking down into the cockpit from the port side *(©Scott Willey)*

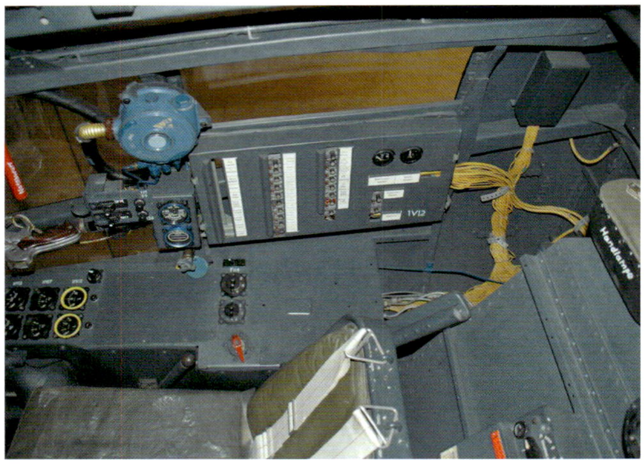

This is the distribution panel on the starboard side of the cockpit *(©Scott Willey)*

The front section of the starboard side console *(©Scott Willey)*

The area above and behind the pilot's seat with the battery visible on the left-hand side *(©Scott Willey)*

Looking straight down onto the seat *(©Scott Willey)*

An overall view forward into the cockpit area *(©Scott Willey)*

The main central element of the instrument panel, which itself seems to be made of an early composite material a bit like Bakelite *(©Scott Willey)*

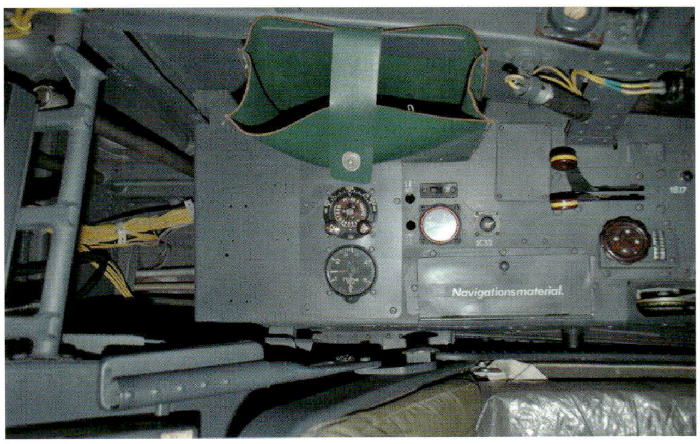

The rearmost section of the port side console, with the map case visible and the racks for the batteries on the far left *(©Scott Willey)*

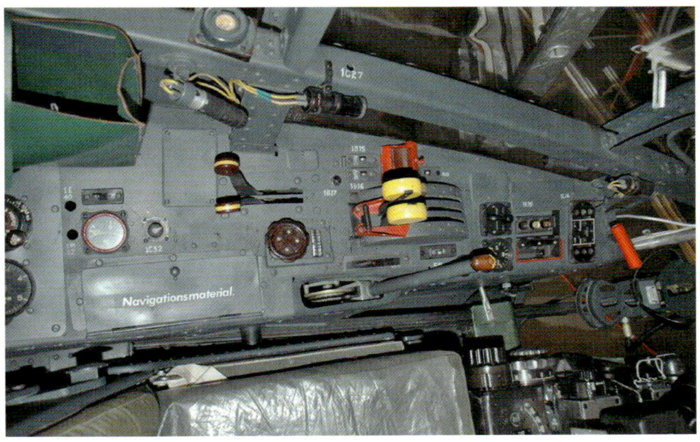

Looking down on the port side console *(©Scott Willey)*

Here is a clearer look at the back corner of the port sidewall, with the battery and rack now very visible *(©Scott Willey)*

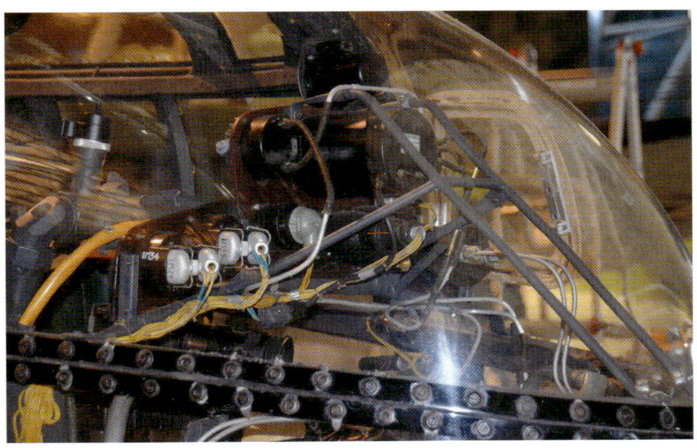

It is also best to view the support frame for the instrument panel and the backs of the instruments themselves from the outside too, so this is that region seen from the starboard side *(©Scott Willey)*

It is best to view the rudder pedals from the outside, as seen here from the port side *(©Scott Willey)*

Here are the rudder pedals viewed more from the front on the starboard side *(©Scott Willey)*

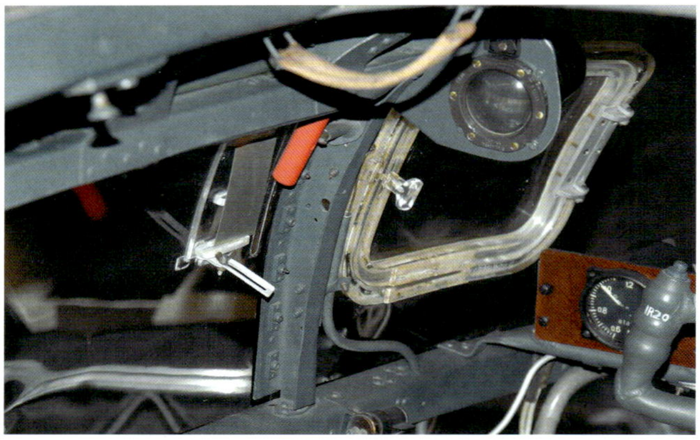

This is the top corner of the port side of the nose, with the compass mounted up under the frame and the bad weather panel clearly visible; it is nearly all made of Perspex, although the latch toggle and the retaining arm at the bottom seen in the manual diagrams do not seem to be on this example *(©Scott Willey)*

This mock-up of the C-3 cockpit confirms that the image at the bottom left probably shows a production or prototype (V21?) machine. Note also that you can just make out that the Lofte bombsight for the C-series was going to be the 7D

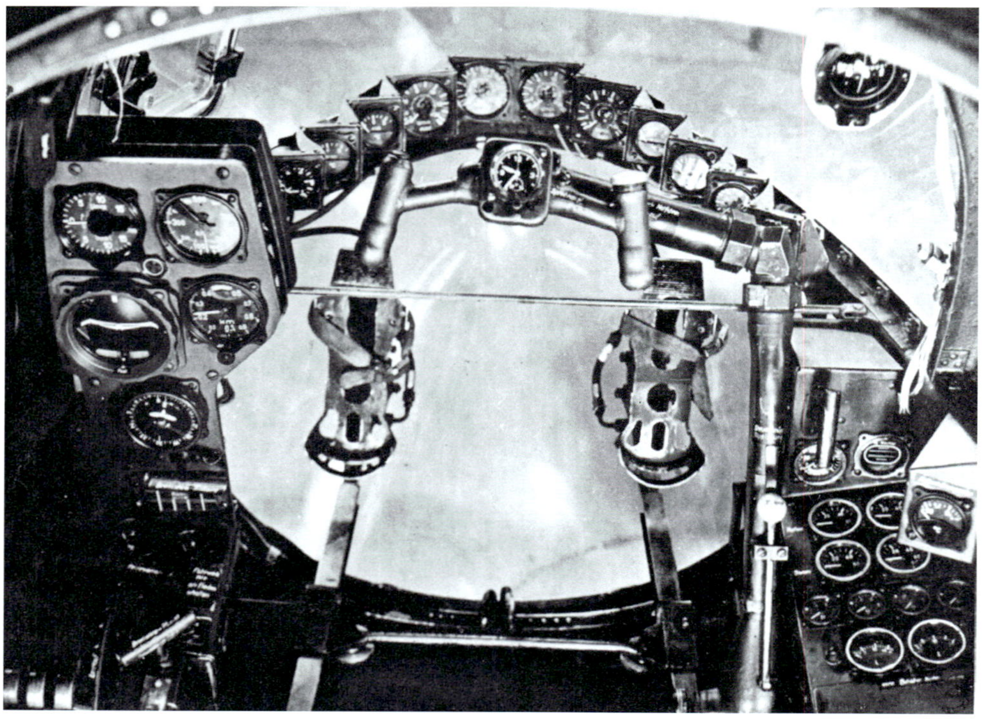

Although few C-series machines were actually ever built, there are some images of the interior and some of the mock-ups, this is one of the former, as it shows the layout of the cockpit within a C-series machine, most likely a C-3 or one of the prototypes

The C-series would have had a revised control yoke to the B-series, as seen in this image

This is the starboard side console in the C-3 mock-up

This is the small stub-panel at the end of the starboard side console; in the C-3 mock-up it would have contained engine controls

This is the vertical instrument panel on the port side of the C-3 cockpit mock-up, which contains the flying controls

Overall view from the front of the C-3 cockpit mock-up

This is the port side console in the C-3 mock-up

This shows the E.370 mock-up and although it is pretty close to the initial machines and has the large access panel in the top, the style, placement and size of the glazed sections are different to what would be used in the prototype and production Ar 234Bs

The first thing to remember with all the skid-equipped prototypes is that the cross-section of the whole of the fuselage is different and this also means that the canopy is different. This shot of the V2 undergoing engine runs show the large hinged canopy access panel that applies to all machines up to the V9

The nose of the V2 viewed from the front, starboard side. Note the large hinged canopy access panel, the fact that the instrument panel does not go across between the side consoles and there are two up-stands that contain the flight instruments on the front of each side console instead. You can probably also see that the nose shape differs from the prototypes after the V9 and the production machines, it is narrower at the bottom

Just to clarify the difference between the prototypes prior to the V9 and the production machines, this montage image shows the V1 on the left and the S10 on the right. Note that the profile of the V1 is much narrower, with the width at the top of the fuselage greater than that at the bottom, thus meaning the fuselage sides are not parallel. The S10 on the other hand has parallel fuselage sides with the curvature at both the top and the bottom of the fuselage being identical. This is all down to the move from skid to retractable undercarriage, as the whole fuselage cross-section had to be increased to take the undercarriage system, and this is how it was done

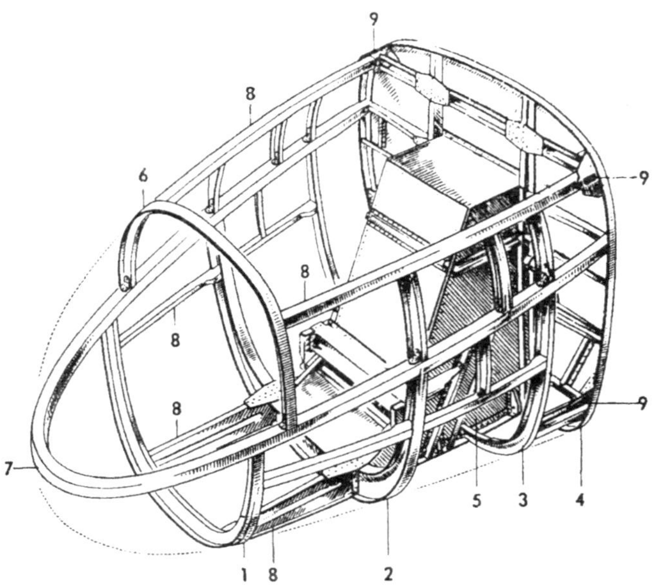

This diagram shows the cockpit/nose components and is applicable to all B-series airframes

Key
1. Spant 1 – Frame 1
2. Spant 2 – Frame 2
3. Spant 3 – Frame 3
4. Spant 4 – Frame 4
5. Bugradschacht – Nose wheel bay
6. Windschirmspant – Windscreen frame
7. Obergurt – Top flange
8. Längersstringer – Longitudinal stringers

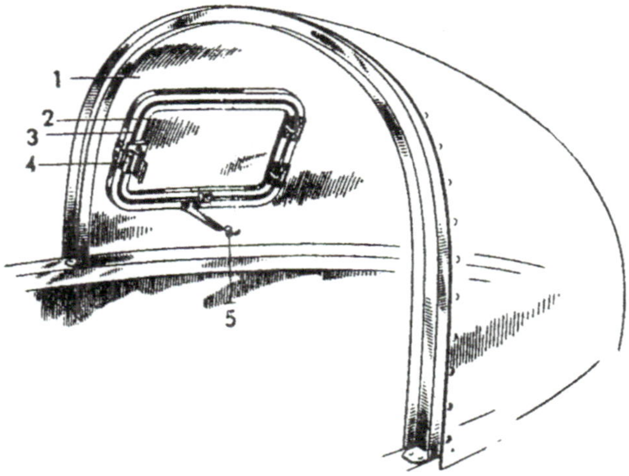

This diagram shows the bad weather panel in the port side of the upper nose glazing in the B-series

Key
1. Windschirm – Windscreen
2. Schlechtwetterscheibe – Bad weather panel
3. Dichtschlauch – Sealing tube
4. Raste für "Zu"-Stellung – Latch to open (literally 'latch for "to" position')
5. Raste für "Offen"-Stellung – Latch for 'open' position

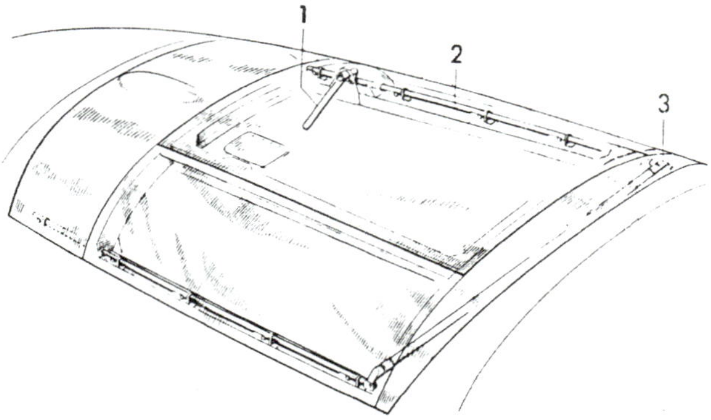

This diagram shows the later style of access hatch, as applies to all machines from the V9 and all aircraft of the B-series

Key
1. Handgriff – Handle
2. Riegelstange – Locking bar
3. Welle – Shaft

Here is a shot of the access hatch in the canopy of NASM's B-2 in the open position; it hinges to starboard *(©Scott Willey)*

Here is a view of the hinge in the back right corner of the access panel, plus you can also see how all the screws holding the Perspex panel in place are countersunk *(©Scott Willey)*

Here is a view of the starboard side of the nose on the NASM example *(©Scott Willey)*

A nice overall shot of the port side of the nose on the NASM example *(©Scott Willey)*

The port side of the nose again, here you can see the foot- and hand-holds, the location of the individual aircraft letter and the electrical connection for the ground power unit. The bad weather panel we showed earlier can been seen in the upper nose panel and the frame for this is glued in situ *(©Scott Willey)*

A close-up of the ground power connection in the port side of the nose *(©Scott Willey)*

Here you can see the battery access panel as a long unit in the middle of this image, the cover also doubles as a foot-hold, while above it is a hand-hold and then a small air scoop and below it is an oblong access panel, with a push-button to open it

This period image from the manual shows how the battery access panel hinges down on opening

From this angle looking back along the port side of the nose you can probably make out the transit joint between the nose and fuselage, if not it is covered with fabric and situated just aft of the battery access panel, and ahead of the oval panel on the lower edge. Note the long panel on the underside, these were access panels for the intended location of nose-mounted cannon, which were never installed on the B-series *(©Scott Willey)*

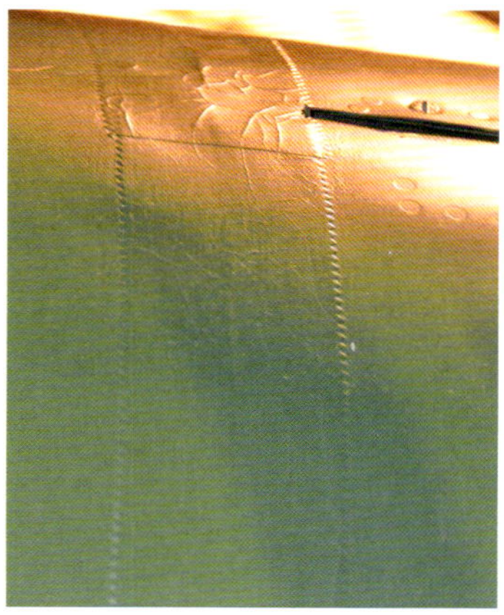

With a bit of contrast from the light, here you can clearly see the pinking done to the fabric strip that sealed the transit joint between the nose and main fuselage *(©Scott Willey)*

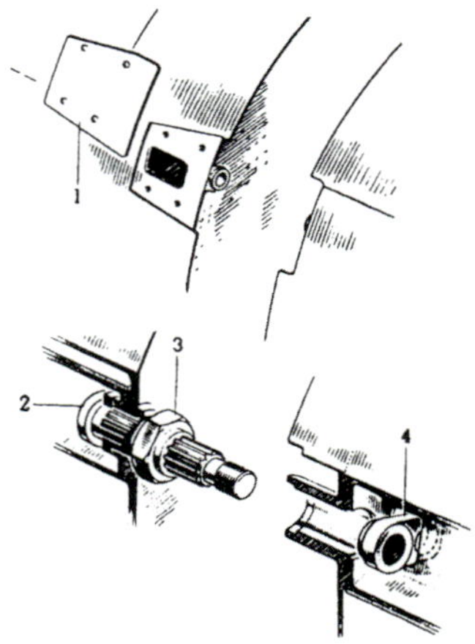

This diagram shows how the nose section joins to the main fuselage

Key
1. Schraubblech – Removable (screw) plate
2. Keilnutenbolzen – Splined bolt
3. Sechskantnabe – Hexagonal boss
4. Mutter – Receiving collar (literally 'mother' e.g. to bring up)

A close-up of the blade antenna, this is probably a sensor panel as it remains unpainted *(©Scott Willey)*

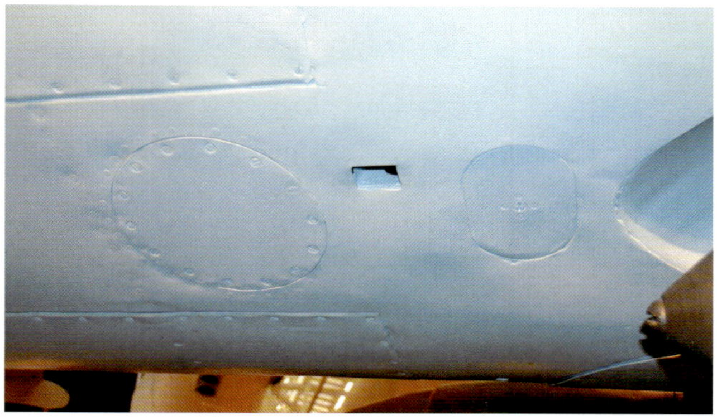

Going under the nose of the B-2 now, to the left you can see the aft section of both of the gun access panels we mentioned earlier (the guns were never installed in the B-series) plus an oval and round access panel, a small square hole, which is probably a hang-over from the armament and right at the back (right) the nose of the ventrally-slung bomb and the contoured recess above it *(©Scott Willey)*

If we now go forward, right up under the nose, you can see the Loft 7C bombsight head to the left and the little blade antenna to the right (starboard) *(©Scott Willey)*

Looking straight up under the nose cone you can see into the cockpit with the Lofte 7C bombsight, rudder pedals and instrument panel, but you can also probably make out the thin black line applied inside the glazing on the centreline; this is not a join it is a datum line for sighting purposes *(©Scott Willey)*

Here is a close-up of the head of the Lofte 7C bombsight, note the heater wire inside the lens *(©Scott Willey)*

This shot is included so you can see the relative position of the little blade antenna that we included in another shot earlier in this section, along with the vent port and various access panels on the lower starboard side of the nose *(©Scott Willey)*

An overall view of the starboard side of the nose, proves this is pretty smooth and lacking the access steps etc. that are on the port side *(©Scott Willey)*

This is the rear of the electrical distribution panel inside the cockpit that is visible through the side glazing on the starboard side, obviously covering this from the outside was considered a waste of time and resources *(©Scott Willey)*

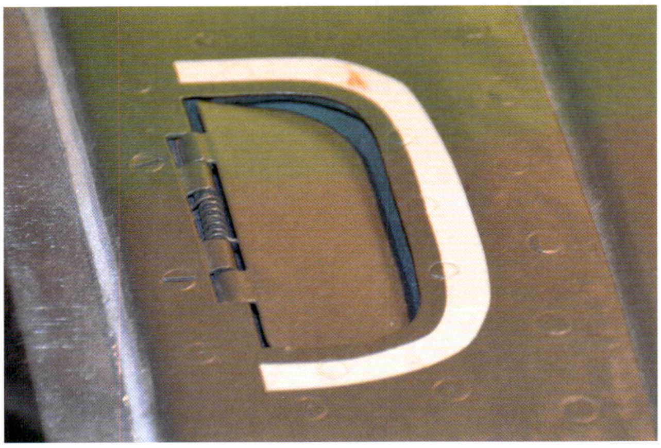

In the centre top of the cockpit area, aft of the access panel, you will find this hand-hold *(©Scott Willey)*

If you go directly forward from the hand-hold on the upper nose, you will find this hinged access panel within the main access panel in the roof of the cockpit *(©Scott Willey)*

A lovely overall shot of the starboard side of the nose in the B-2, showing all the screws attaching the clear panels to the black framework, but also just how much of the interior is visible in this 'goldfish bowl' of a cockpit *(©Scott Willey)*

From directly in front you can see how glare would have been an issue due to the complex curves and the extensive glazing of the nose region *(©Scott Willey)*

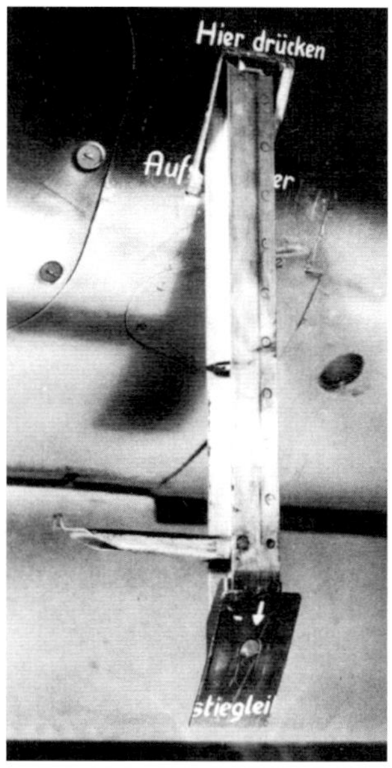

The revised nose of the C-3 and C-4 also meant that the access step arrangement was revised, with this fold-down ladder extending out of the port side of the nose/ forward fuselage, just aft of the access panel for the nose-mounted gun that is visible on the left; this is the installation in the V21

The C-series had a totally revised nose section, as seen here with the mock-up of the C-3. You can also clearly see the gun port low on the fuselage side, as the C-3 and C-4 were to have an MG 151/20 cannon either side of the nose

The revised nose of the C-3 and the C-4 coupled with pressurisation meant that the crew access door was also changed, as seen here. This is again the V21, but this installation applies to the C-3 and C-4 as well as all projected versions based on them

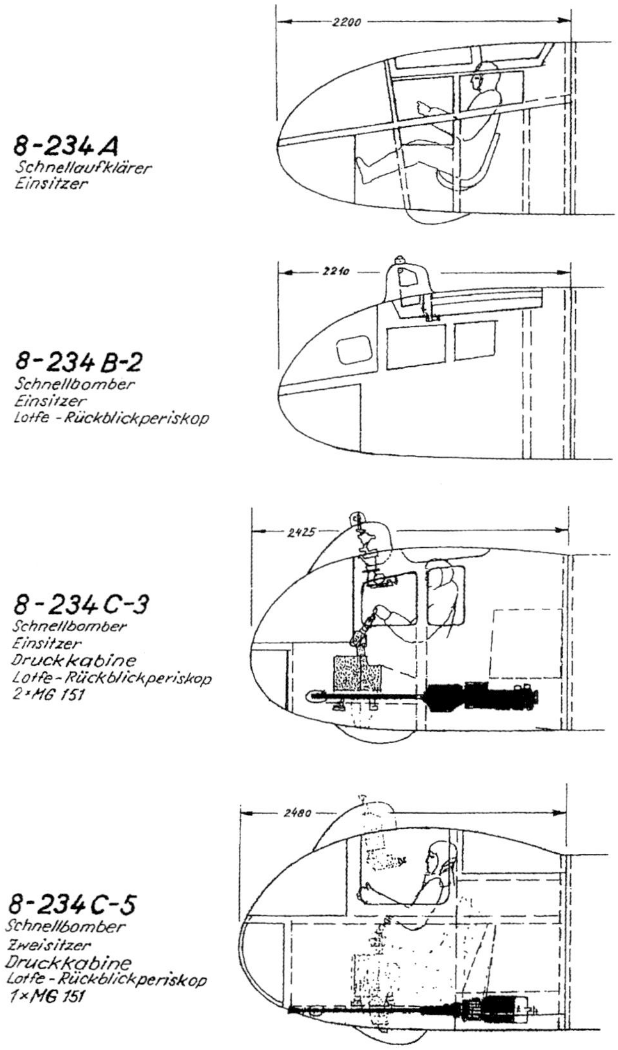

An interesting diagram showing the evolution of the forward cockpit section from the original A-series through the B and on to the C-3 and projected C-5, which shows all the real major changes in the front end of the Ar 234 series

This diagram shows all the various components that go to make up the entire fuselage assembly

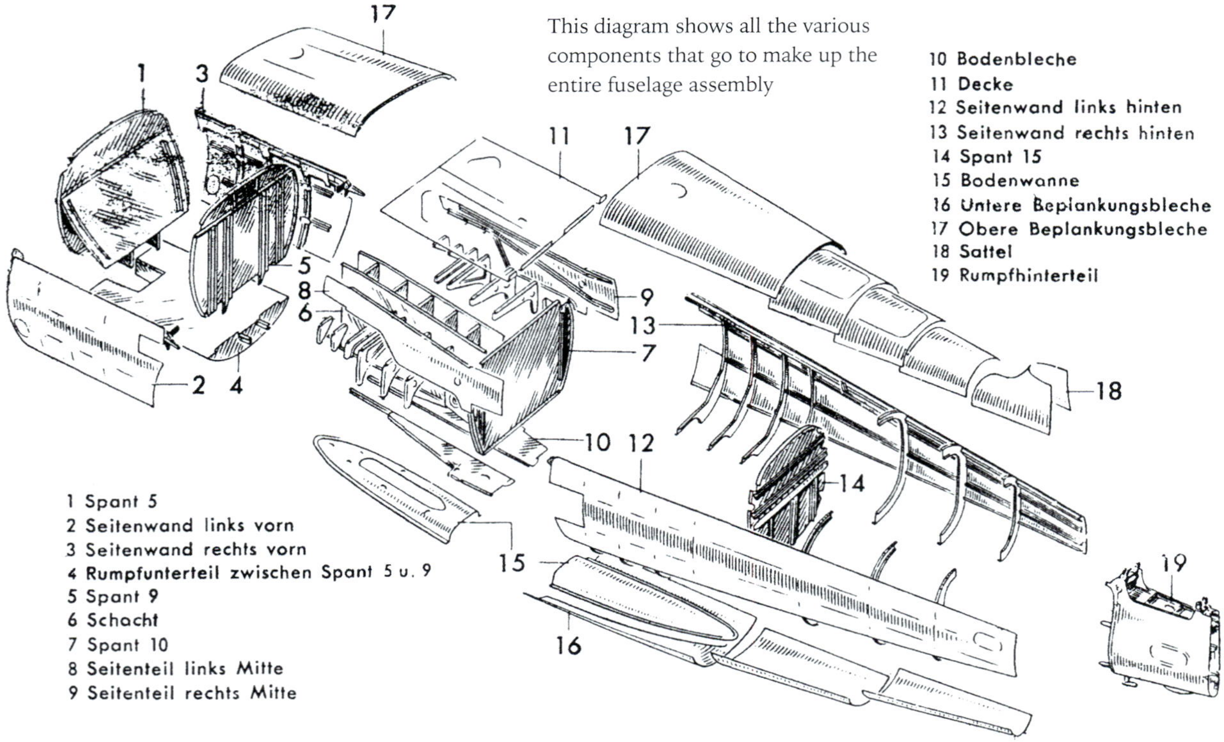

This is the port side of NASM's B-2, the panel you can see on the top is the aft camera bay, the forward one is just visible ahead of it. The larger panel to the extreme left is the panel above the aft fuel cell, with the round panel probably to get to the pumps and drains for the tank. The braking parachute housing can be made out under the fuselage to the right *(©Scott Willey)*

This is the starboard fuselage side, with the aft camera access panel visible to the left, the forward bay just ahead of it and the big panel to the right for the fuel tank *(©Scott Willey)*

This period photo of the V13 during construction clearly shows the two camera access bays at the rear of the fuselage, the access panels ahead of this for things like the fuel and oil systems, with the gentleman actually sitting in the bay for the front fuel cell. Note how small the inboard flaps sections are, plus the access panels for the control linkage in the aft fuselage side

A look back towards the tail of NASM's machine, you can just make out the round access panel for the aft fuel tank plus the two panels for the cameras behind that. Once again the fact that many panels are proud of the rest of the skin is of note *(©Scott Willey)*

Here is a closer look at how the parachute cable attaches under the tail *(©Scott Willey)*

Here is the dorsal spine of the forward fuselage section, the big panel here is for access to the front fuel tank *(©Scott Willey)*

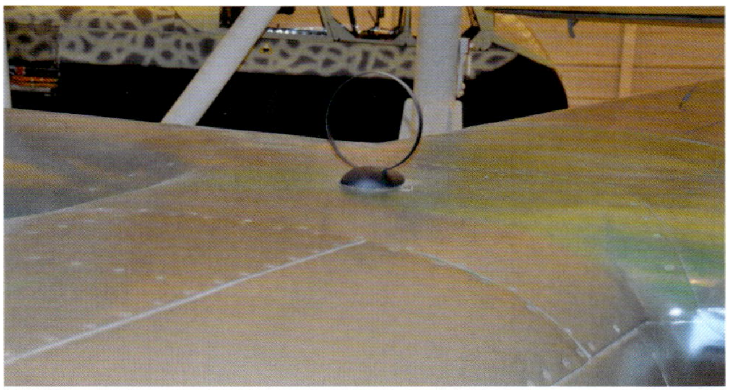

The mid-upper section of the fuselage above the wings, with a D/F loop in this location on the NASM example, but no sign of a Peil G.IV D/F loop and cover on this particular machine. Note how all the panels are screwed down and how many of them are proud of the rest of the airframe skin *(©Scott Willey)*

Up under the tail you have a braking parachute, the unit itself is under the square cover further back, with it linked to the anchor point under the tail via a steel cable *(©Scott Willey)*

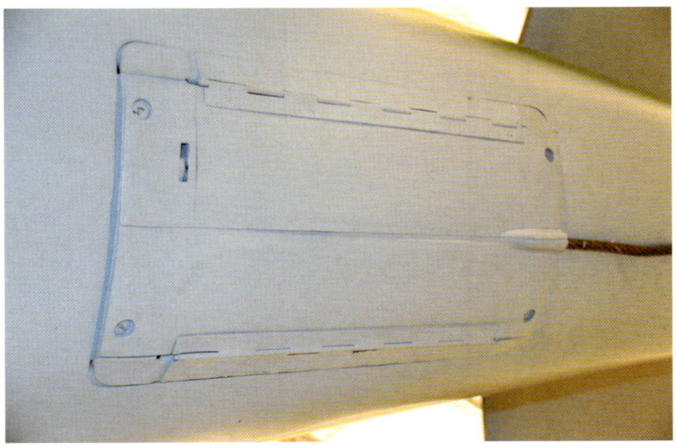

Here are the doors for the braking parachute under the rear fuselage, with the cable to the tail on the right *(©Scott Willey)*

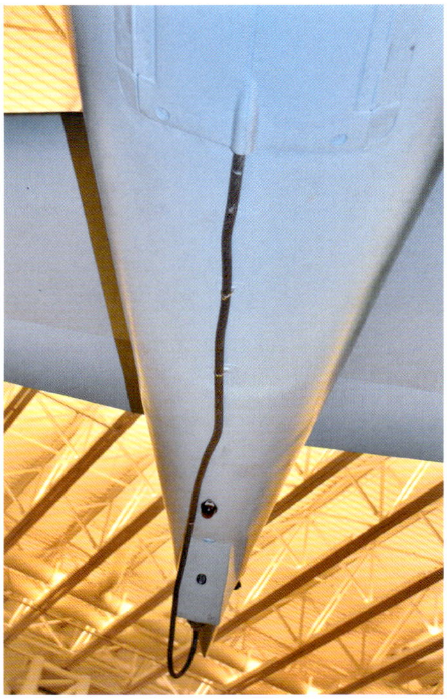

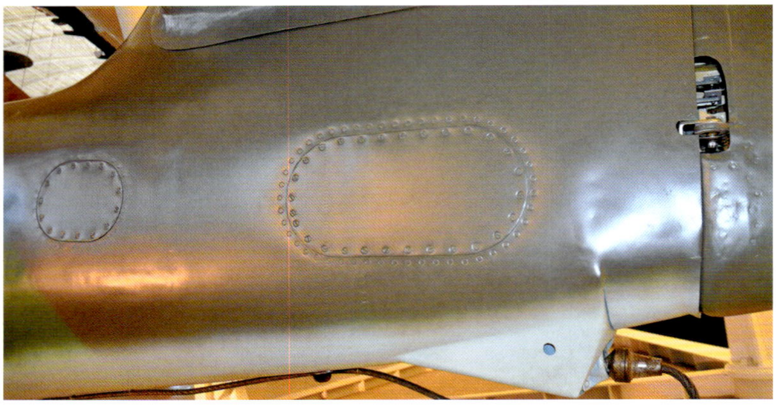

Up under the tail on the port side you will find these two large access panels, which relate to the control linkage within the fuselage at this point *(©Scott Willey)*

Looking back towards the rear under the fuselage you can see the cable running to the mounting underneath the tail, plus the red formation light that the cable bypasses *(©Scott Willey)*

Here is a close-up of the red formation light under the rear fuselage, with the brake parachute cable on its left *(©Scott Willey)*

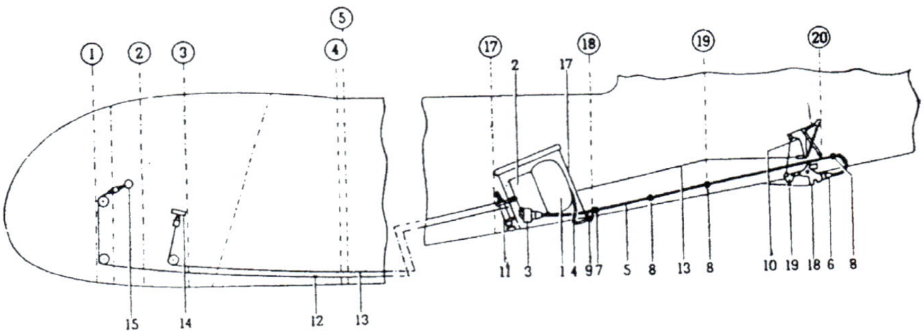

This diagram shows the braking parachute installation

Key

1. Bänderschirm – Braking parachute (literally ‘ribbons’ (or ‘bands’), ‘umbrella’ (or ‘Parasol’))
2. Packtasche mit Seilen – Pack, parachute chord
3. Seilanschlußglocke – Cable connection cover
4. Reißleine – Release chord
5. Bremsschirmseil – Parachute cable
6. Anschlußöse – Connecting eyelet
7. Seilhalterungsöse – Eyelet, rope holding
8. Seilhalterungsöse – Eyelet, rope holding
9. Schelle – Clamp
10. Öffnungsvorrichtung – Opening mechanism
11. Abwurfvorrichtung (Sperre) – Release device (lock)
12. Seilzug für Öffnen – Cable for opening (release)
13. Seilzug für Abwurf – Cable for discarding (detaching)
14. Handriff für Abwurf – Handle for opening (release)
15. Handgriff für Öffnen – Handle for discarding (detaching)
16. Bremmsschirmkasten – Parachute box
17. Bremsschirmgehäuse – Braking parachute housing
18. Seilkupplung – Cable clutch
19. Anzeigeschraube – Indicator screw

The parachute cable is kept in place by wire ‘snap loops’ as seen here; there are three along its length *(©Scott Willey)*

This is the forward camera access panel on the dorsal spine, viewed from the rear on the starboard side *(©Scott Willey)*

This is the aft camera access panel on the dorsal spine, again viewed from the rear on the starboard side *(©Scott Willey)*

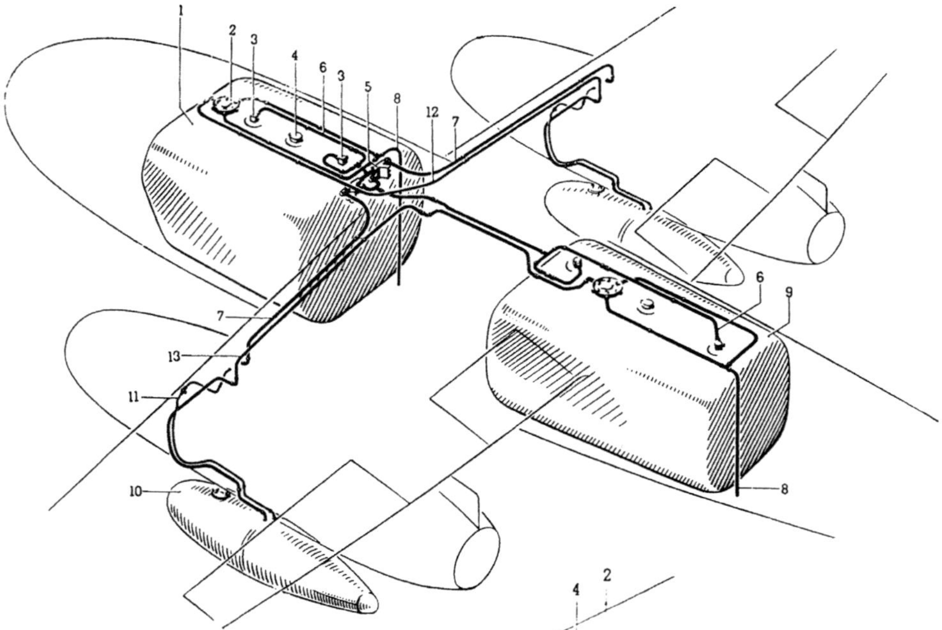

This diagram shows the fuel system fitted to the Ar 234B-series

Key

1. Vorderer Kraftstoffbehälter – Front fuel tank
2. Behälterfüllkopf – Fuel tank filler
3. Behälterkraftstoffpumpe – Fuel pump
4. Tauchrohr für Kraftstoffvorratsmessung – Dipstick tube
5. Ventilbatterien mit Brandhahn – Valve cluster with fuel cock
6. Vorlaufleitungen zu den Ventilbatterien – Supply lines to the drop tanks
7. Vorlaufleitungen zu den Triebwerken – Supply lines to the engines
8. Abtropf- und Entlüftungsleitungen – Drip and ventilation pipes
9. Hinterer Kraftstoffbehälter – Rear fuel tank
10. Zusatzbehälter für Kraftstoff – Drop tanks
11. Druckluftleitung zwischen Lader und Zusatzbehälter – Compressed air lines between main and drop tanks
12. Umpumpleitung zum vorderen Kraftstoffbehälter – Recirculating line from front fuel tank
13. Umpumpleitung zum hinteren Kraftstoffbehälter – Recirculating lines from rear fuel tank

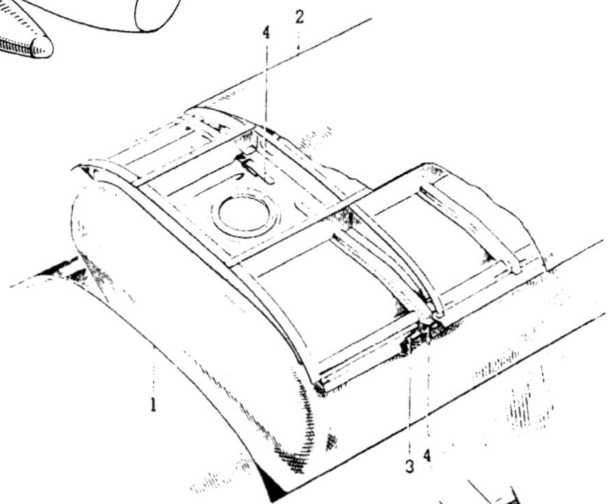

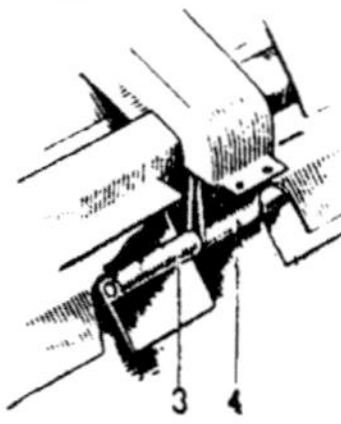

This diagrams shows how the fuel tank is suspended in the fuselage, both tanks being the same

Key

1. Sackbehälter – Fuel cell (literally 'bag container')
2. Rumpfdeckel – Access panel (literally 'hull cover')
3. Aufhängeschlaufen – Suspension loops
4. Aufhängeriemen – Hanging straps

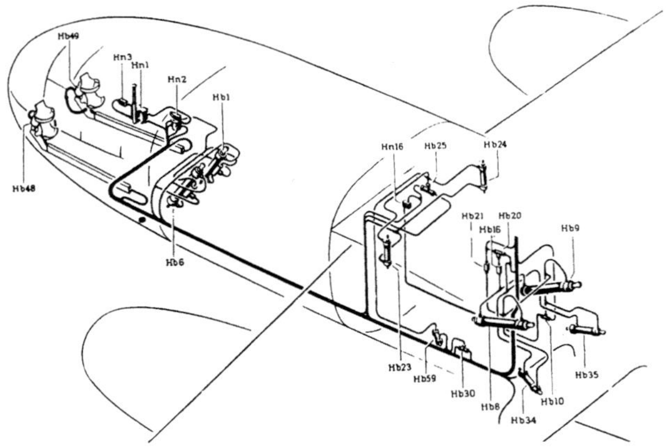

This diagram shows the hydraulic system in the Ar 234B, with Hb 8 & 9 operating the main undercarriage legs, Hb 1 & 6 the nose leg, Hb 23 & 24 the ailerons and Hb 48 & 49 the rudder pedals to the elevators via Hb 34 & 35

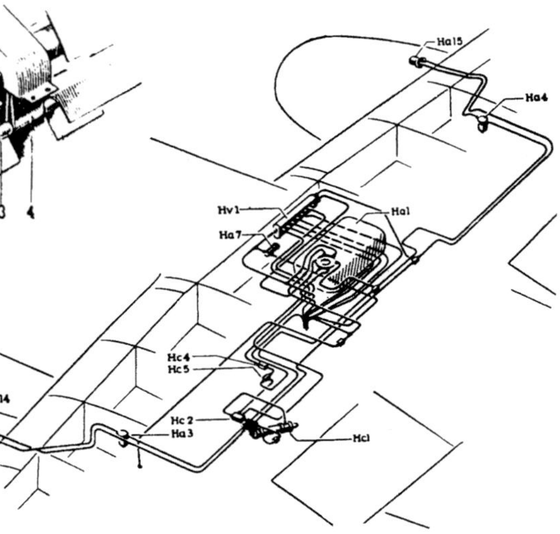

This diagram shows the oil pressure system in the Ar 234B, with the header tank (Ha 1) in the fuselage, the accumulator (Hv 1) ahead of it and the relief valve (Mc 1) in the port wing, accessible via an access panel underneath. Ha 14 and 15 are the sensors in each engine gearbox, while Ha 3 and Ha 4 look to be filter units. All the remaining units are links and switches

Note: None of the surviving documents for the Ar 234 include a pneumatic system diagram

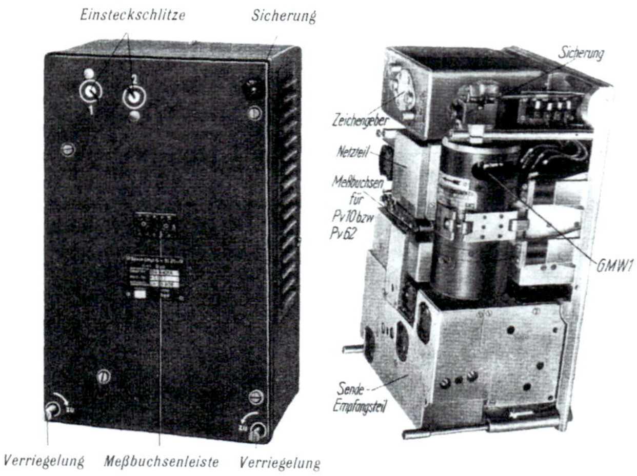

The IFF system installed in the Ar 234 was the FuG 25A, which responded to Freya, Würzburg and Jadgschloss systems. This image from the manual shows the unit with and without cover

Here is the rod antenna for the FuG 25A situated under the tip of the port wing and seen here on NASM's B-2 *(©Scott Willey)*

A closer look at the FuG 25A antenna *(©Scott Willey)*

Now there is a bit of confusion with the Ar 234, because in service you will see images that confirm the fitment of this, what looks to be a D/F (direction finding) loop on the dorsal spine, either up near the point where the wings meet the fuselage, as here on the NASM machine, or further aft towards the tail. The problem is that sources vary as to the use of this loop, as some state it is for the FuG 25A system (for which we have already seen the rod antenna under the port wing?), while others state it is a D/F loop even though the Ar 234B and C would have had the Peil G.IV system installed (confirmed by the schematics for the B-2, which show this on the dorsal spine under a clear panel); either way, check your references, as in-service Ar 234s had a mix of fitment and location for D/F loop and/or Peil D/F system *(©Scott Willey)*

The base of the FuG 25A and the antenna itself seems to be rubber-coated *(©Scott Willey)*

This period photo of the tail of the V10 clarifies where the D/F loop could be situated, when farther back on the dorsal spine

Very little remains about the Peil G.IV (surpressed) direction finder system as far as images go, this poor period shot does show the unit though, which would have been mounted in the dorsal spine of the Ar 234, just ahead of where the D/F loop seen elsewhere in this section was often positioned. The cover is clear plastic, the radiating arms are bare metal and the container is probably RLM 02; the antenna itself, inside the unit is actually dark brown with the metal straps around it in gloss black going by those examples of Luftwaffe WWII-era D/F loops I have seen (e.g. Ju 87G)

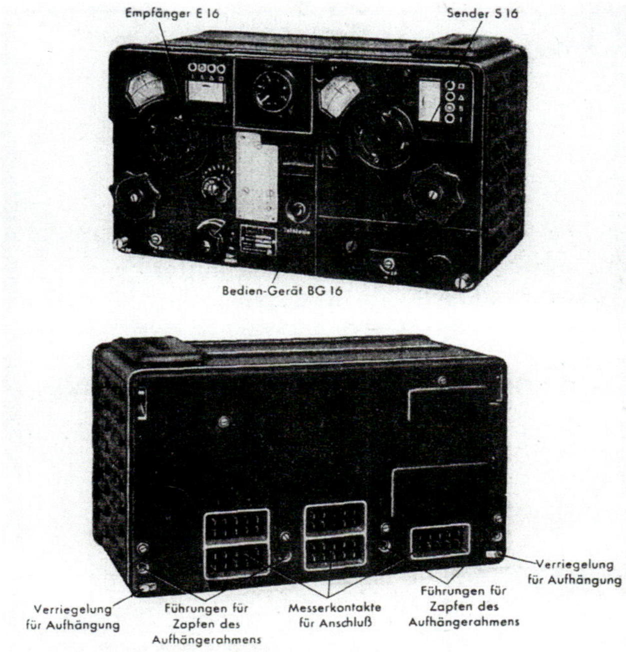

The radio used in the Ar 234 was the FuG 16, either as the Z or ZY version. This is the transmitter/receiver unit itself

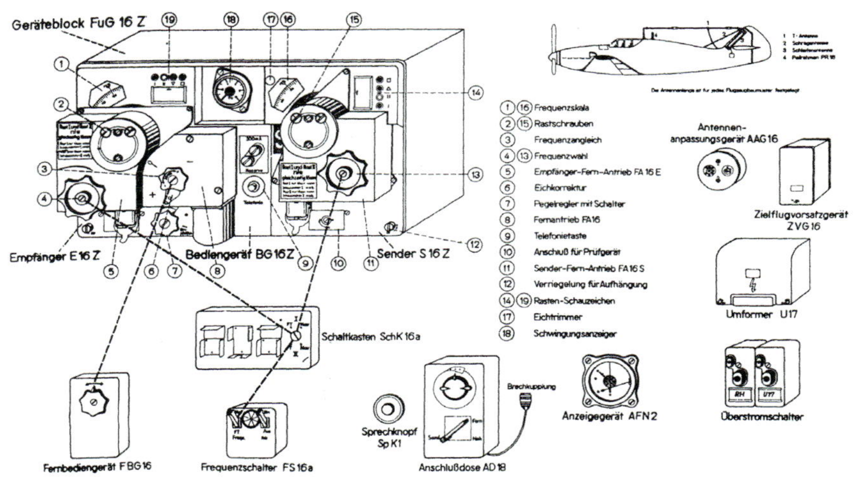

Here is the standard installation of the FuG 16Z in a single-seat fighter

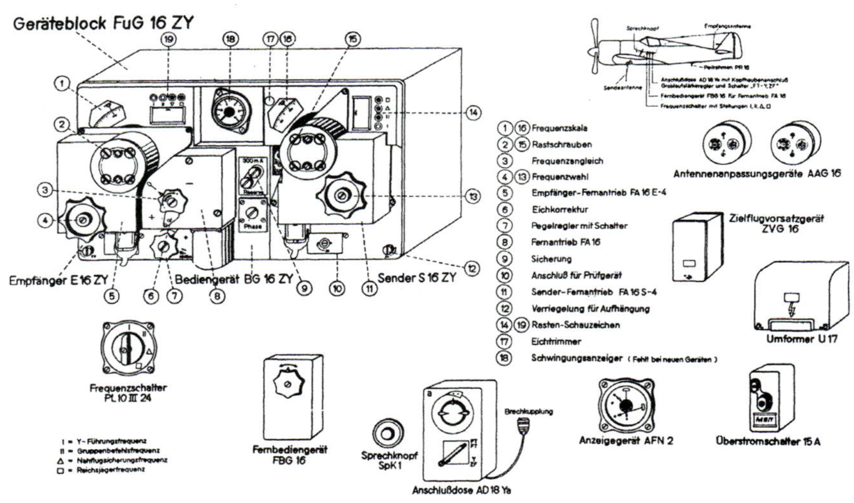

This is the installation of the FuG 16ZY system in a single-seat fighter

The transmitting aerial for the FuG 16Z and ZY ran from the top of the vertical fin as seen here on NASM's B-2 *(©Scott Willey)*

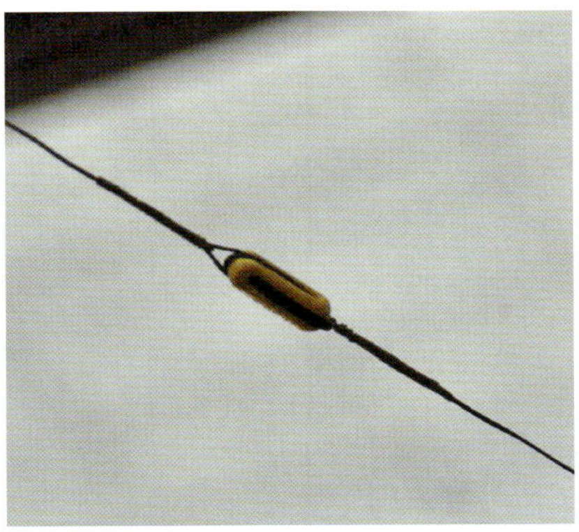

Just after the join to the fin, the lead has this ceramic insulator inserted into it *(©Scott Willey)*

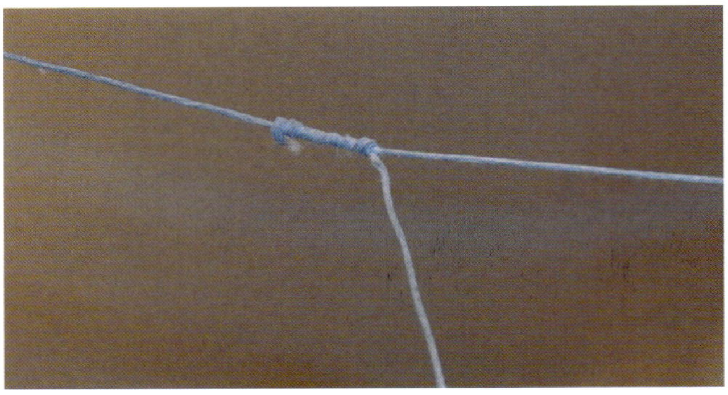

The lead then splits as seen here, with the lower one entering the dorsal spine ahead of the vertical fin and the other end going down to the dorsal spine at a point parallel to the wing trailing edge *(©Scott Willey)*

Here is the pick-up for the lead on the dorsal spine, as you can see it is just a simple hook and loop arrangement, the lead does not go inside the fuselage at this point, it did that already nearer the vertical fin *(©Scott Willey)*

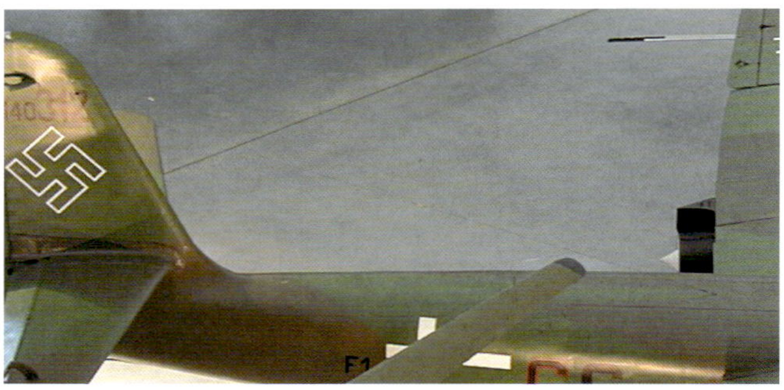

This overall shot of NASM's B-2 shows the route of the aerial lead from the fin to the dorsal spine, with two insulators visible, fore and aft of the split in the wire *(©Scott Willey)*

Very, very few images exist of the FuG 218 Neptun radar installation in the Ar 234B-2/N, this one, although of poor quality shows the prototype installation. Note how the antenna arms come out through the nose glazing *(via Internet)*

The question remains, where is the receiver aerial for the FuG 16, as this would either be a 'washing line' antenna under the aft fuselage or a 'Morane Mast' under the starboard wing, neither of which the Ar 234 has? The answer is this, the antenna is inside the leading edge of the vertical fin. Under the panel you can see up the front of the fin is a simple wire from top to bottom, looking a bit like a heater element, and this is the receiver for the FuG 16Z or ZY system. This is why the front half of the leading edge of the fin on the Ar 234 has that fabric covering along the joint you may be able to see here on NASM's machine, with the zig-zag edges; there is a good chance, as I have never seen the type apart, that the leading edge cover at this point may therefore not be metal, it may be plastic or even wood? *(©Scott Willey)*

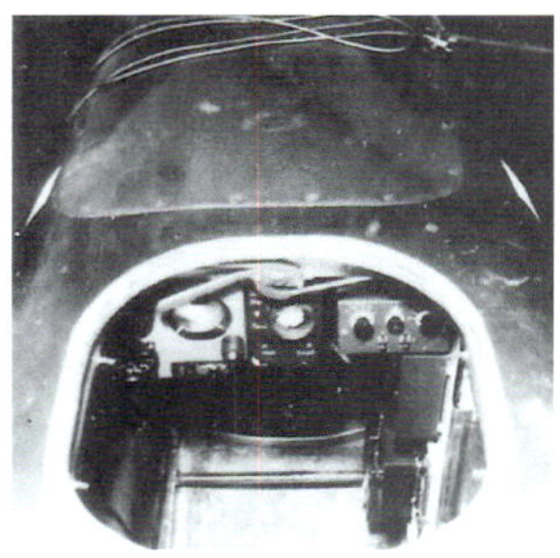

Along with the radar antenna on the nose of the B-2/N, the camera bay in the aft fuselage was used to house a radar operator. This photo, although poor quality, shows this set-up in one of the prototypes and you are looking aft with the compartment at the bottom thus being the forward ex-camera bay, and the aft camera bay cover can be seen at the top. Note the revised shape of the access panel in comparison with those originally used over the camera bay and note that this was first covered with a solid plate, which was bolted from the outside(!), but later received a Perspex cover over it *(via Internet)*

This photo shows the centreline skid underneath the V1 during construction

This front view of the V1 on its trolley clearly shows that initially, the outrigger skids under each nacelle were not supported by the trolley in any way

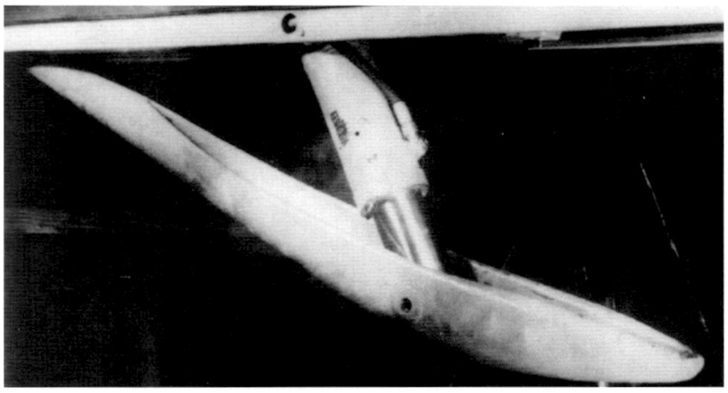

Here is a close-up of the outrigger skid under one nacelle, these were revised slightly from the V5 onwards

From the V3 onwards the trolley was revised, with the outrigger skids also being supported by additional arms added each side of the main trolley body. Here you can see the slightly revised central skid and the port outrigger frame bolted to the trolley, plus the starboard skid itself resting on the new supporting arm in the background

left: This is another view of the trolley from the V3 onwards, clearly showing the new supporting arms for the outrigger skids under the engines

The V3-onwards style trolley viewed towards the front, aircraft and trolley separated via a standard bomb release mechanism

At the front of the trolley used on the V3 onwards you have the 360° castoring wheel, plus the foot-step assembly that is only fitted on the port side; many times this image is published flipped horizontally, thus seeming to show this foot-step on the starboard side

The skids under each nacelle were slightly modified with the V5 and V7 onwards, as seen here they are slightly deeper, probably to give a better lead-in on striking the ground initially

The trolley under the V5 viewed from the rear, the pipes from the back of the skid are the brake lines, which snap on release and thus activate the brakes to slow the trolley. The pads under the outrigger skids are probably wooden blocks

The V6, which was powered with two BMW 003s had a similar layout of both skids and trolley, as seen here in this view from the starboard side. The only difference is probably the size of the outrigger skids, as the 003 nacelles were deeper than those for the 004

An overall view of the revised trolley on the V5 from the front, you can see the bomb release unit in the middle, under the skid

All of the V-series machines had a braking parachute in a spring-mounted box at the back of the trolley, as seen here on the V5. The only exceptions to this were on the initial V1 flights, where first there were two parachutes, one mounted on either side of the main body of the trolley, towards the rear axle housing. This was then revised to move these two parachutes slightly forward, to balance the trolley on its descent (it was actually dropped from the aircraft once airborne at this stage), before finally being moved to the rear of the trolley to slow the unit after separating just at the point of take-off

The four-engine prototypes used a similar trolley to the twin-engined prototypes, as seen here under the V6. However, a close study of the various shots of those machines with the four separate nacelles seems to point to the fact that the tubes for the outrigger support arms are of heavier gauge and look to have edges, which could mean they are made of a diamond-shaped cross-section, due to the increased weight outboard of them caused by the additional engines? The outermost skids were not supported in any way

The V9 was the first test airframe to have a tricycle, fully-retractable undercarriage fitted, as seen in this period image

The lack of any bombsight etc., and the fact this period image focuses on the nose wheel, probably denotes that this shows the V9 or one of the other early V-series machines with the retractable undercarriage. Note the cross-thread pattern to the tyre

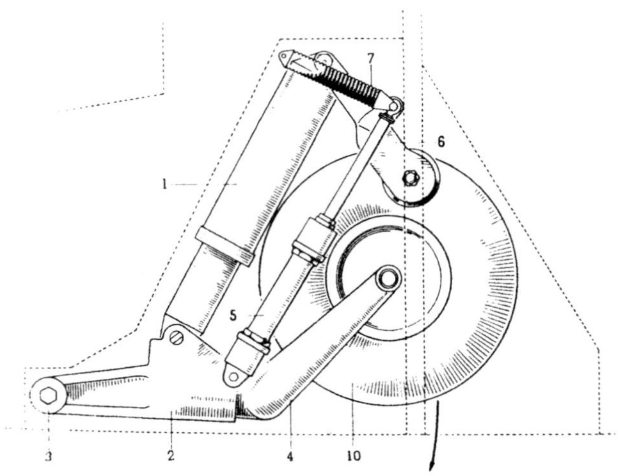

Here is the nose wheel in the fully retracted position

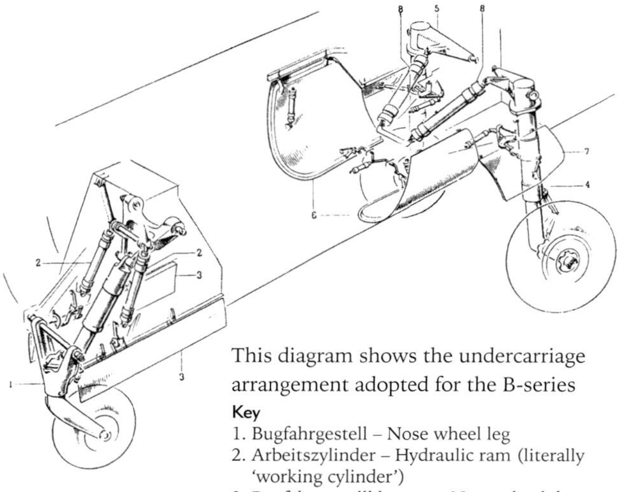

This diagram shows the undercarriage arrangement adopted for the B-series

Key
1. Bugfahrgestell – Nose wheel leg
2. Arbeitszylinder – Hydraulic ram (literally 'working cylinder')
3. Bugfahrgestellklappen – Nose wheel door
4. Linkes Hauptfahrgestell – Left main undercarriage leg
5. Rechtes Hauptfahrgestell – Right main undercarriage leg
6. Große Hauptfahrgestellklappen – Large main undercarriage door
7. KleineHauptfahrgestellklappen – Small main undercarriage door
8. Arbeitszylinder – Hydraulic ram (literally 'working cylinder')

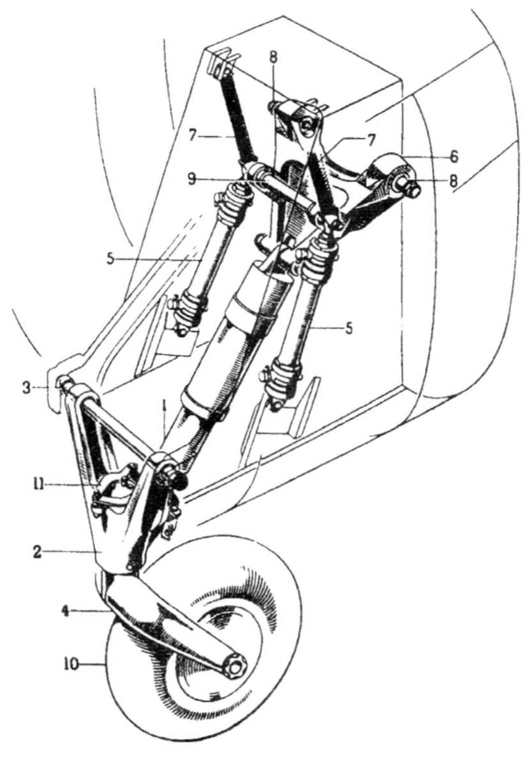

A more detailed diagram of the B-series nose wheel unit

Key
1. Federbein – Strut
2. Anschlußbrücke – Wire bridge
3. Anschlußrohr – Connection tube
4. Bugradgabel – Nose wheel yoke (castoring)
5. Arbeitszlinder für Bugfahrgestell – Hydraulic ram for nose oleo
6. Schwenkbeschlag – Pivot point
7. Federzylinder – Spring
8. Lagerbolzen – Bearing bolt
9. Lagerrohr – Bearing tube
10. Bugrad – Nose wheel
11. Spurzwang – Up-lock assembly

This diagram shows the nose wheel undercarriage doors

Key
1. Bugfahrgestellklappen – Nose wheel doors
2. Klappenlager – Hinge (literary 'fold bearing')
3. Klappenbügel – Hinged bar
4. Falle – Catch
5. Klinke – Ratchet
6. Sprungfeder – Spring

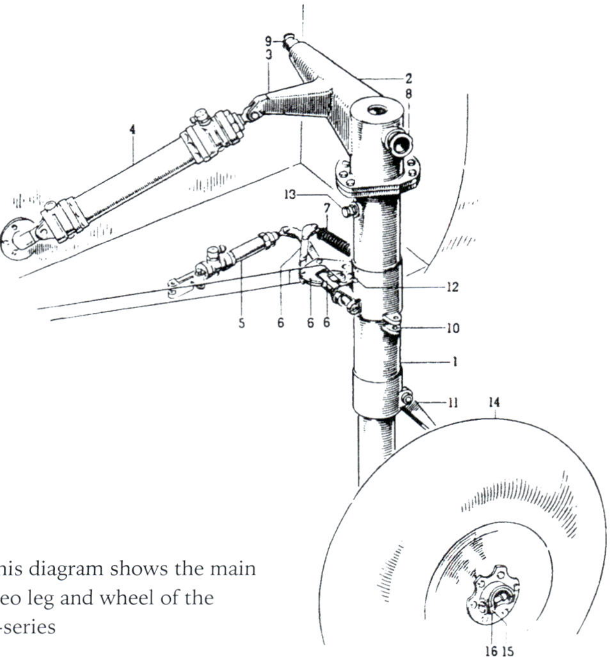

This diagram shows the main oleo leg and wheel of the B-series

Key
1. Federbein – Oleo strut
2. Schwenkachse – Swivel axis (casting)
3. Schwenkachsenhebel – Arm swivel axis actuating
4. Arbeitszylinder für Hauptfahrgestell – Hydraulic cylinders for main undercarriage
5. Verriegelungsvorrichtung für Hauptfahrgestell – Locking device for main undercarriage
6. Verriegelungsvorrichtung – Locking device linkage
7. Druckfeder – Compression spring
8. Steckachse – Through axle
9. Riegelbeschlag der Steckachse für Bajonettverriegelung – Bolt fitting (literally 'Bolt fitted the front axle for bayonet locking')
10. Anlenkstelle für Klappenbetätigung – Mount for linkage to main undercarriage door
11. Lenkhebel – Compression linkage arms
12. Schmiernippel – Grease nipple
13. Füllverschraubung – Connector (threaded for hydraulic fluid renewal)
14. Laufrad – Wheel
15. Laufradachse – Wheel axle
16. Achskappe – Axle (hub) cap

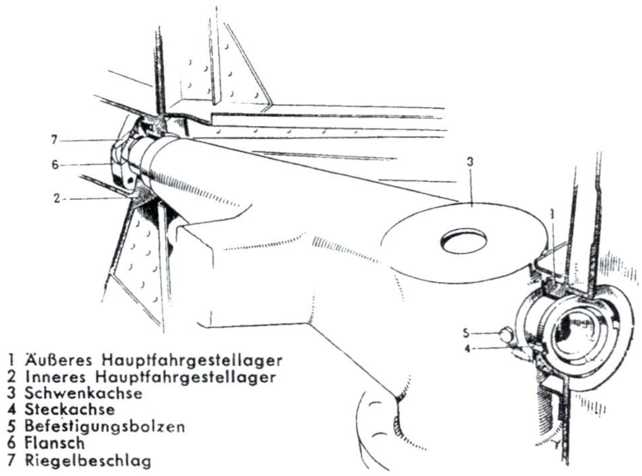

Here is a close-up of the swivel axis casting at the top of each main oleo leg

An overall view from the front of the nose wheel on NASM's B-2 *(©Scott Willey)*

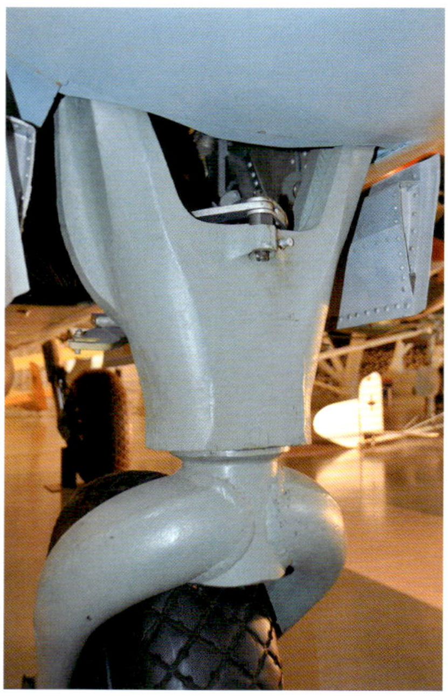

A close-up of the upper section of the nose wheel casting *(©Scott Willey)*

A vew from the rear of the nose wheel assembly *(©Scott Willey)*

A look up into the front of the nose wheel well on the NASM example *(©Scott Willey)*

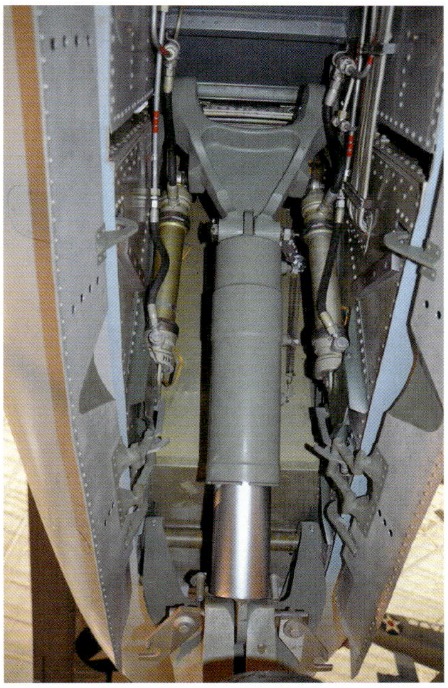

A overall look at the mid and front section of the nose wheel well *(©Scott Willey)*

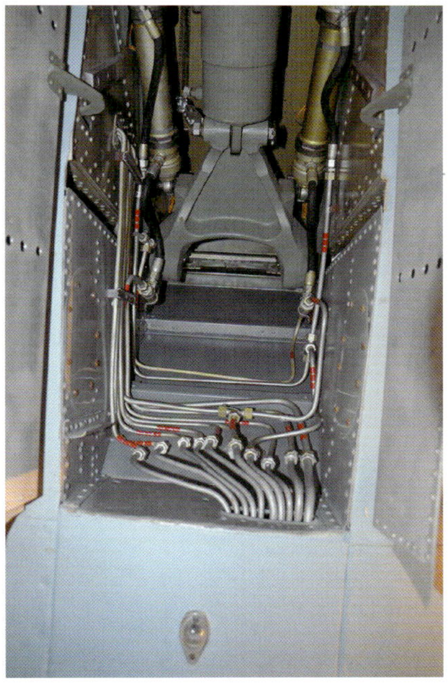

The rear area of the nose wheel well *(©Scott Willey)*

This diagram shows the main wheel undercarriage doors

Key

1. Große Hauptfahrgestellklappen – Large main wheel doors
2. Kleine Hauptfahrgestellklappen – Small main wheel doors
3. Arbeitszylinder für große Hauptfahrgestellklappe – Hydraulic operating ram for the large main wheel doors
4. Arbeitszylinder für kleine Hauptfahrgestellklappe – Hydraulic operating ram for the small main wheel doors
5. Lagerbolzen für große Hauptfahrgestellklappe – Hinge pins for the undercarriage doors
6. Verriegelungszylinder – Latching cylinder
7. Stroßstange – Bumper
8. Klinke – Pin ratchet
9. Drücker – Bracket
10. Einstellschraube – Adjustment screw
11. Führung – Guide
12. Druckstange – Plunger rod
13. Zapfen am Pratzenträger – Pins on the undercarriage doors

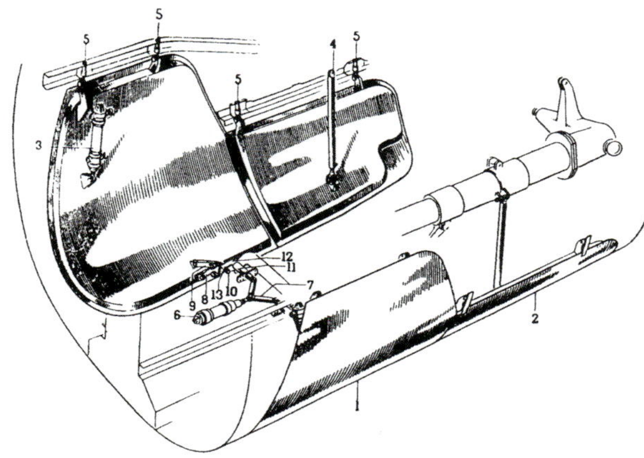

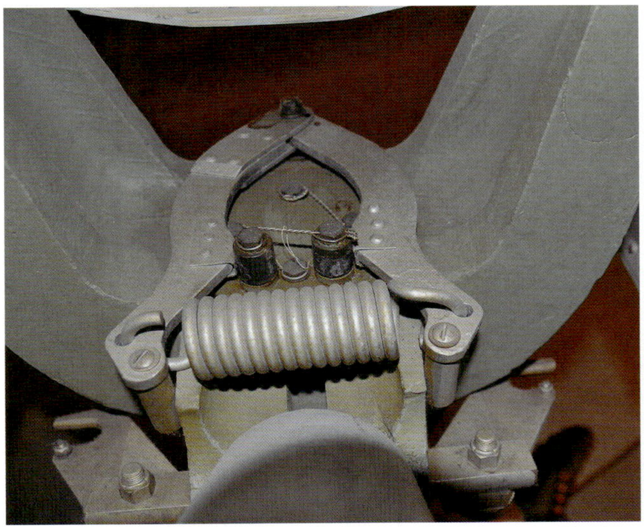

This mechanism atop the yoke of the nose wheel assembly is to dampen the castoring of this unit and stop the whole thing rotating once the weight of the airframe is off it, so it can retract into the wheel well without jamming or damaging the airframe; the front of the aircraft is to the top of this image *(©Scott Willey)*

Here is the back of the damper on the nose oleo, viewed from behind, looking forward *(©Scott Willey)*

Here you can see the nose wheel door along with the hinges and linkage (©Scott Willey)

An overall view of the nose wheel, this is 630x220mm and as you can see, is welded steel (©Scott Willey)

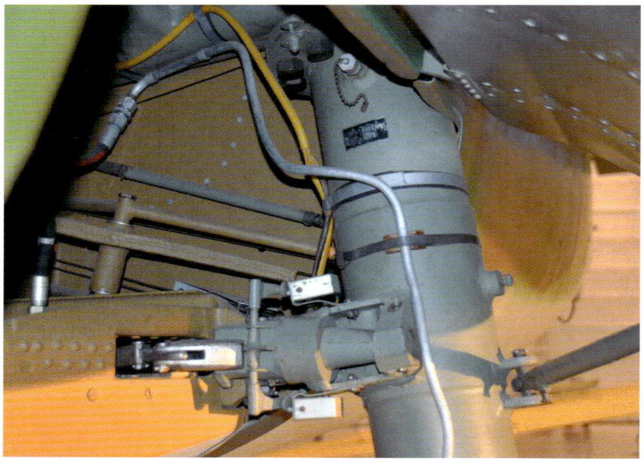

The top section of the port oleo leg, viewed from the front (©Scott Willey)

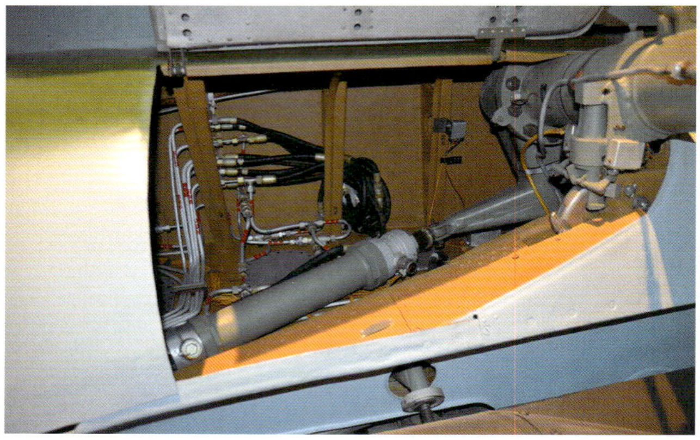

A view up into the port main undercarriage well, the front of the aircraft is to the left of the picture and the original colour of this area is reproduced; it was a yellow-tan colour (©Scott Willey)

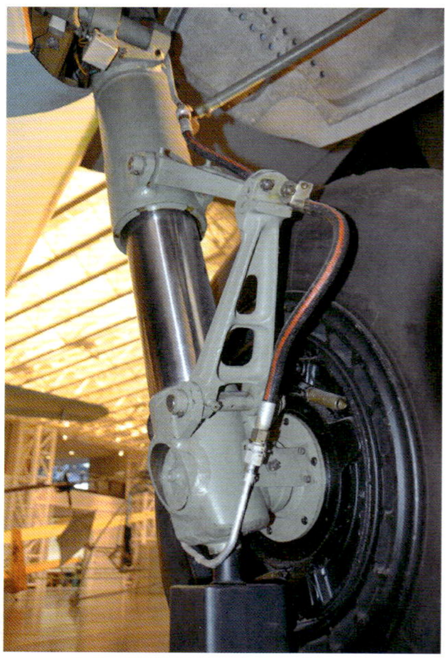

The compression linkage arms on the port oleo leg, these are on the front unusually with the brake hydraulic lines running through them (©Scott Willey)

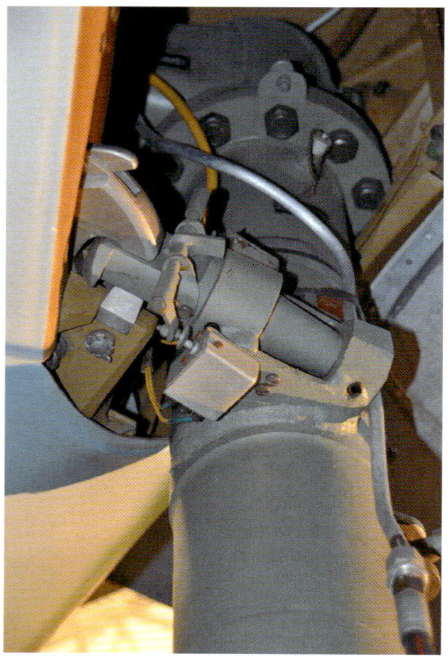

A look up at the top of the port oleo leg from the inside, highlighting the electric up-lock and other items fitted here (©Scott Willey)

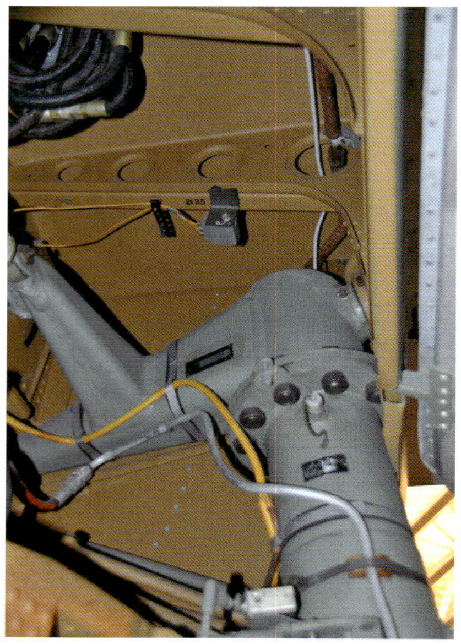

The rear of the port main undercarriage well, once again in the reproduction of the original colour of this area (it was not RLM 02 or unpainted), with the pivot point casting dominating the area (©Scott Willey)

The port main undercarriage unit viewed from the front *(©Scott Willey)*

This is the smaller undercarriage door, ahead of the main one, which only opens during retraction and extension of the undercarriage and remains closed the rest of the time *(©Scott Willey)*

A view up inside the main undercarriage door on the port side, this was never painted originally, apparently *(©Scott Willey)*

This is the main undercarriage door, which is physically linked to the oleo leg and thus remains open whilst the gear is down; this is the port side viewed from the rear looking forward *(©Scott Willey)*

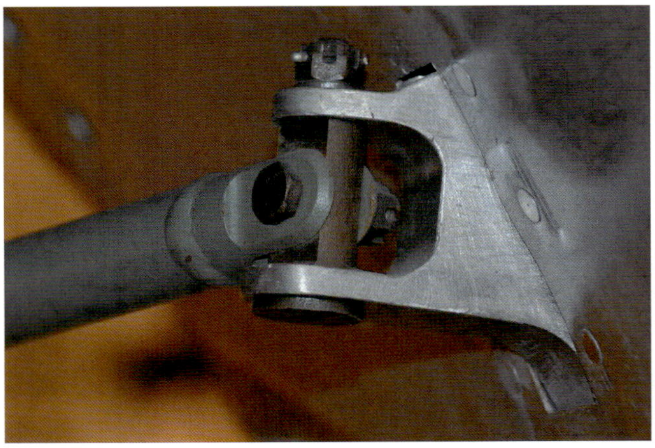

This is the linkage on the inside of the main door with the oleo *(©Scott Willey)*

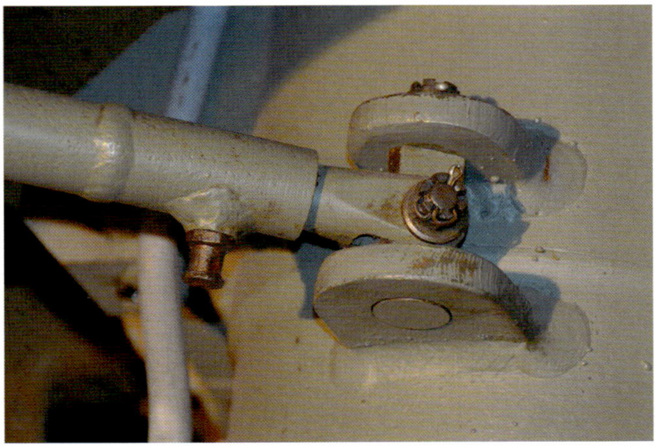

While this is the linkage point on the oleo itself for the main undercarriage door *(©Scott Willey)*

The main wheel hub with the brake line coming through the axle stub *(©Scott Willey)*

Overall view of the 935x345m main wheel *(©Scott Willey)*

The nose wheel, viewed from the inside looking forward. If these are original tyres is doubtful, so the tread pattern may not be accurate either; the same applies to the main wheel tyres *(©Scott Willey)*

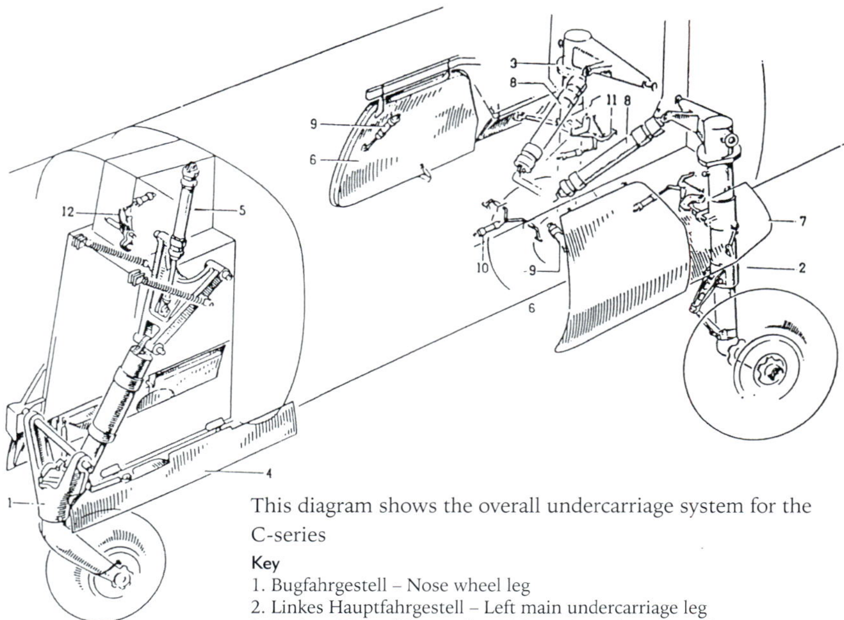

This diagram shows the overall undercarriage system for the C-series

Key

1. Bugfahrgestell – Nose wheel leg
2. Linkes Hauptfahrgestell – Left main undercarriage leg
3. Rechtes Hauptfahrgestell – Right main undercarriage leg
4. Bugfahrgestellklappen – Nose wheel door
5. Arbeitszylinder für Bugfahrgestell – Hydraulic ram for nose wheel leg
6. Grosse Hauptfahrgestellklappen – Large main undercarriage door
7. Hauptfahrgestellklappen – Small main undercarriage door
8. Arbeitszylinder für Hauptfahrgestell – Hydraulic ram for main undercarriage leg
9. Arbeitszylinder für Hauptfahrgestellklappen – Hydraulic ram for main undercarriage door
10. Entriegelungszylinder für Hauptfahrgestellklappen – Locking cylinder for main undercarriage door
11. Hauptfahrgestellverriegelung – Main undercarriage leg 'up' lock
12. Bugfahrgestellaufhängung – Nose wheel leg 'up' lock

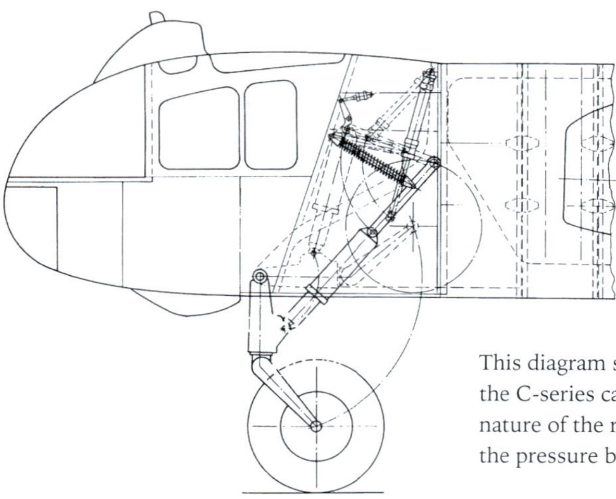

This diagram shows the revision to the front undercarriage unit in the C-series caused by the increased weight, and the pressurised nature of the revised cockpit section (note how it all remains behind the pressure bulkhead)

This close-up of the tail of the V2 shows how the initial prototypes were fitted with horn linkage rudder and elevators

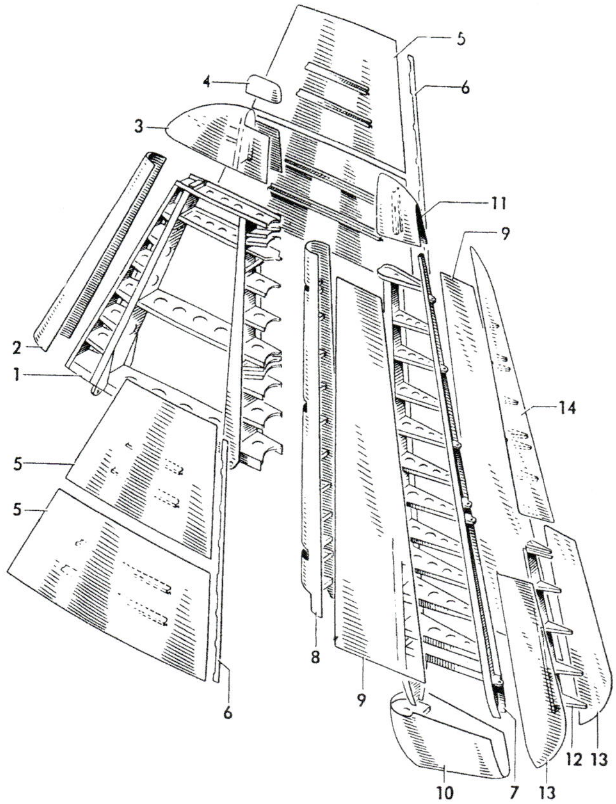

1 Seitenflossengerüst
2 Seitenflossennase aus Sperrholz
3 Seitenflossenrandkappe
4 Heckleuchtenverkleidung
5 Beplankung der Seitenflosse
6 Verstärkungsleisten
7 Seitenrudergerüst
8 Seitenrudernase
9 Beplankungsblech des Seitenruders
10 Untere Endkappe des Seitenruders
11 Obere Endkappe des Seitenruders
12 Seitentrimmrudergerüst
13 Beplankungsbleche des Seitentrimmruders
14 Seitenausgleichruder

This component diagram from the B-2 manual lacks the horn-balance on the rudder but does show the split trim tab (13 and 14)

This shot of NASM's machine shows the trim tab restricted to the lower section of the rudder *(©Scott Willey)*

An overall shot of the starboard side of the rudder, note the small formation light on the top aft section of the fin *(©Scott Willey)*

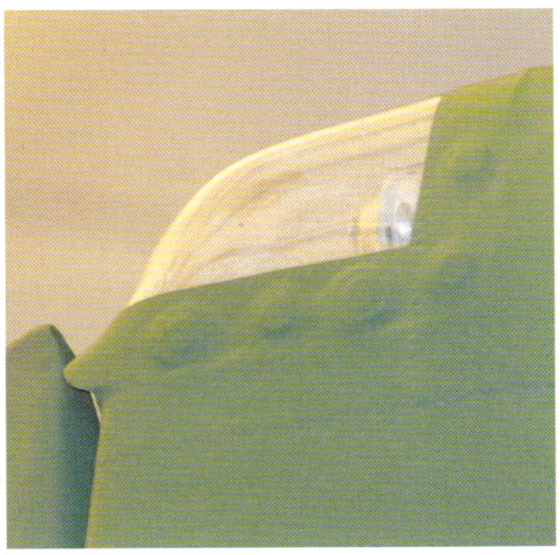

Here is a close-up of the formation light atop the vertical fin *(©Scott Willey)*

Here is the rudder and trim tab viewed from the starboard side *(©Scott Willey)*

A close-up of the horn linkage at the top of the rudder on NASM's machine *(©Scott Willey)*

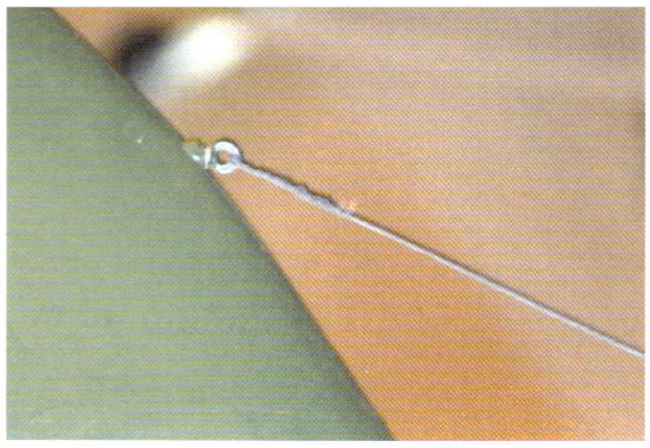

The aerial lead attaches to the top of the fin via this eyelet *(©Scott Willey)*

In this shot you can see that the leading edge fillet on the vertical fin has the join line sealed with doped fabric; once again cut with a zig-zag edge to stop fraying *(©Scott Willey)*

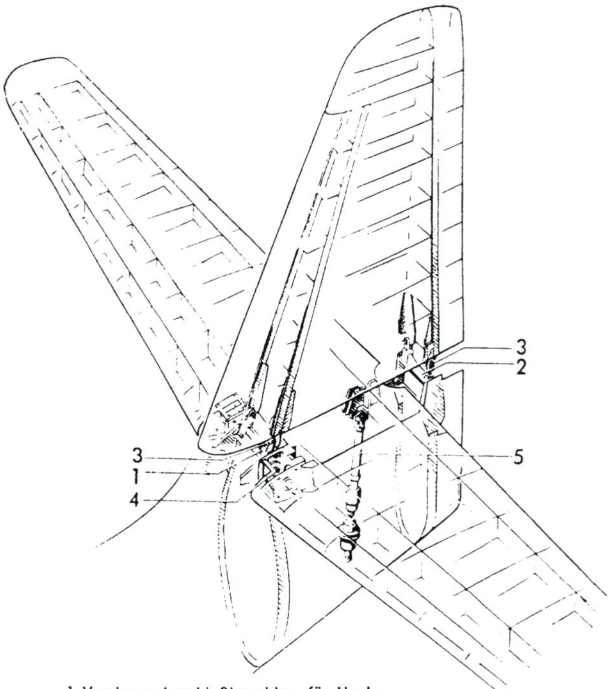

1 **Vorderer Anschlußbeschlag für Heckleitwerk**
2 **Hinterer Anschlußbeschlag für Heckleitwerk**
3 **Anschlußbolzen für Seitenflosse**
4 **Anlenkbolzen für Höhenflosse**
5 **Verstellspindel für Höhenflosse**

This diagram shows how the vertical fin mounts to the aft fuselage/tailplanes

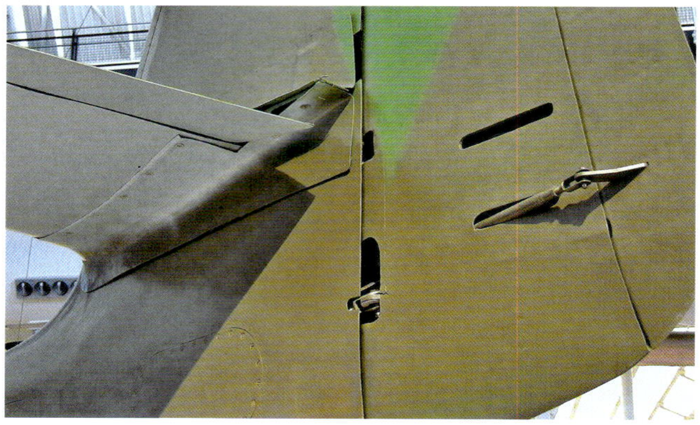

The linkage for the trim tab on the rudder only projects on the port side *(©Scott Willey)*

Detail of the root fillet, seen here on the starboard tailplane of NASM's machine *(©Scott Willey)*

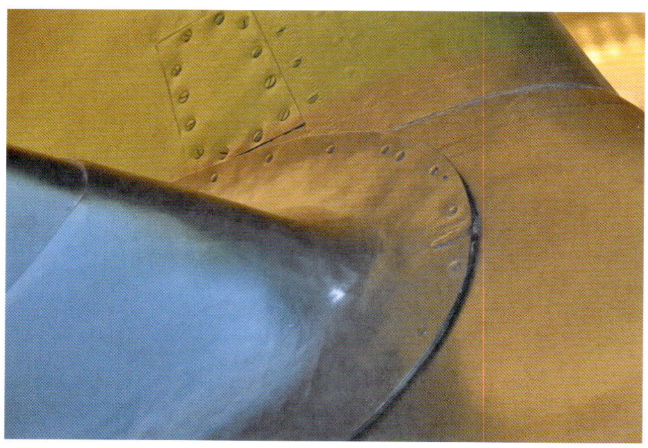

A close-up of the tailplane fillet *(©Scott Willey)*

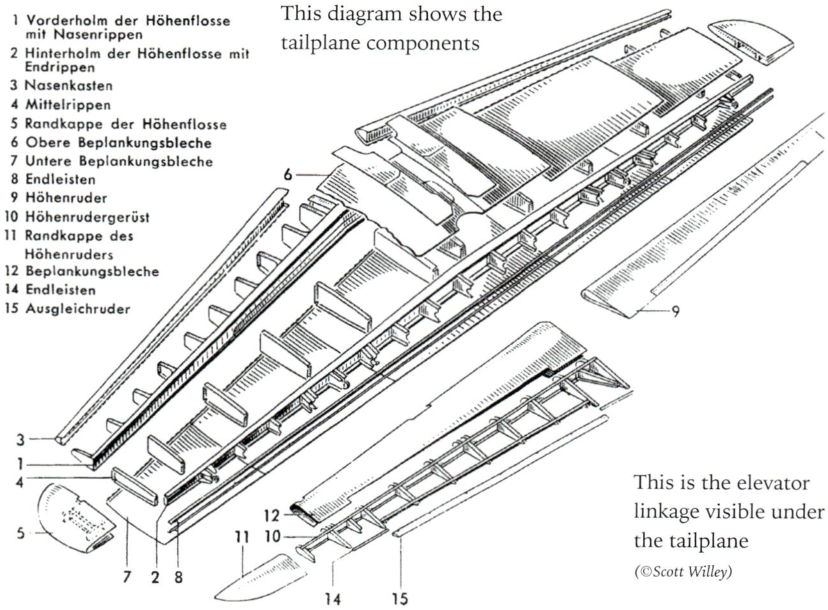

This diagram shows the tailplane components

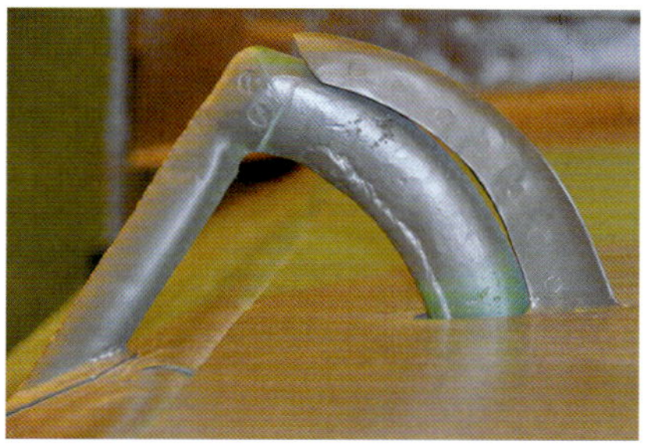

The elevators have large horn linkage, this is the unit above the starboard tailplane *(©Scott Willey)*

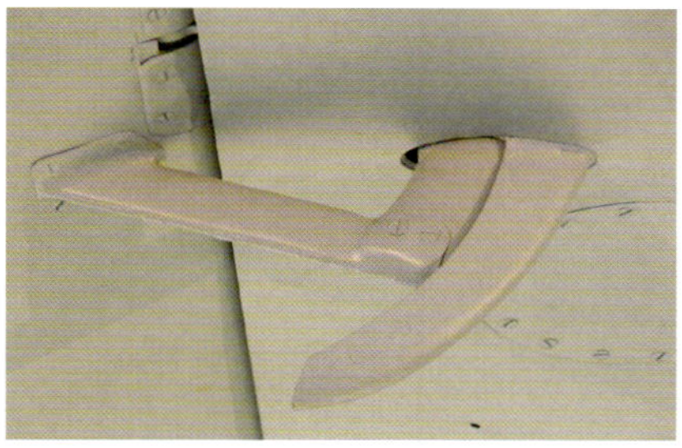

This is the elevator linkage visible under the tailplane *(©Scott Willey)*

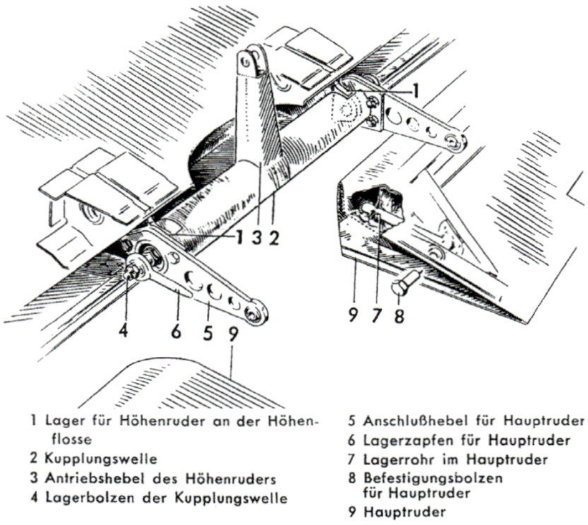

This diagram shows how the elevators mount across the tailplane/vertical fin joint

An overall shot of the starboard tailplane on NASM's B-2 *(©Scott Willey)*

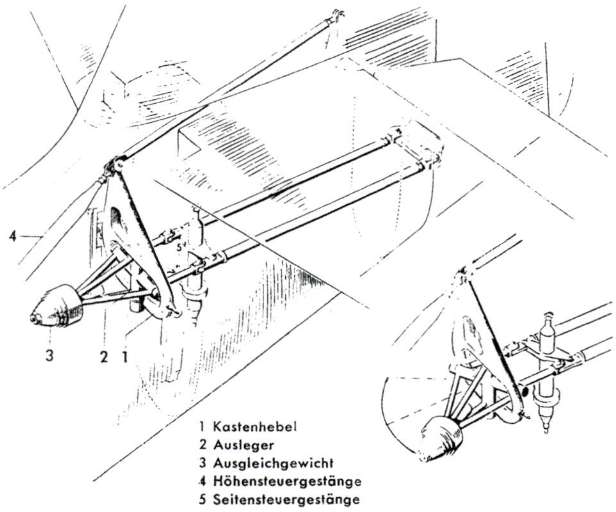

The rudder is counterbalanced inside the rear fuselage, as shown in this diagram

Just to clarify (or maybe confuse) things, this is the tail of C-3 W/Nr.250012 found dumped at the end of WWII, note the split trim tab on the rudder, which appears in the B-2 manual, but was never adopted by the B-series, and the total lack of horn linkage on either elevators or rudder

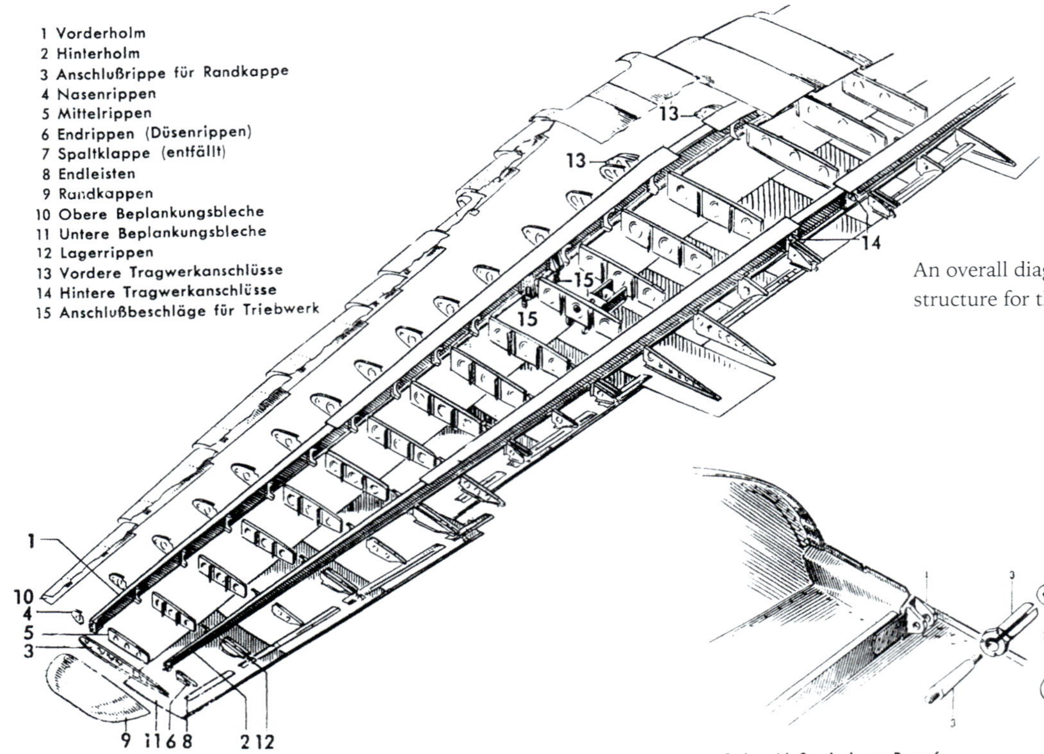

An overall diagram of the wing structure for the B-series

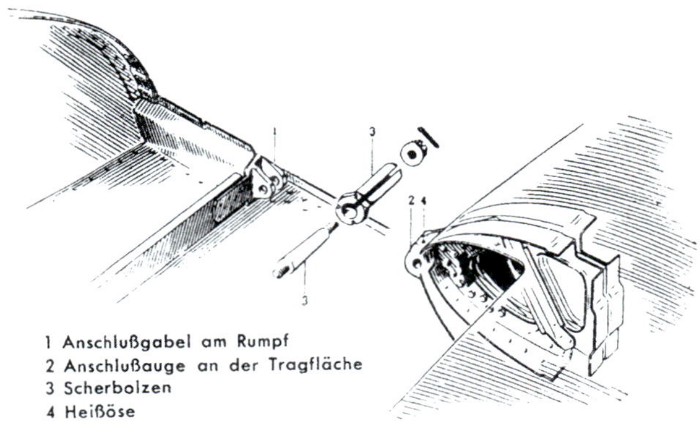

This is the wing-to-fuselage front attachment

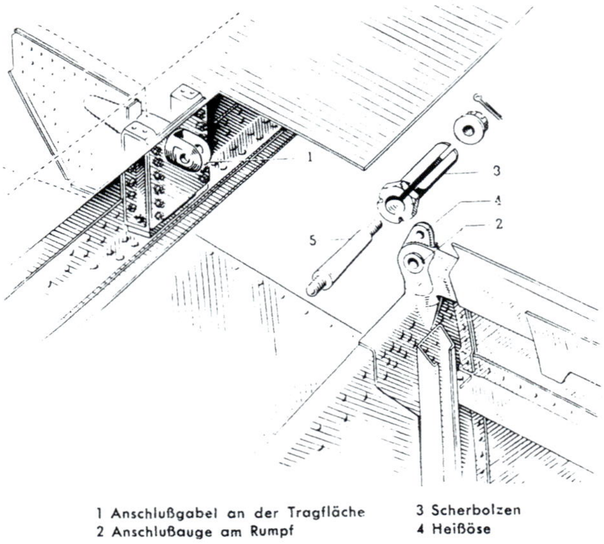

This is the wing-to-fuselage rear attachment

A overall view of the underside of the port wing on the NASM example *(©Scott Willey)*

The upper surface of the port wing on the NASM machine *(©Scott Willey)*

A look along the starboard wing of the NASM machine, note the kink in the outboard leading edge *(©Scott Willey)*

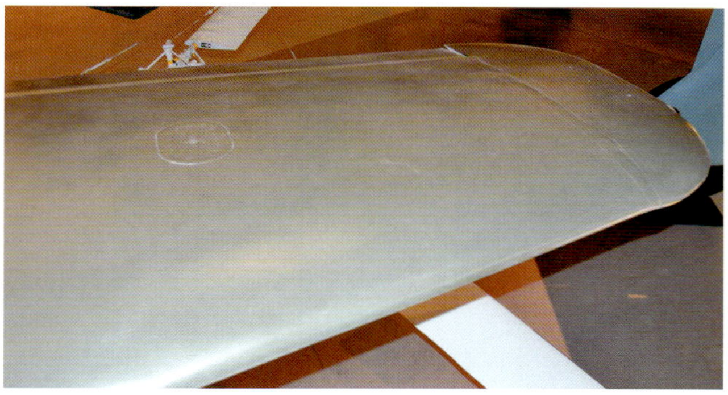

The outer edge and tip of the port wing *(©Scott Willey)*

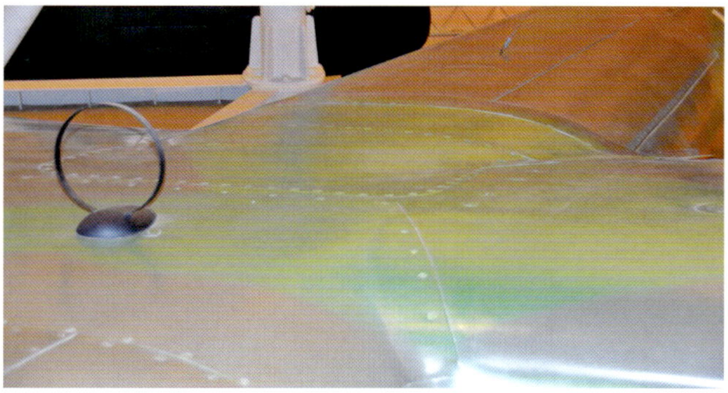

Here you can see how the wing merges with the centre-section of the fuselage *(©Scott Willey)*

This is the access panel that was just partially visible on the extreme right of the above photo *(©Scott Willey)*

The red tip light on the port wing, viewed here from the front *(©Scott Willey)*

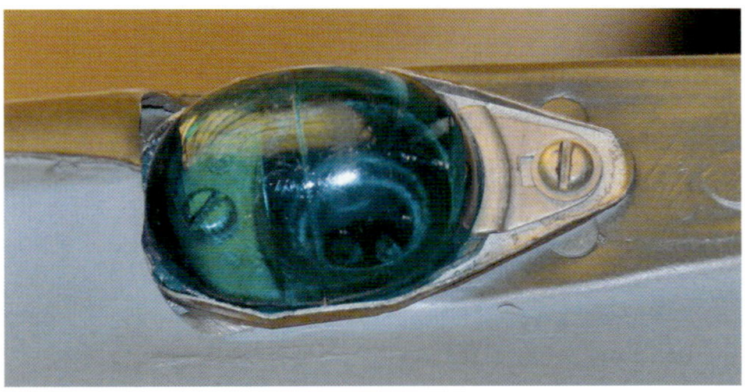

This is the green light on the starboard wing tip *(©Scott Willey)*

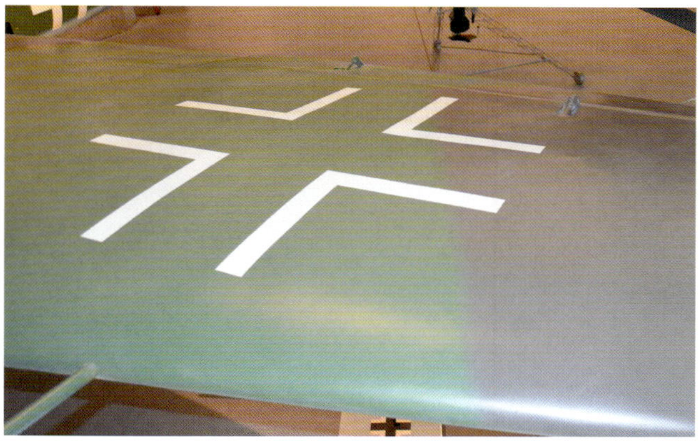

Inboard of the tip of the port wing, where you can see the linkage for the aileron and trim tab *(©Scott Willey)*

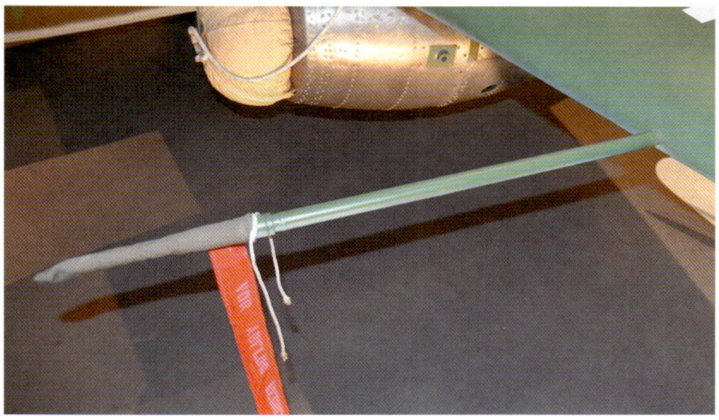

The pitot is situated in the port wing on the B-series *(©Scott Willey)*

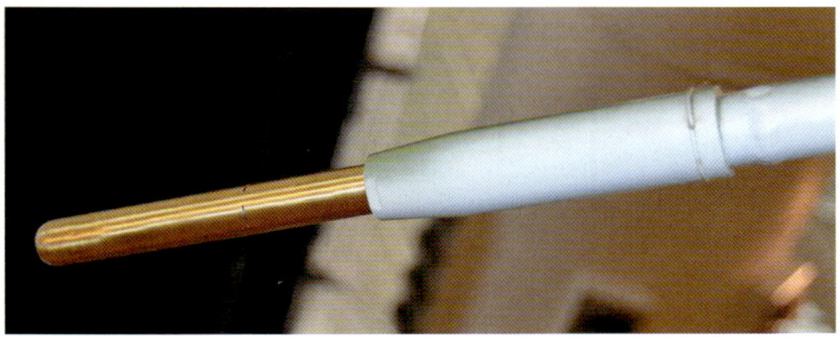

The tip of the pitot tube, which always remains unpainted *(©Scott Willey)*

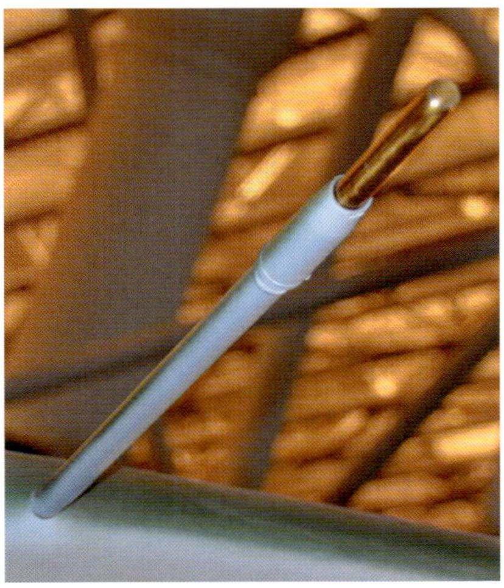

The underside of the pitot tube *(©Scott Willey)*

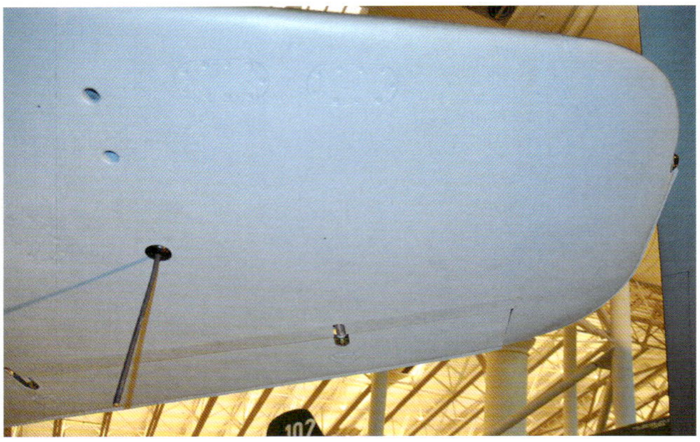

Under the tip of the port wing you have the IFF rod antenna, plus two holes forward of it *(©Scott Willey)*

Here is a close-up of the two holes, probably relating to jacking or tie-downs *(©Scott Willey)*

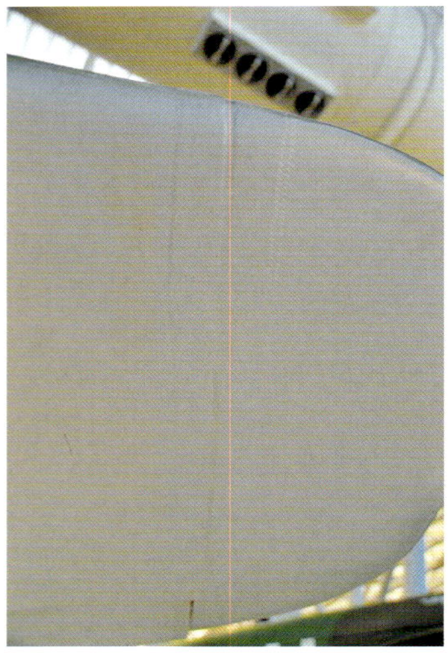

Hopefully you can just make out here that the join line for the tip section is covered with doped fabric; in this instance cut with a zig-zag edge to stop fraying *(©Scott Willey)*

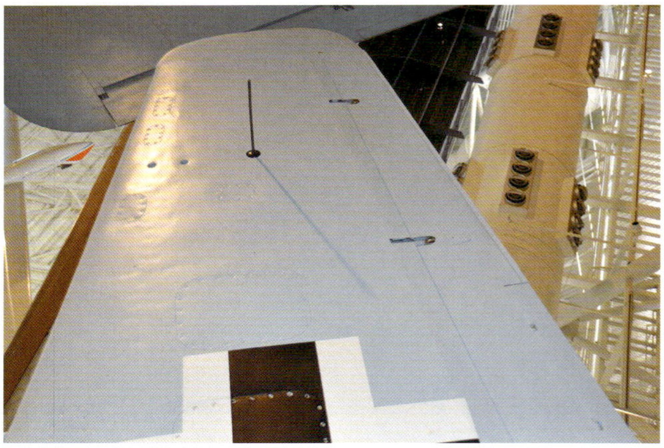

A look up under the outer section of the port wing highlighting the rod antenna, markings and the various access panels in this region *(©Scott Willey)*

A look inboard under the port wing, again showing the cross plus the various access panels; note that all the latter are attached with screws *(©Scott Willey)*

This is the underside of the port wing showing the section inboard of the engine; note the two large access panels. The stencil on the panel should be ignored, as it is a NASM note relating to a modification made to the flap up-locks inside that panel *(©Scott Willey)*

This is the section of the port wing underside just outboard of the engine nacelles, with the rocket pod just visible to the top *(©Scott Willey)*

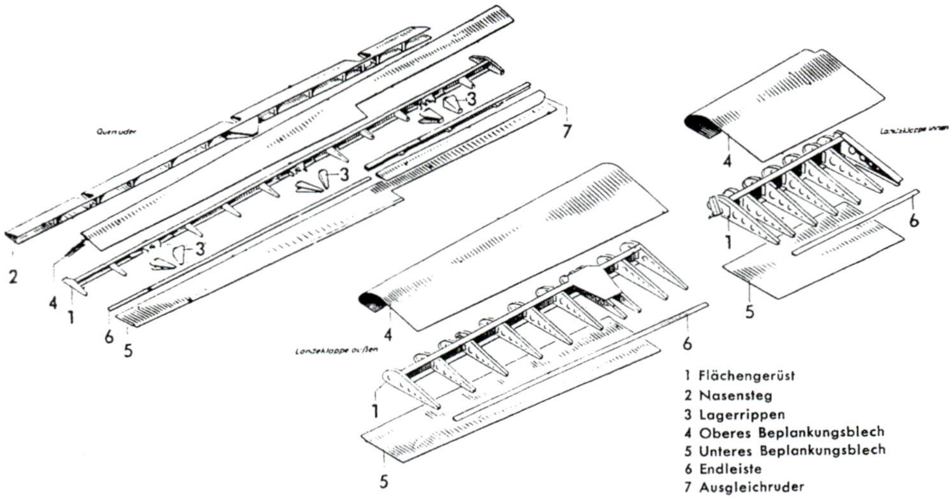

This diagram shows the components of the ailerons, trim tab and flaps of the B-series

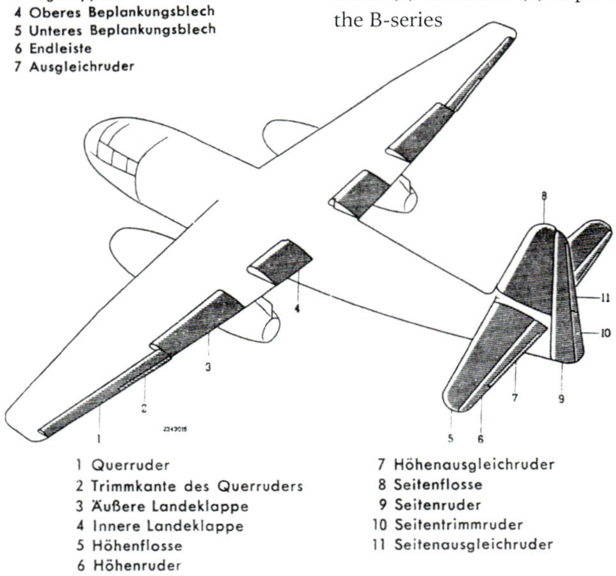

This diagram shows the ailerons (1), trim tabs (2) and outer (3) and inner (4) flaps of the B-series

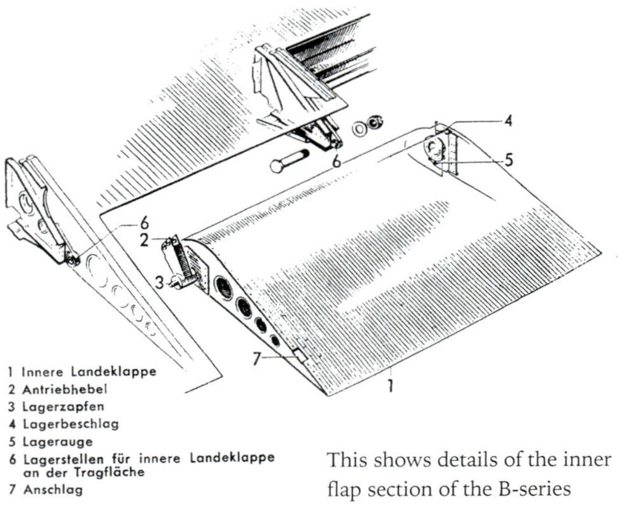

This shows details of the inner flap section of the B-series

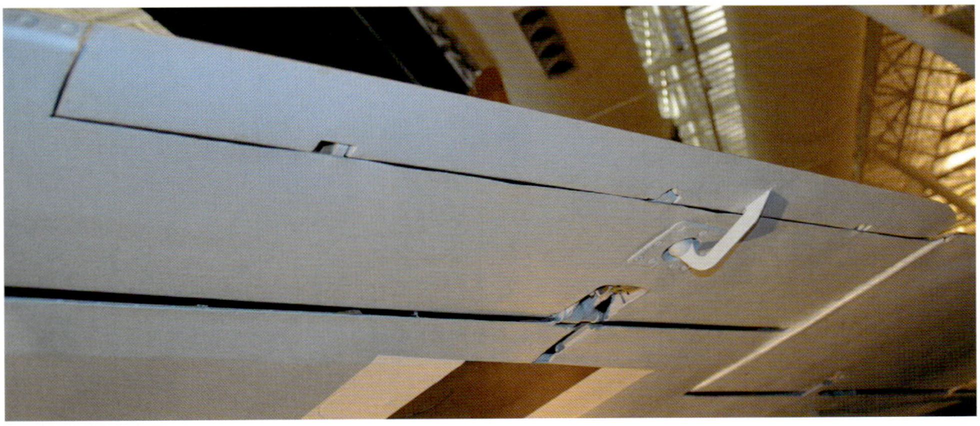

An overall view of part of the aileron and the entire trim tab on the port wing of NASM's Ar 23B-2 *(©Scott Willey)*

This is a view of the underside of the aileron and trim tab of the starboard wing of NASM's B-2 *(©Scott Willey)*

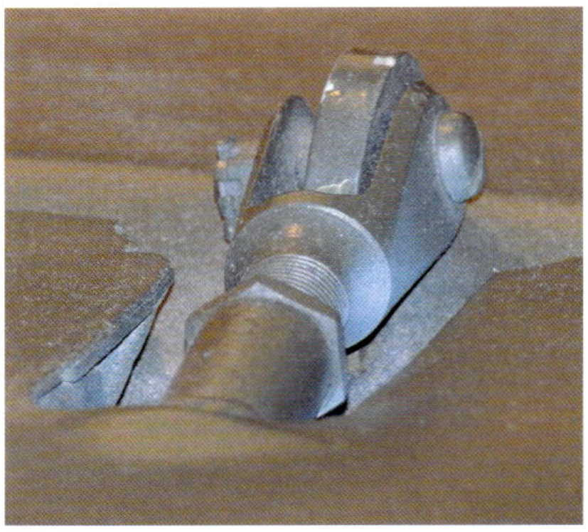

This is the linkage for the aileron, visible on the upper surface *(©Scott Willey)*

A top view of the port wing on NASM's machine, showing the linkage to both aileron and trim tab, plus the gap at the hinge line *(©Scott Willey)*

This diagram shows all the various control linkage

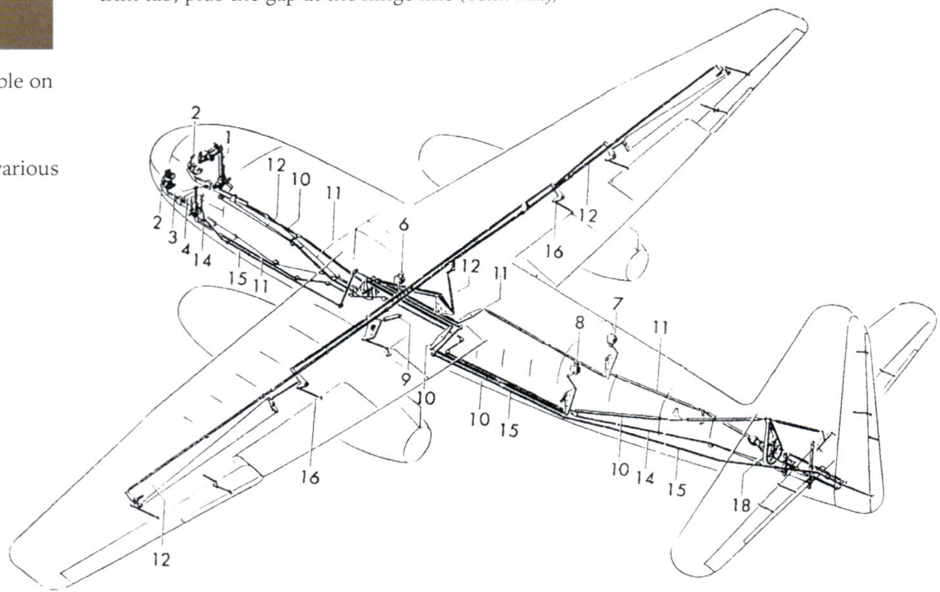

1 Steuersäule mit Handrad
2 Seitensteuerpedale
3 Handgriff für Höhenflossenverstellung
4 Handrad für Seitenrudertrimmung
6 Rudergetriebe für Querruderantrieb (Dreiachsensteuerung)
7 Rudergetriebe für Seitenruderantrieb (Dreiachsensteuerung)
8 Rudergetriebe für Höhenruderantrieb (Dreiachsensteuerung)
9 Arbeitszylinder für Landeklappenantrieb
10 Höhensteuerung
11 Seitensteuerung
12 Quersteuerung
14 Höhenflossenverstellung
15 Seitenrudertrimmung
16 Landeklappensteuerung
17 Steuerung für Kupplung zwischen Landeklappe und Querruder
18 Heckruder-Gewichtsausgleich

This is the linkage for the trim tab, again visible on the upper surface *(©Scott Willey)*

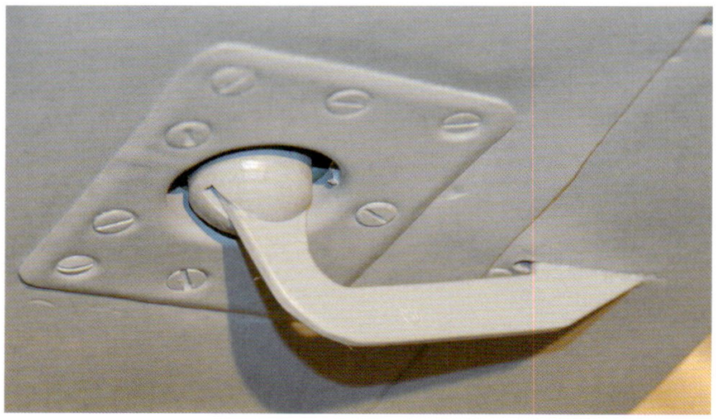

This is the trim tab linkage visible on the underside *(©Scott Willey)*

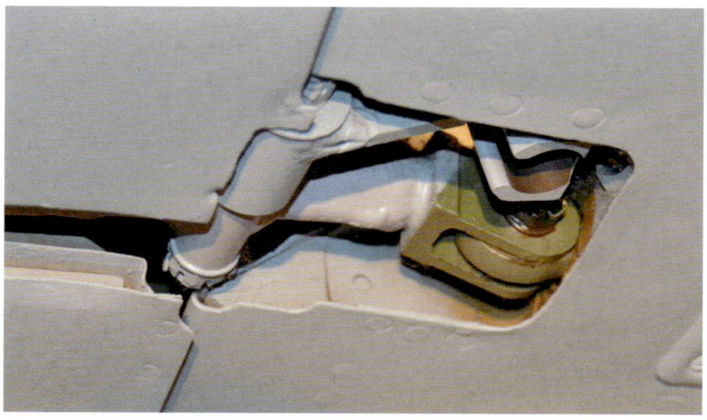

This is the linkage for the aileron visible on the underside *(©Scott Willey)*

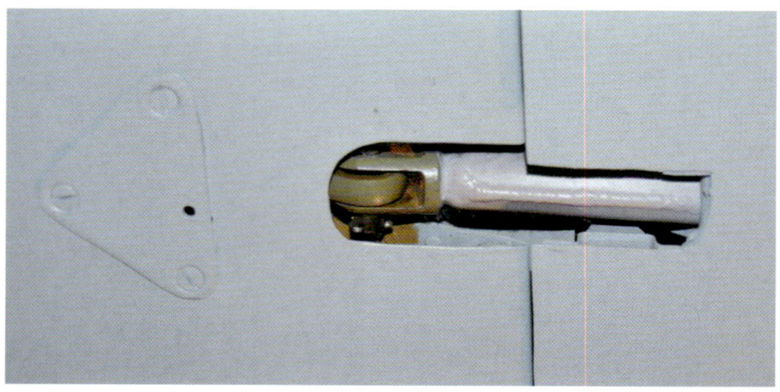

The outermost linkage for the aileron can only be seen on the underside *(©Scott Willey)*

This shot shows the ailerons (outboard) and flap (inboard) from the underside of the trailing edge of the port wing *(©Scott Willey)*

An overall view of the outboard flap section of the port wing *(©Scott Willey)*

This is the innermost hinge of the outboard port flap, which can only be seen on the underside *(©Scott Willey)*

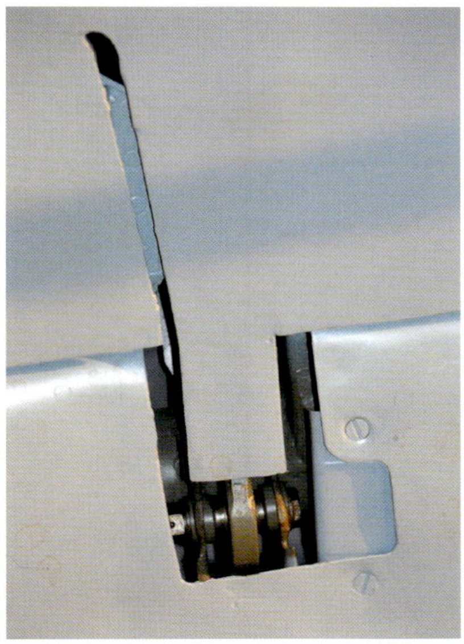

Here is a close-up of one of the hinges under the outboard port flap *(©Scott Willey)*

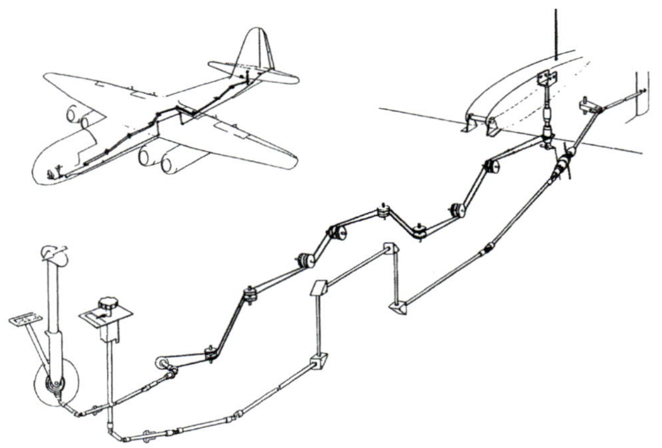

This diagram shows the adjustment linkage for the rudder and its trim tab in the C-series

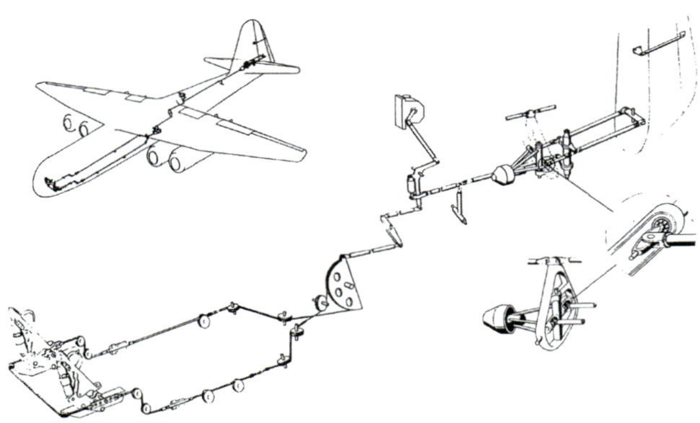

This diagram shows the control linkage for the rudder in the C-series

This is Jumo 004 W/Nr.040 as fitted to the port side of the V2

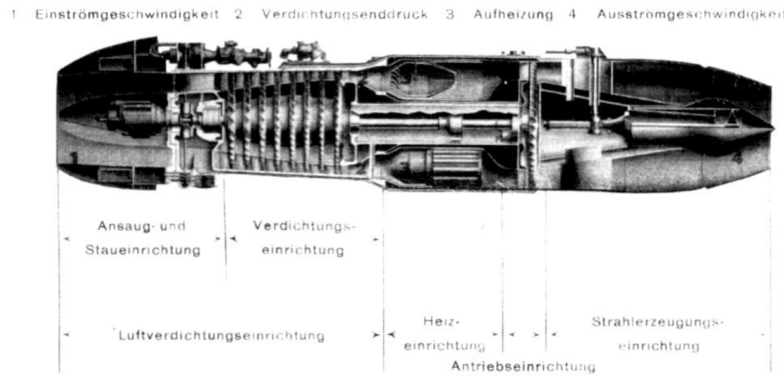

This is a cutaway of the Jumo 004 from the service manual

This is the left side of one of the 004s taken from W/Nr.140173 after capture and sent to Power Jets Ltd for evaluation *(©British Official)*

This is the right side of one of the 004s taken from W/Nr.140173 after capture *(©British Official)*

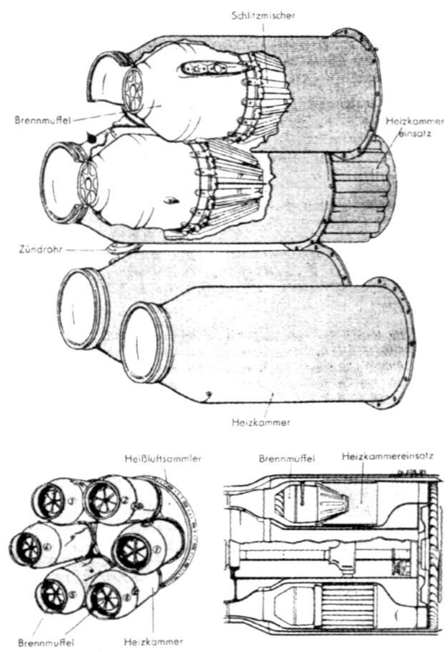

This diagram from the manual shows the combustion chambers on the 004

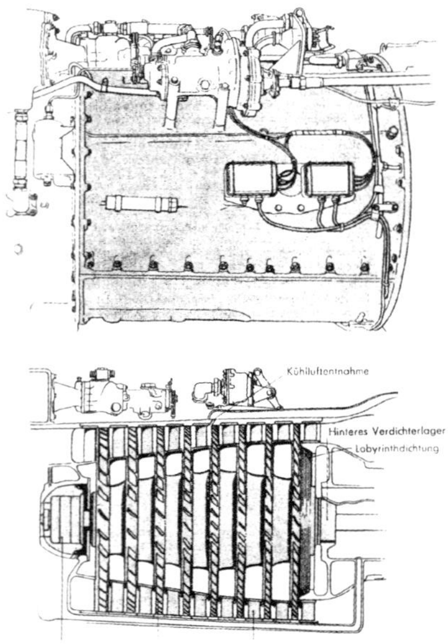

This is the compressor stage of the 004

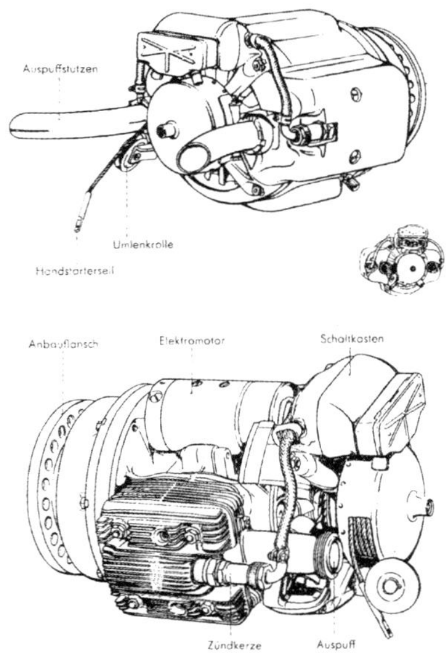

At the very front of the 004, in an aerodynamic fairing was this two-stroke Reidel starter engine, which spun up the engine prior to ignition

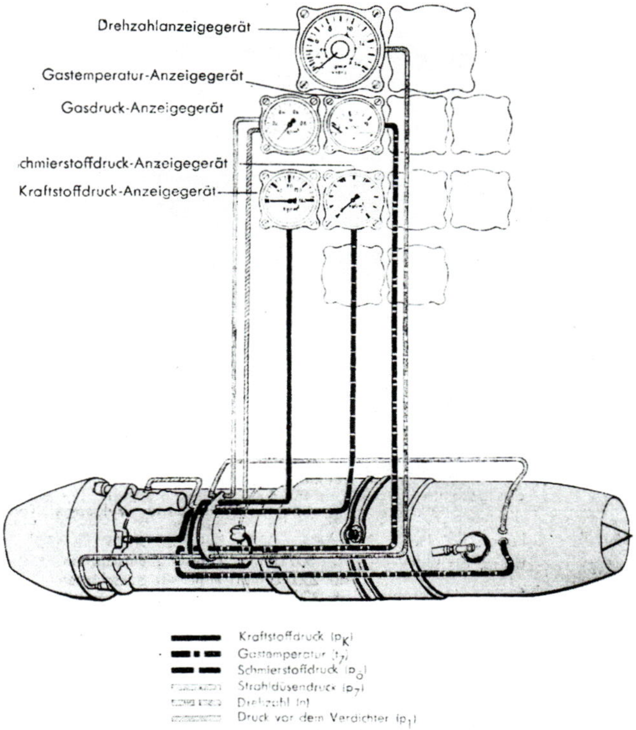

This diagram shows the operating systems for the 004

Key
Drehzahlanzeigegerät – RPM indicator (literally 'speed display')
Gastemperatur-Anzeigegerät – Gas temperature gauge
Gasdruck-Anzeigegerät – Gas pressure gauge
Schmierstoffdruck-Anzeigegerät – Lubricant pressure gauge
Kraftstoffdruck-Anzeigegerät – Fuel pressure gauge

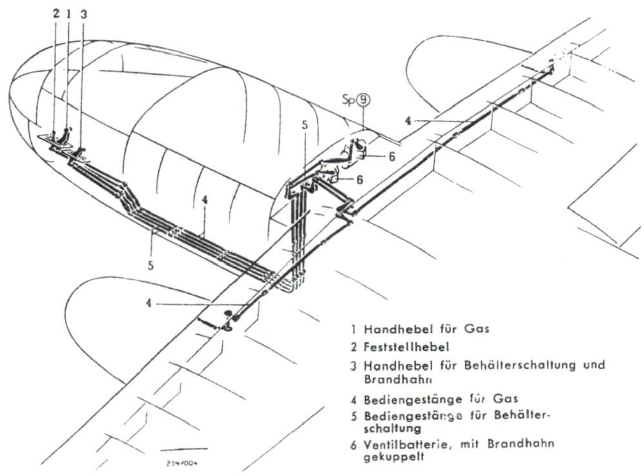

This diagram shows the engine control linkage for the 004-powered B-series. The controls for the C-series are identical, save for another set of linkage on each side for the additional (outer) engine

Here you can see the twin BMW 003s fitted onto the port wing of the V19

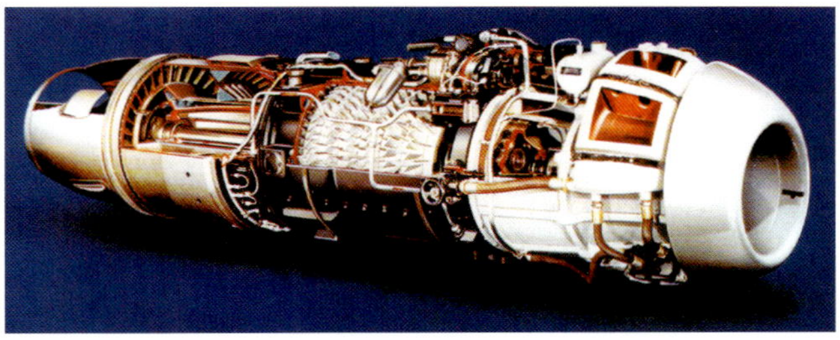

The other engine intended for the Ar 234 was the BMW 003, as shown in this post-war colour cutaway

Although neither are of great quality, this is the HeS 011A intended for the D-series...

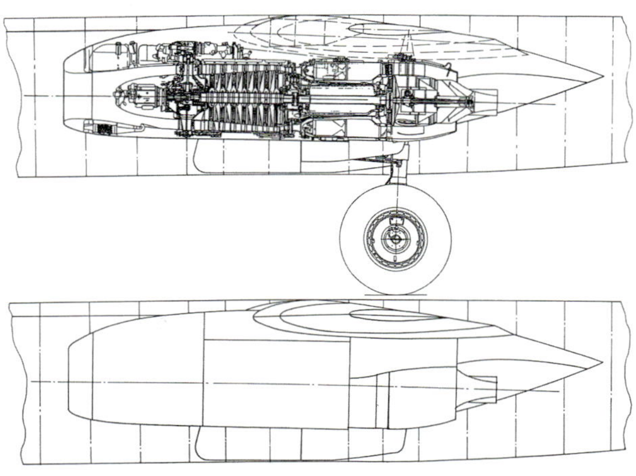

This period diagram shows the instillation of twin BWM 003As in the C-series

...while this is the right side of the HeS 011A

This montage of two images of the port nacelle on the V1 shows how it differed from the later production nacelles, especially around the front

An overall view of the port nacelle on the V5

This is the port nacelle of the V9 with the large bomb rack unique to this prototype underneath

This is the starboard nacelle on the NASM B-2 *(©Scott Willey)*

Here is the port nacelle of NASM's B-2 *(©Scott Willey)*

This is the front inboard side of the port nacelle on NASM's example *(©Scott Willey)*

Here is the rearmost section of the starboard nacelle on NASM's machine *(©Scott Willey)*

A close-up of the NASM example, showing the intake scoop on the starboard side of the upper cowl; this is the port engine, so the intake is inboard, but is the same on the starboard engine, thus making the intake on that side outboard *(©Scott Willey)*

A nice top down view on the join between nacelle and wing on the port side of the NASM machine *(©Scott Willey)*

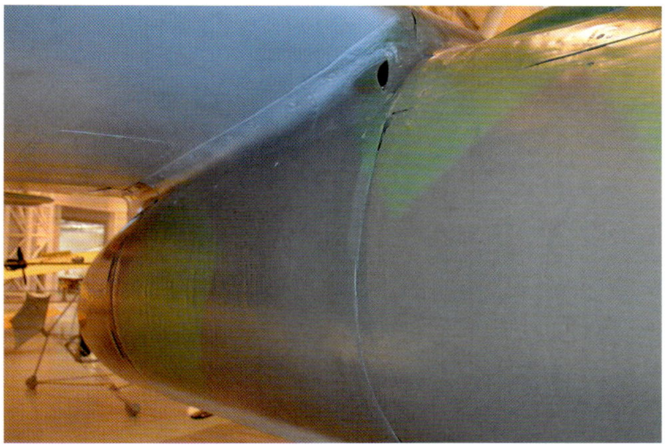

This is the inboard mid-section of the port nacelle on the NASM machine *(©Scott Willey)*

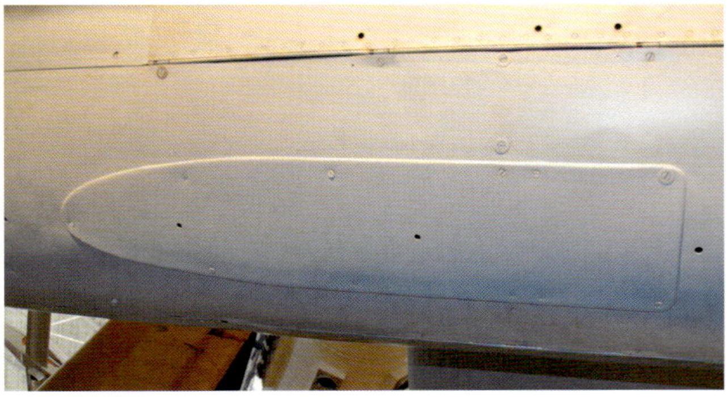

This plate under the nacelle on NASM's machine covers where the ETC rack would usually go; the front is to the left in this photo *(©Scott Willey)*

Moving forward under the nacelle, you can see this access panel, note also the piano-hinge for the main mid-section panel, whilst the upper front cowl is held on with screw-fasteners *(©Scott Willey)*

An overall view of the exhaust area on the port engine, note the louvres in the front edge of this area and the 'onion' in the exhaust itself *(©Scott Willey)*

Here is a close-up of one of the louvres in the exhaust section of the cowling *(©Scott Willey)*

A look up into the exhaust outlet, showing the 'onion' that changes the size of the outlet, plus the last stage of the engine further back inside *(©Scott Willey)*

Not all seams are neat and tidy, this is the upper seam of the fillet between engine exhaust and wing trailing edge and as you can see, it is just a hole *(©Scott Willey)*

A useful shot of the join between nacelle and wing on the inboard section of the port side *(©Scott Willey)*

A look into the front of the Jumo in the NASM machine *(©Scott Willey)*

This is the aerodynamic bullet covering the Reidel starter motor, with the ring pull to start it visible in the front *(©Scott Willey)*

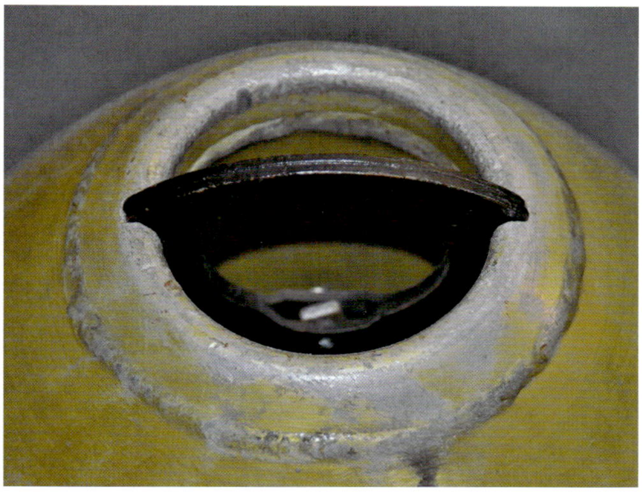

Here is a close-up of the Reidel unit's own starter pull-cord; the entire black unit is held and pulled, like starting a mower *(©Scott Willey)*

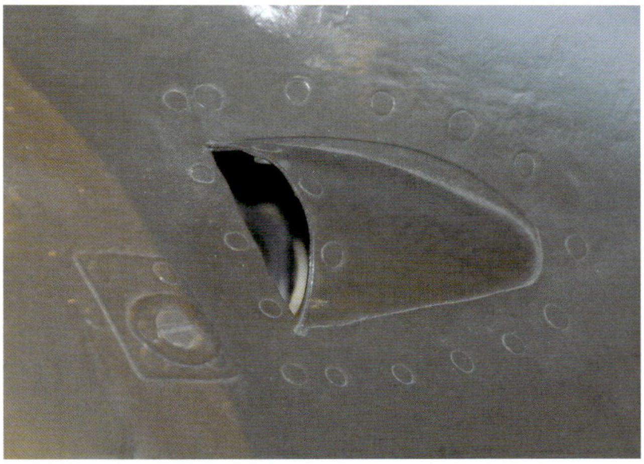

This is a close-up of one of the intakes just under the wing root/leading edge *(©Scott Willey)*

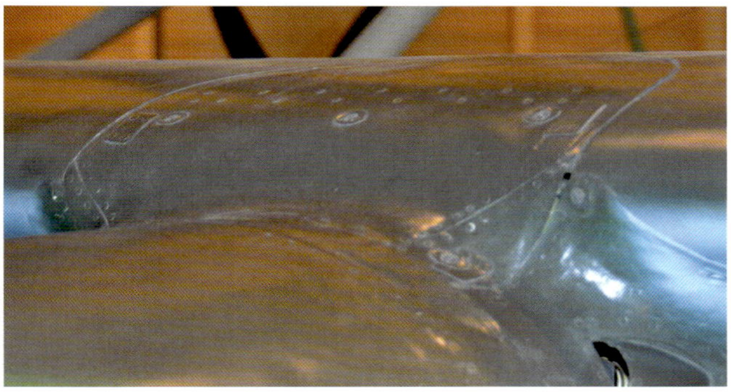

Here is the hump on the upper cowl where it joins the wing, with the intake visible just below the wing; there is one on either side of the nacelle *(©Scott Willey)*

Note the tiny slits around the front of the nacelle *(©Scott Willey)*

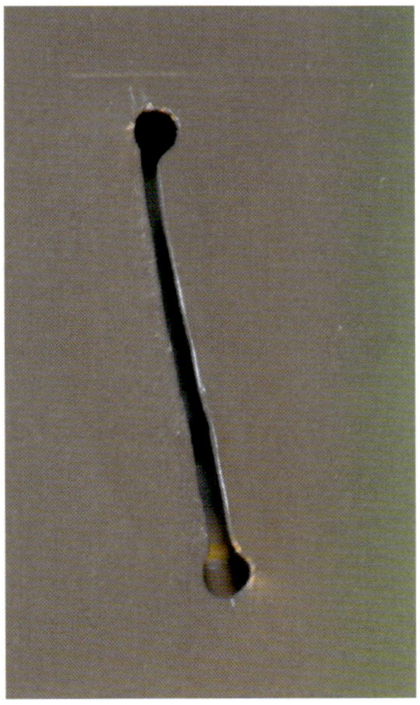

Here is a close up of one of these slits, the holes drilled at the ends stop such slits from 'creeping' and causing a fracture *(©Scott Willey)*

A nice wartime shot of a groundcrewman sitting astride the front of a 004 on a 8./KG76 machine at Burg in the winter of 1944/45, note the red band around the front of the cowl

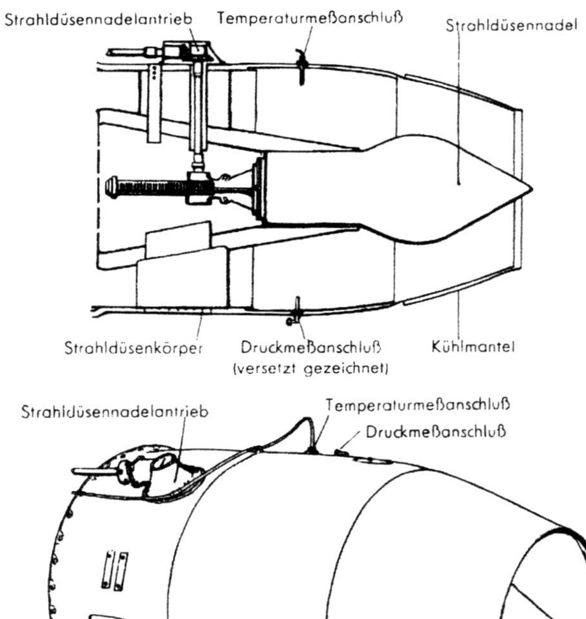

This diagram shows how the 'onion' operates in the exhaust section of the nacelle

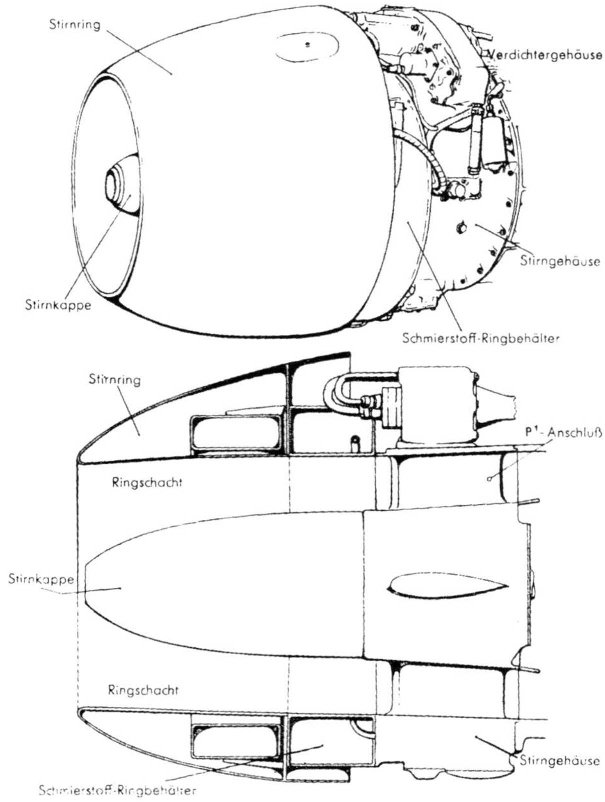

A nice diagram showing the construction of the front cowl section along with all the elements within this area

Some Ar 234s received an installation of a single BWM 003 under each wing, as shown in this shot of the V17

The early BMW 003s did not have the Reidel starter of the 004, and in the early machines there was a large boss installed that allowed a shaft to be coupled to an external engine, which would then spin up the jet before ignition. This is the separate twin 003 installation of the V6

This is the V8 and this time you can see the exhaust region on the coupled 003 installation, although the fairing between the exhausts has not been installed yet

Viewed from the front, you can see how much narrower and deeper the BMW 003 engine was when installed on its own

Here is a front shot of the coupled BMW 003s in the V8, note the projections in the centre of each, which is the pick-up for the external starting system and which is only on the early four-engine prototypes

A nice front view of the 003A-1s installed in the V19, see how these engines lack the housing that projected from the middle of the intake on the V8. The sway braces of the ETC rack are visible in the bottom panel

This view of the 003s in the V19 show how much bigger the twin installation was, plus the larger intake and pronounced 'hump' to the cowl top

Viewed from slightly above, the cowls of the V19 highlight the sweeping curves of the upper cowlings

An overall view of the Walter 109-500 (Ri 202b) rocket pod fitted under the starboard wing of NASM's example *(©Scott Willey)*

Viewed from the rear, you can see the various access and connection points, as well as the supporting framework *(©Scott Willey)*

If you look at the other side of the rocket pod, you will find these filler and access points, as well as their associated stencils *(©Scott Willey)*

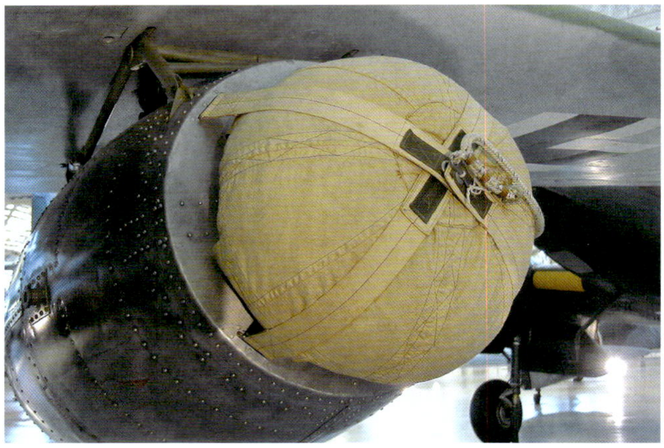

A close-up of the parachute pack on the front of the unit *(©Scott Willey)*

Note the rope lanyard connected between the wing and the front of the parachute pack *(©Scott Willey)*

This is a close-up of the connection between the lanyard and the wing alongside the rocket pod *(©Scott Willey)*

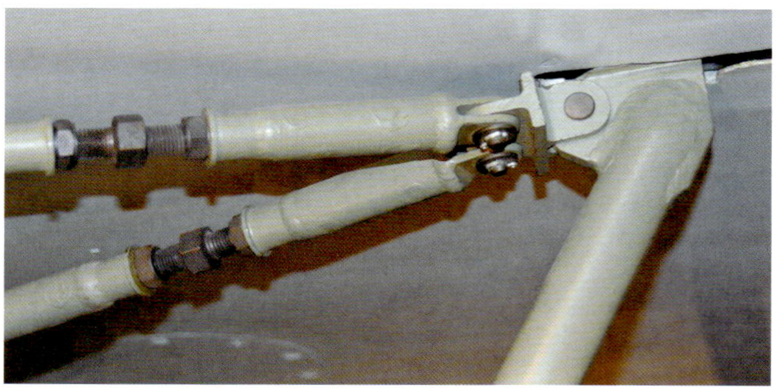

The rear of the pod has this three-point pick-up, with the screw-threads allowing a degree of adjustment to get the rocket exhaust gases at the correct angle *(©Scott Willey)*

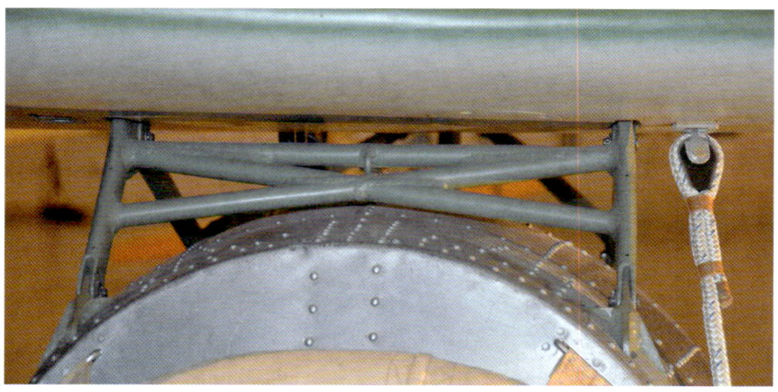

This view from the front shows the cradle fitted to the pod to allow attachment to the wing, this drops away with the pod when it is ejected after take-off *(©Scott Willey)*

Looking forward from the aft connections, you will find this electrical connector fixed into a socket in the wing underside *(©Scott Willey)*

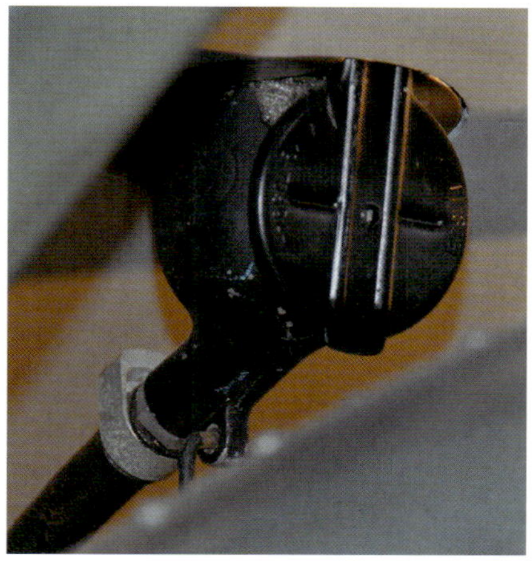

Here is a close look at that electrical connector, viewed from the front this time *(©Scott Willey)*

Here is the underside of the pod *(©Scott Willey)*

This is the exhaust outlet of the pod, viewed from the underside *(©Scott Willey)*

The number of the pod is stencilled above the aft section, forward of this you can also see the pressure gauges that can be seen in more detail in the next image *(©Scott Willey)*

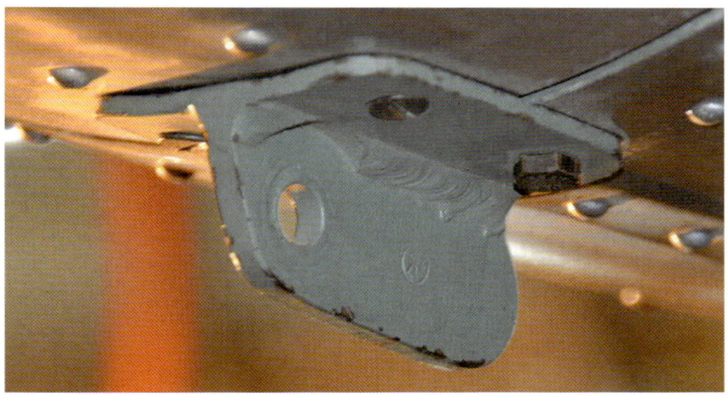

This is the lug you can see in the above shot and it is probably to mount the pod to a handling trolley prior to installation *(©Scott Willey)*

Two pressure gauges, for the propellants, situated inside the pod on the right side, with holes in the outer skin to allow them to be checked from the outside *(©Scott Willey)*

There are also these tube lugs on either side of the pod, again hinting that these relate to a handling trolley *(©Scott Willey)*

Please note that the Ar 234 had many projected armament and ordnance options, but very few of these were actually even tested, let alone adopted in service. What follows therefore confines itself to those tested or used/intended for the variants that were actually built.

It was planned to arm the Blitz with twin MG 151/15 or MG 151/20 cannon in a rearward-firing 'Magirus' installation in the aft fuselage, but no production Bs ever had this installation

The V21 actually had the twin cannon installed in the rear fuselage, this is the unit in its mounting frame seen from the front

below: These are the mounting blocks for the barrels of the MG 151/20 in the lower, aft fuselage of the V21

The twin MG 151/20s of the V21 seen from the side

The V21's MG 151/20 assembly viewed from the rear

Here you can see the blast port in the side of the rear fuselage of the V21

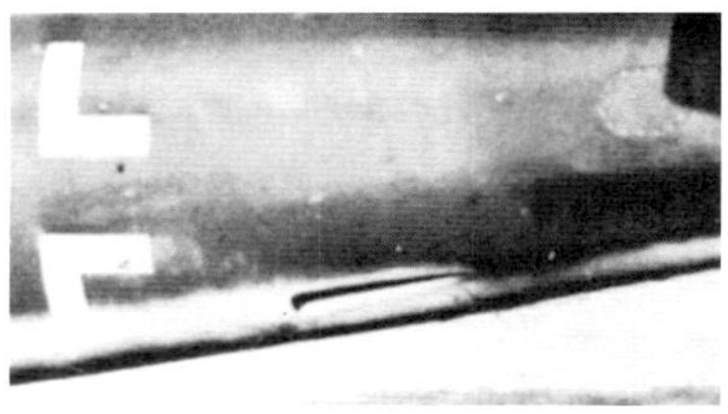

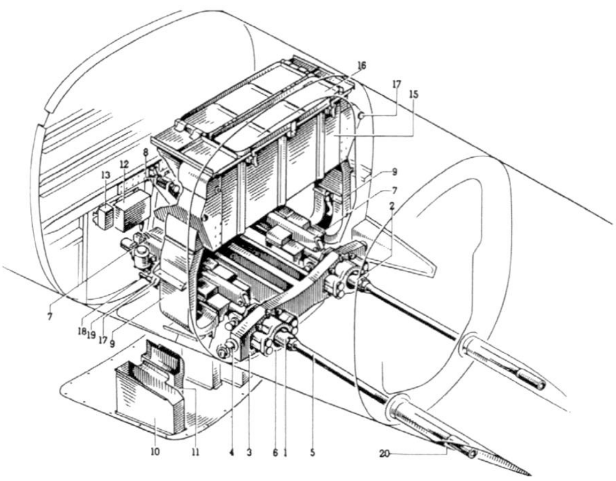

This diagram shows the MG 151/20 installation intended for the C-3

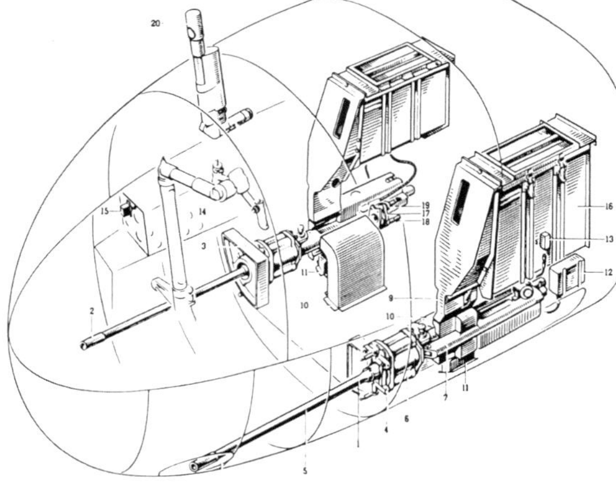

This diagram shows how the MG 151/20s would have been installed in the nose of the production C-3s. This installation was also intended for other versions, but none of these ever saw fruition

The bomb rack mounted under the nacelles of the V9 was a lot larger than that intended for the production machines, this is a view of the one under the port engine, viewed from the outside

Here you can see the size of the rack under the port nacelle of the V9

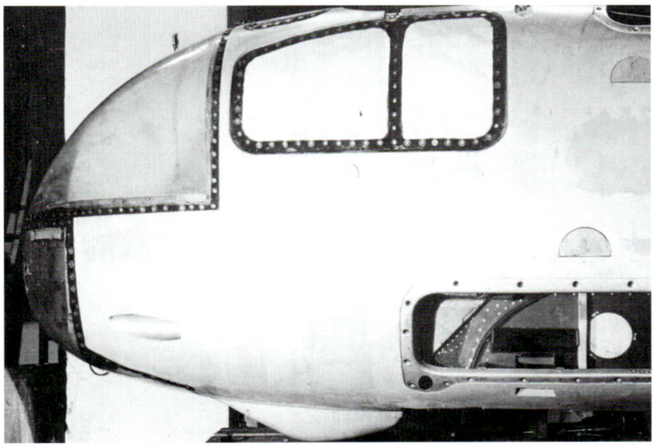

The C-3 series was also to have a single MG 151/20 cannon on either side of the nose, and here you can see the bay with the ejector chute visible on the post side of the nose

The V9 did most of the initial trials with bombs, this shot shows it fitted with SC500s under the fuselage and each nacelle

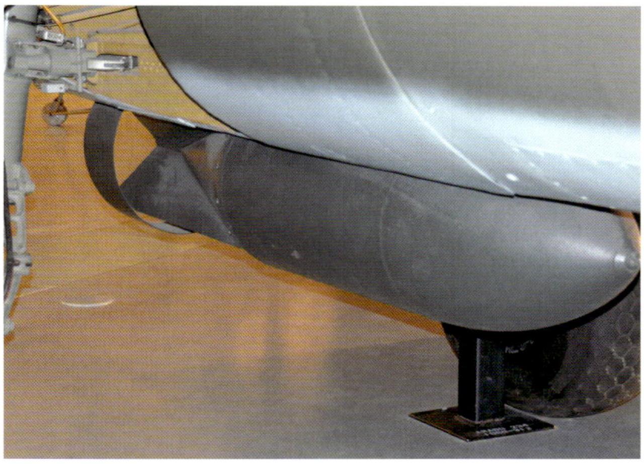

This is the SD500 under the belly of the NASM example, viewed from the front *(©Scott Willey)*

This is the NASM example's SD500 viewed from the starboard rear *(©Scott Willey)*

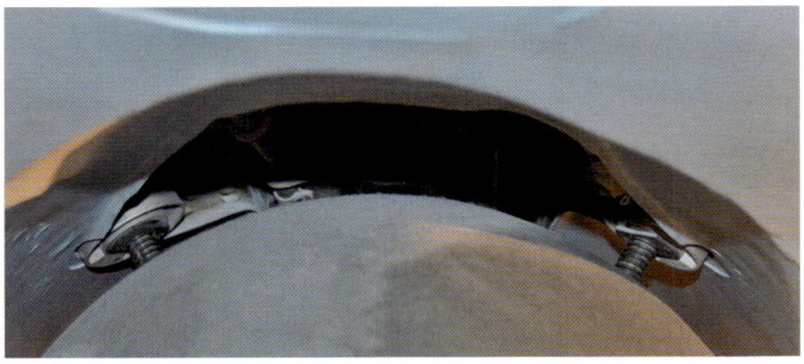

With a bomb on the centreline rack it is steadied by screw-adjusters at four points: front and aft, port and starboard. Here you can just see the forward ones on the NASM example *(©Scott Willey)*

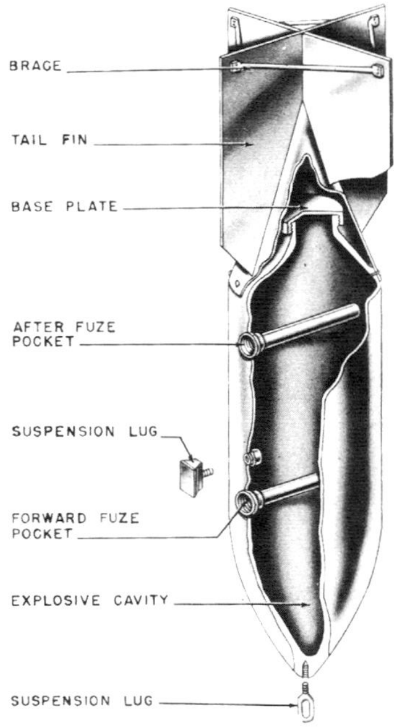

This is an SC250, which had a thinner wall thickness than the SD version

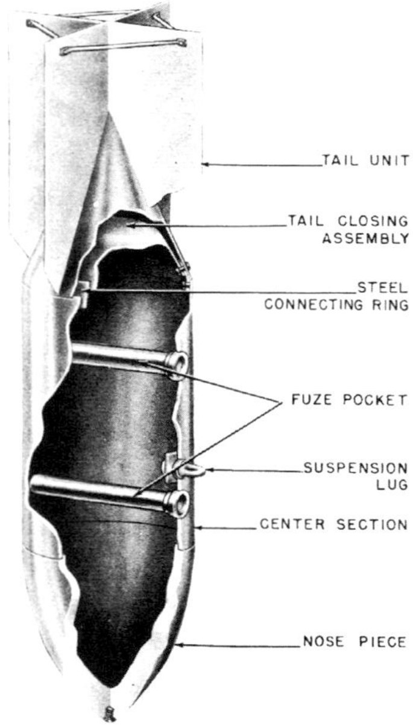

This is an SC500

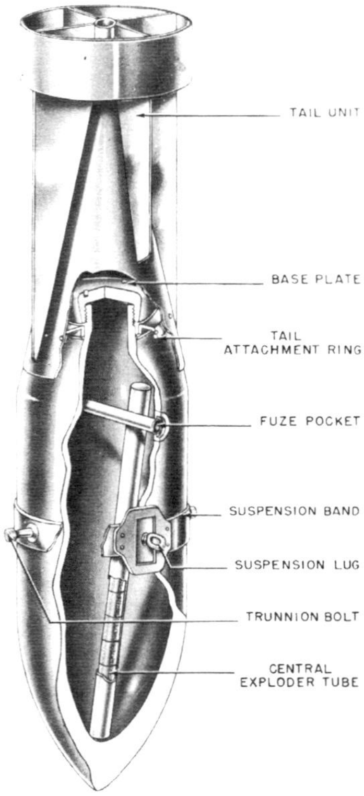

This is an SD500

The centreline rack could also carry an SC1000 'Hermann', as seen here under the V9, viewed from the port rear

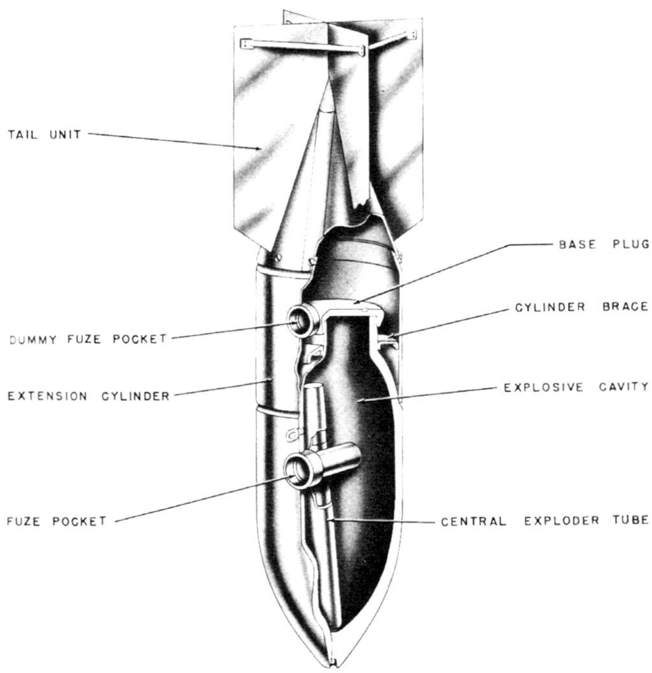

This is an SD250

This is the SC1000 under the V9 viewed from the port front

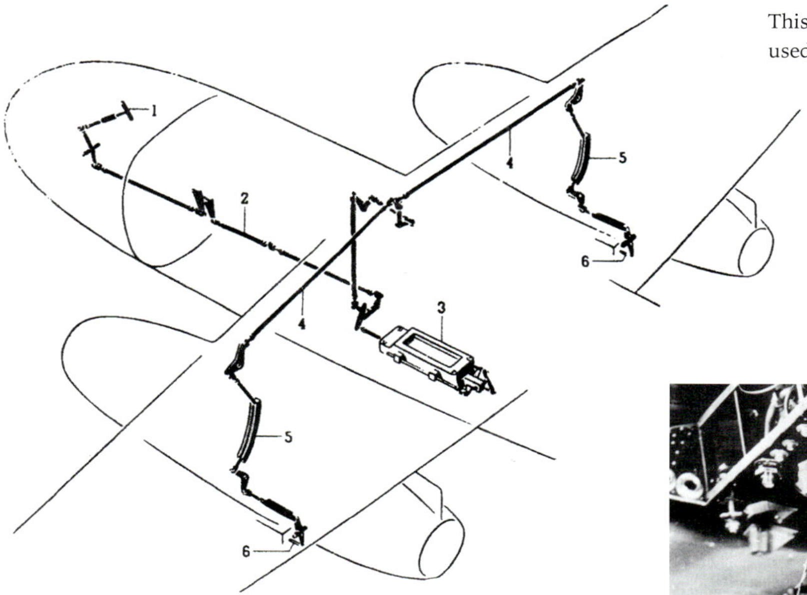

This diagram shows the bomb release system used in the B-series

Key
1. Bombennotzug – Bomb release (handle)
2. Bombennotwurfanlage im Rumpf – Bomb release cable in fuselage
3. Schloßträger im Rumpf – Bomb carrier in fuselage
4. Bombennotwurfanlage im Flügel – Bomb release cable in wings
5. Bombennotwurfanlage am Triebwerk – Bomb release cable in engine nacelle
6. Notwurfstößel am ETC- Bomb release mechanism in ETC

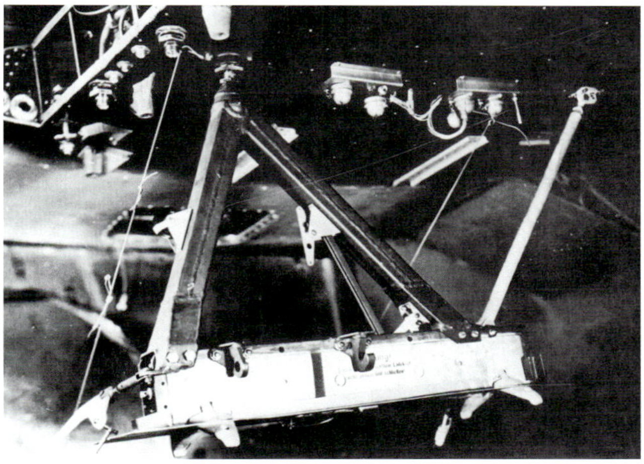

The rack under production machines was probably an ETC 502 (Schloss 502A-1); this period photo shows one of these suspended between the engines of the C-series prototype

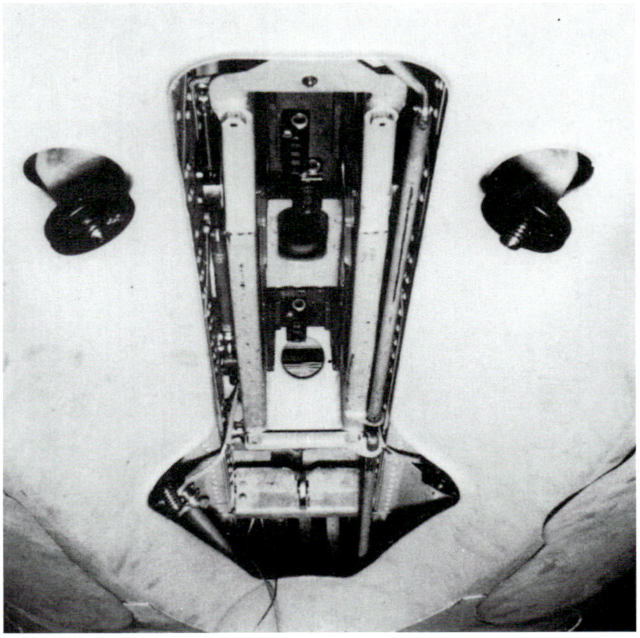

This is the centreline Schlosslafette 1000/500X1BZ carrier

This gives you a good idea of the shape of the rear of the recess on the fuselage underside *(©Scott Willey)*

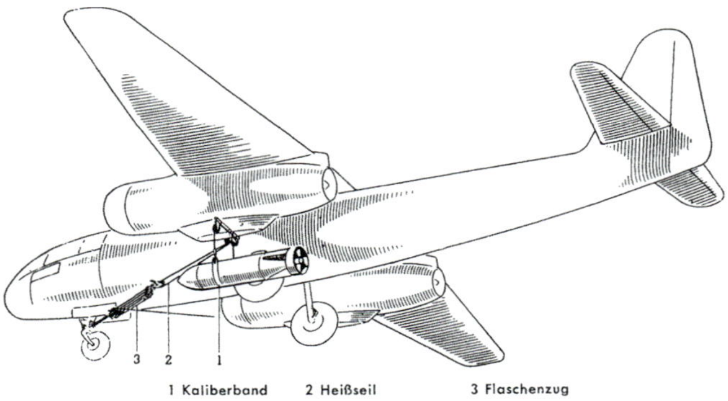

To hoist a bomb up under the nacelle rack, this system of cables and pulleys was used

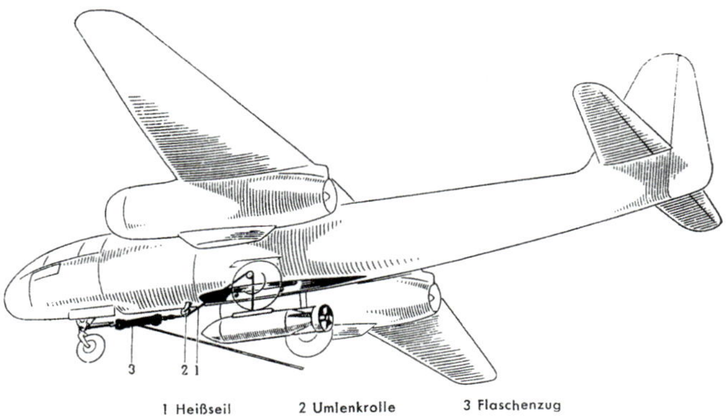

To hoist a bomb underneath the fuselage, this is the system used

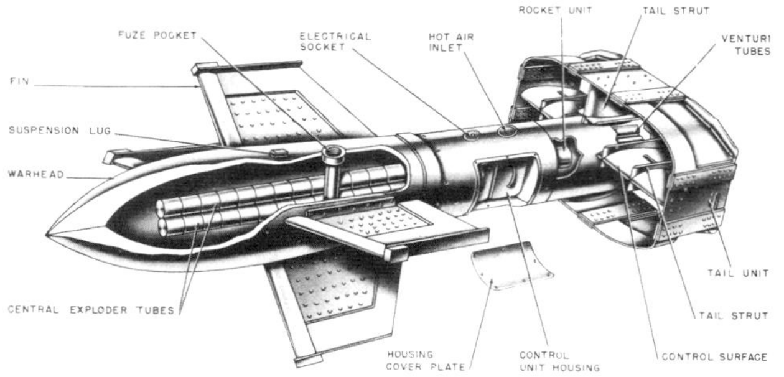

Numerous other weapons were considered for the centreline rack of modified versions of the Ar 234, including the Fritz X

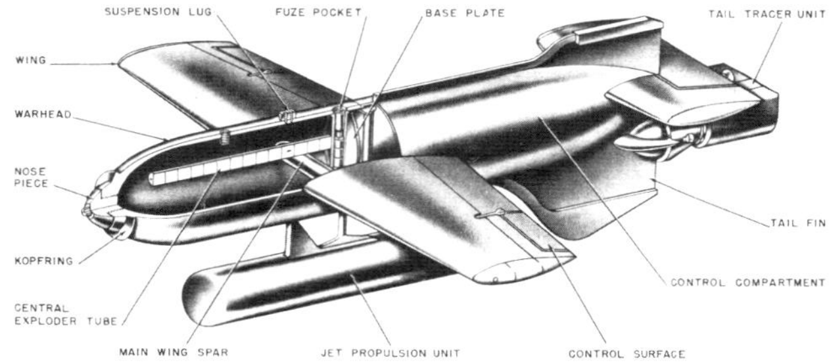

Another potential weapon the Ar 234 could have carried was the Hs 293, although both this and the Fritz X would have required considerable modification

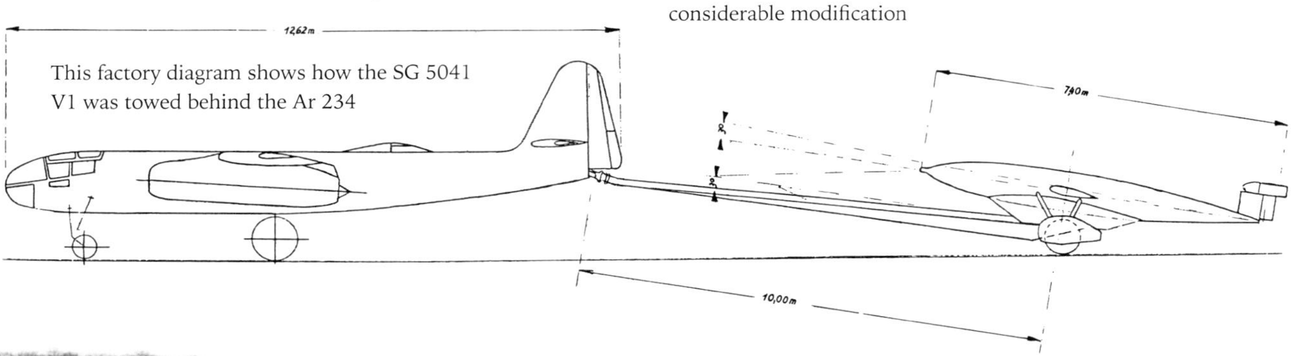

This factory diagram shows how the SG 5041 V1 was towed behind the Ar 234

The Fieseler SG 5041 V1 was tested behind an Ar 234 in early 1945, this is the more complex prototype, production ones would have been simpler

At least two styles of drop tank could be carried by the Ar 234, this is the first type, which is pressed steel with a prominent seam down each side and around the tail cap

The farthest one in this photo is the second type of drop tank that could be used, it is of similar shape to the first (which is also in the foreground here), but it is less complex in its construction and lacks the mounting pads on the sides, etc.

Here you can see the first style of drop tank under the port nacelle rack on the V9

The sight mounted above the cockpit on the NASM example is a PV 1B *(©Scott Willey)*

The sighting head on the top of the PV 1B can be rotated fore or aft, as it was intended for the Ar 234 to have both forward and rearward firing armament, although none was ever fitted to the B-series *(©Scott Willey)*

Looking in the front of the PV 1B you can see the lens plus the ring of wires, which are a heating loop to stop the sight from freezing *(©Scott Willey)*

The PV 1B sight could be used to aim rearward firing guns, with a graticule being visible once the sight was rotated aft, although the field of view then was inverted

Stamped on top of the PV 1B sighting head is its device number (Gerät-Nr), issuing number (Anforderz), the manufacturer (Hersteller) and construction number (Werke-Nr.)

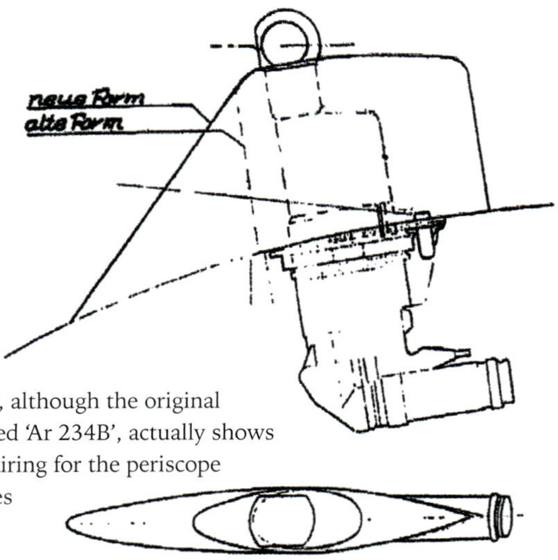

This diagram, although the original page is entitled 'Ar 234B', actually shows the revised fairing for the periscope in the C-series

The other type of sights used on the Ar 234 were the RF 2B and RF 2C, the former is seen here and it was purely a rearward-looking periscope, with the eyepiece visible in the cockpit roof underneath

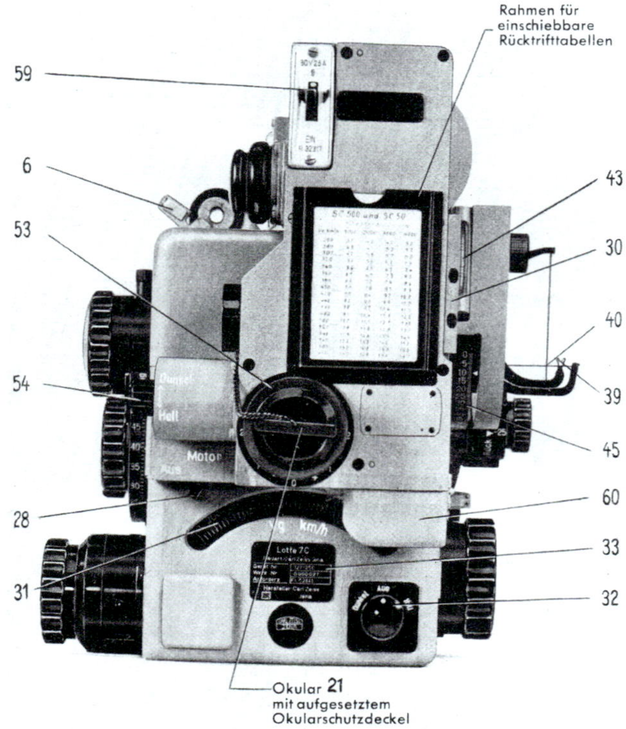

The Lofte 7C sight viewed from above

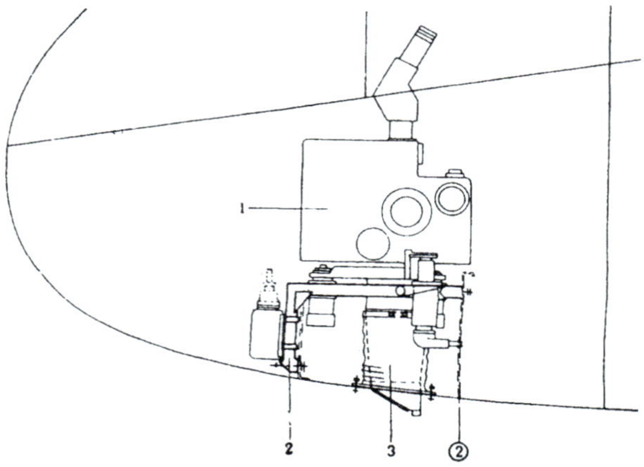

The bombsight on the Ar 234 was situated in the nose/cockpit floor, as seen in this diagram

Key
1. Lofte – Bomb sight
2. Rahmen – Frame
3. Dichtsack (Dichtschlauch) – Sealing bag (sealing hose)

The head of the sight projects below the nose of the aircraft, as seen here in this shot of the NASM B-2. Once again note the ring of heating wire to keep the lens free from mist and frost *(©Scott Willey)*

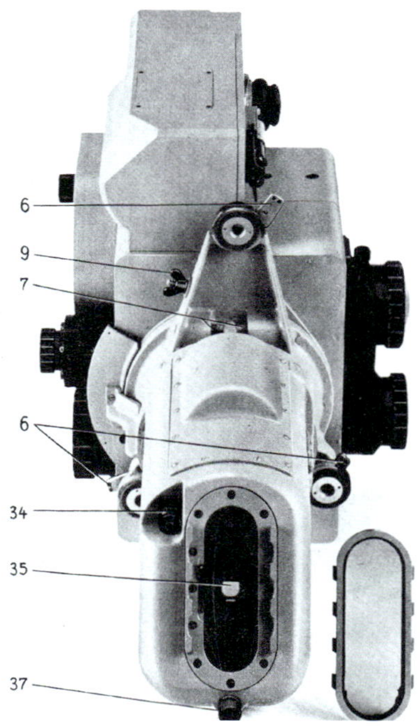

The Lofte 7C seen from below

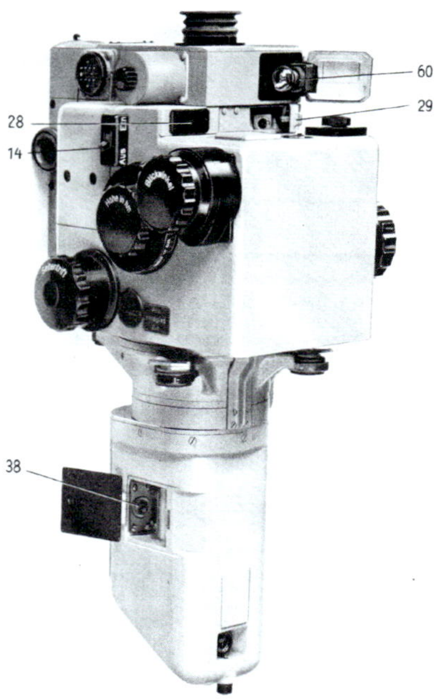

The Lofte 7C viewed from the front of the left side

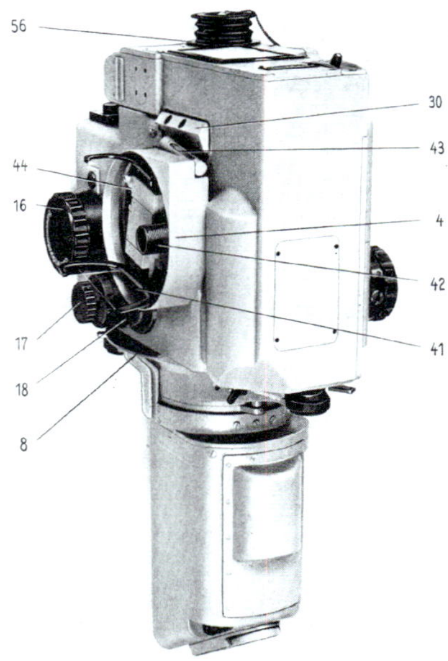

The Lofte 7C viewed from the right side

This is the forward Rb 50/30 camera in the E.370 mock-up

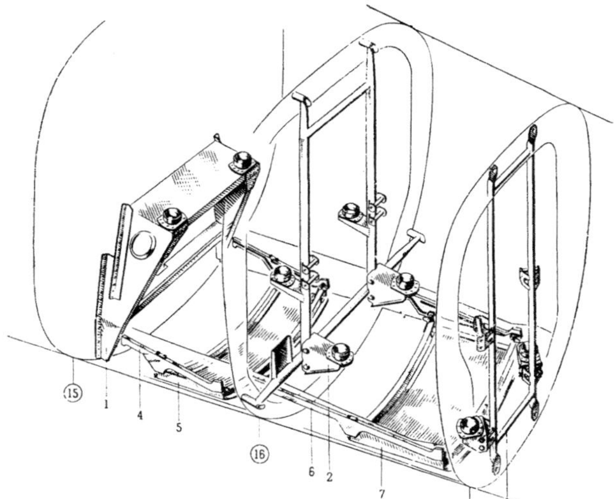

This diagram shows the camera mounting frames built into the rear fuselage

Key

1. Befestigungsgrundlagen am Spant 15 – Mounting bases at frame 15
2. Befestigungsgrundlagen am Spant 16 – Mounting bases at frame 16
3. Befestigungsgrundlagen am Spant 17 – Mounting bases at frame 17
4. Schienen für vorderen Schieber – Rails for front shutter door
5. Vorderer Schieber – Front shutter door
6. Schienen für hintern Schieber – Rails for rear shutter door
7. Hinterer Schieber – Rear shutter door

This is a view of both camera in the E.370 mock-up from underneath; forward is at the bottom of the image

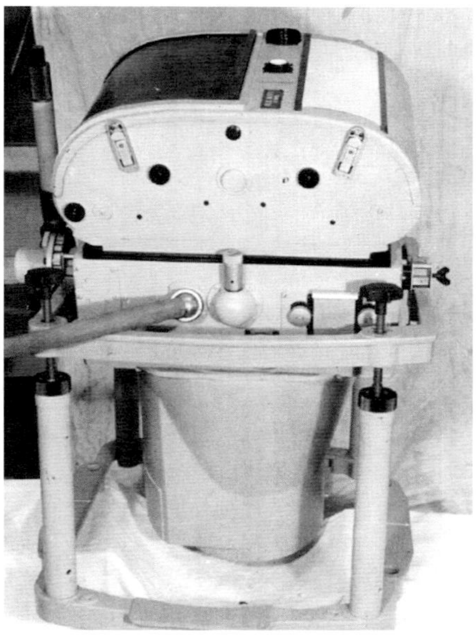

This is an Rb 50/30 camera in its mounting frame

This is a view of the aft Rb 50/30 camera in the E.370 mock-up

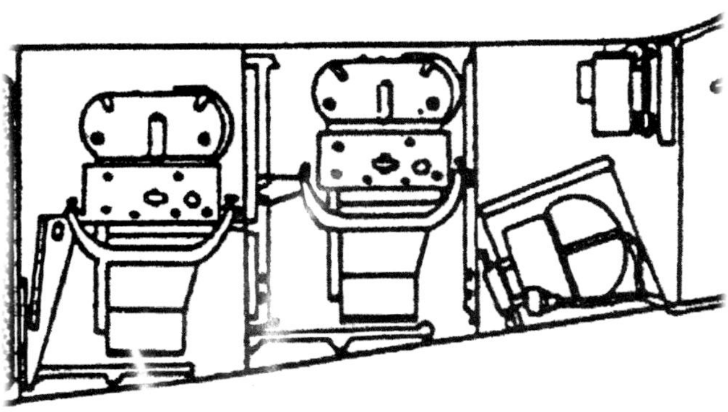

This diagram is listed as showing the Rb 75/30 camera installation in the back of the C-series, but it also applies to the B-series

This shot shows the two camera bays in the rear fuselage, the front of the aircraft is at the bottom of the image

To give you an idea of the size of the film cassette, here you can see a groundcrewman lifting one up to his colleagues on top of T9+GH prior to a sortie

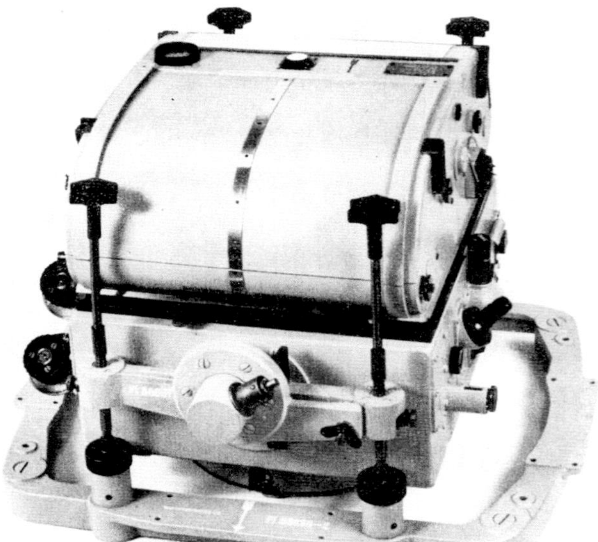

This is an Rb 20/30, which was sometimes used as a twin fitment or in combination with an Rb 50/30 or Rb 75/30

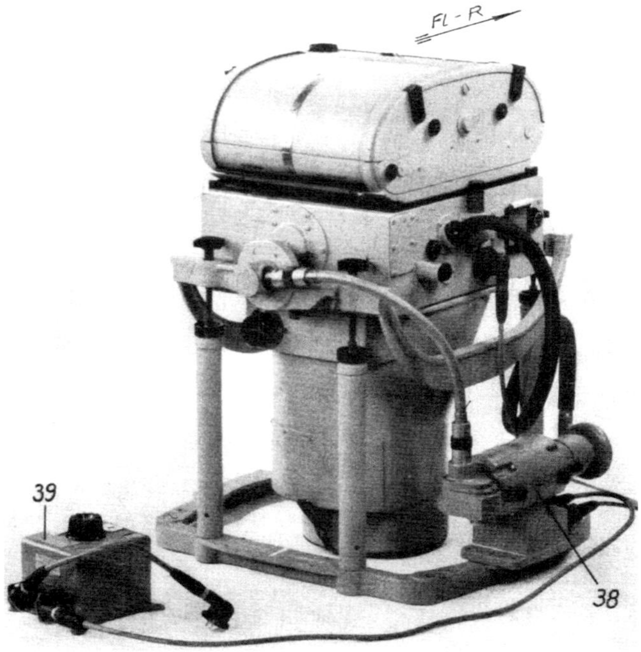

This is an Rb 75/30 complete with the motor and control box, the latter being installed in the cockpit via a much longer control cable

This well-known shot of the Ar 234 V5, after being hit by an Fw 190 at Orainenburg in August 1944, clearly shows one of the Rb 75/30 cameras

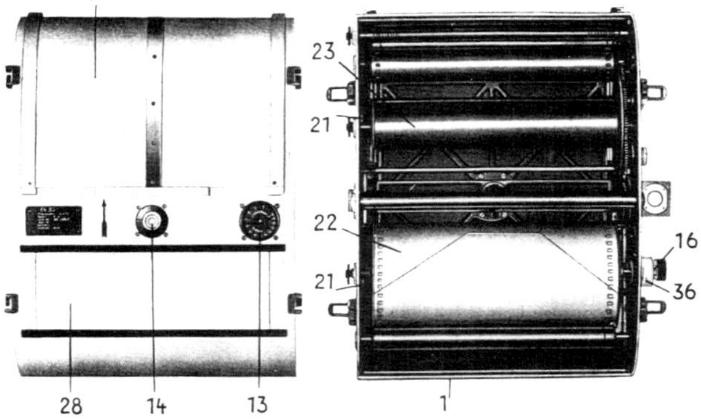

This is a standard Fk 30 film cassette, as used by all camera types fitted to the Ar 234

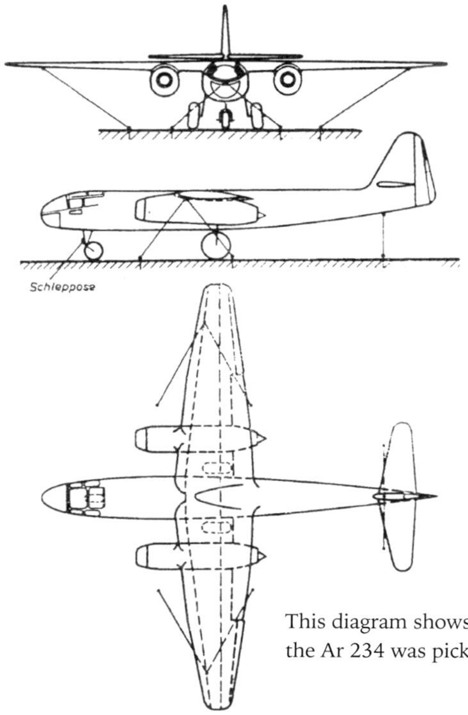

This diagram shows how the Ar 234 was picketed

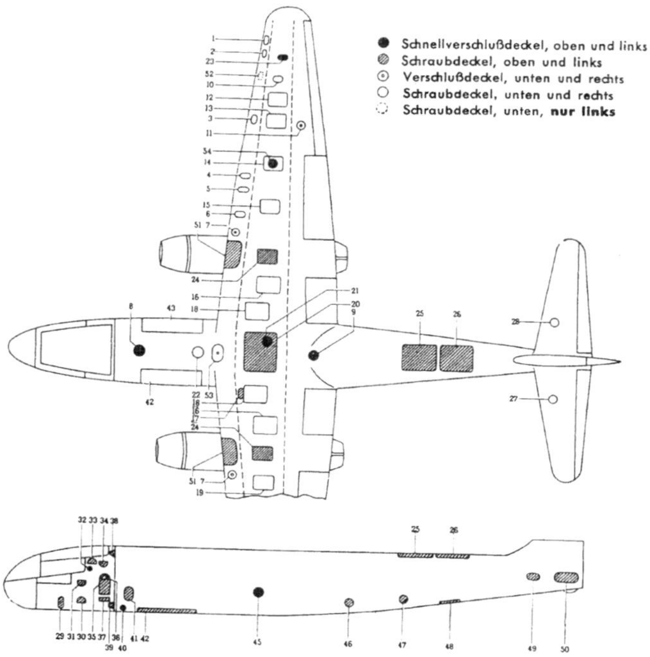

All the various access panels on the B-series, those on the port side being just mirror images of those on the starboard

Key

- Schnellverschlußdeckel, oben und links – Quick-release panels, top and left
- Schraubdeckel, oben und links – Screw-locking access panels, top and left
- Verschlußdeckel, unten und rechts – Hinged access panels, bottom and right
- Schraubdeckel, unten und rechts – Screw-locking access panels, bottom and right
- Schraubdeckel, unten, nur links – Screw-locking panels, underneath, left only

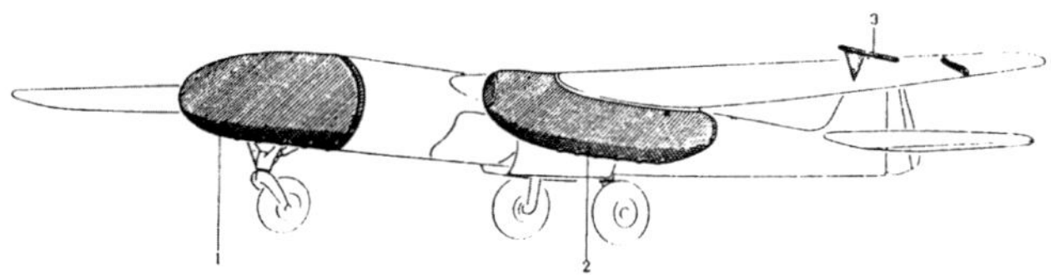

This diagram shows the various tarpaulins used: the literal translation of 'Bezug' is 'respect', but in this instance it means to protect

Key

1. Bezug für Kabine – Cover for cockpit
2. Bezug für die Triebwerke – Cover for engine
3. Bezug für Staurohr – Cover for pitot

The engines of the Ar 234 needed to be changed often, with only a 10 hour operational life, so to do this they used a special crane as shown here. It is unlikely with the worsening situation for Nazi Germany in 1945, that this was often available, though!

To get the ski-equipped early V and projected A-series machines back up on the trolley, these tower jacks were used: they work like a gasometer, only via hydraulic pressure

Evolution

Prototype, Production and Projected Variants

The evolution of the Ar 234 series involved a large number of prototype machines as well as pre-production and production series airframes. What follows therefore is a list of all those airframes that were actually built, or for which at least one existed along with a production order from the Luftwaffe. We appreciate that the Ar 234 had many projected designs as well as a vast number of advanced developments of the basic design, but none of these ever saw production or operational use and thus all of them fall outside the scope of this title.

As you would expect with a subject now 70+ years old, there is much contradiction in both period and subsequent documentation, so we have based all our drawings, where possible, on existing photos and when not, on the most likely layout based on other developments from other aircraft manufacturers in Nazi Germany at that time.

Ar 234 V1 (W/Nr.130001)

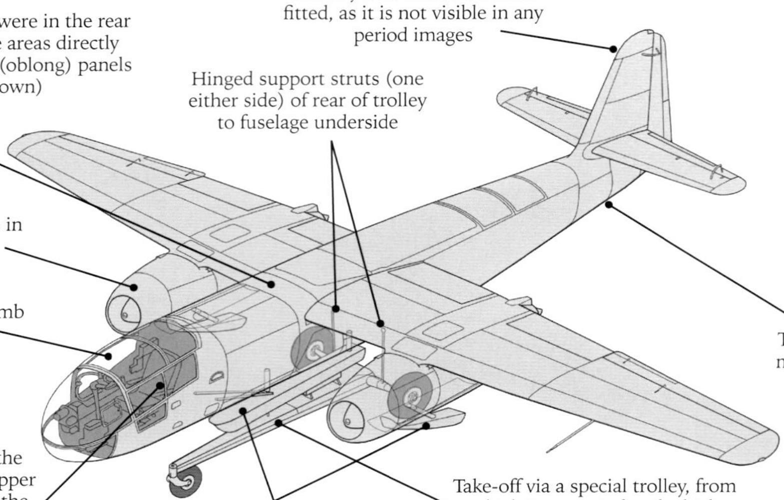

Note
This machine carried the code TG+KB and first flew on the 30th July 1943. This machine was painted in a splinter pattern of RLM 70/71 over RLM 65, the demarcation between upper and lower colours was via a soft wavy line along both fuselage and engines. It was badly damaged on landing on its third flight on the 29th August 1943 and never flew again.

Ar 234 V2 (W/Nr.130002)

Identical to the V1 (W/Nr.130001) except:

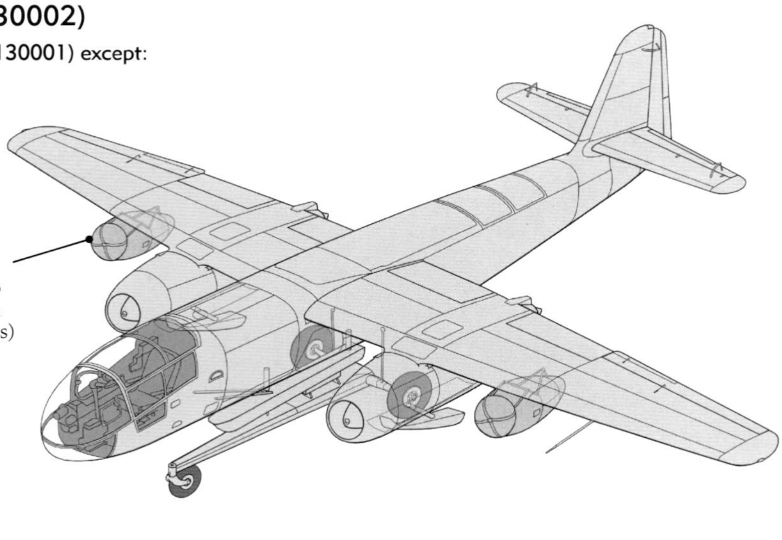

Note
First flew 13th September 1943, coded DP+AW. This machine was painted in a splinter pattern of RLM 70/71 over RLM 65 and again the demarcation was via a wavy soft line. It was lost on its fifth flight on the 2nd October 1943 when the port engine caught fire and burnt through the control rods, killing the pilot Flugkapitän Selle.

Ar 234 V3 (W/Nr.130003)

Same as the V1 (W/Nr.130001) except:

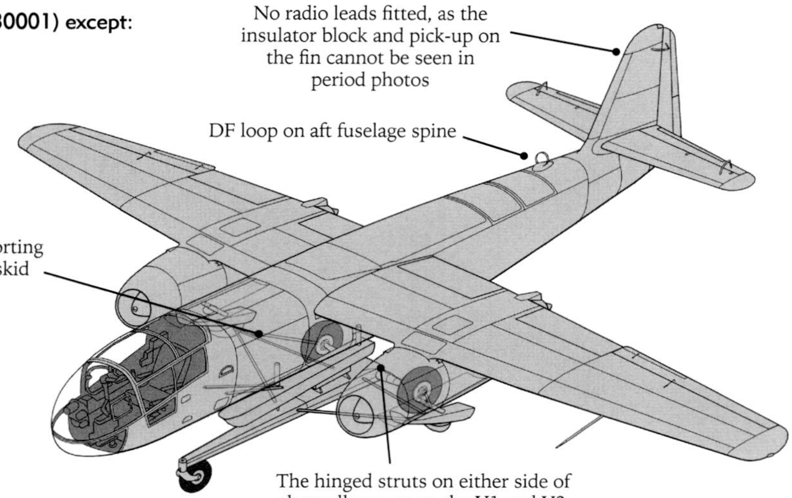

Note
This machine first flew on the 29th September 1943 and carried the code DP+AX. It was painted in a splinter pattern of RLM 70/71 over RLM 65 and again the demarcation was via a wavy soft line. It was intended to have both a pressurised cockpit and an ejection seat, but neither of these were actually ever installed.

No surviving photos show this prototype with Walter 109-500 pods fitted, although it most probably could have carried/used them

Ar 234 V4 (W/Nr.130004)

Same as the V3 (W/Nr.130003) except:

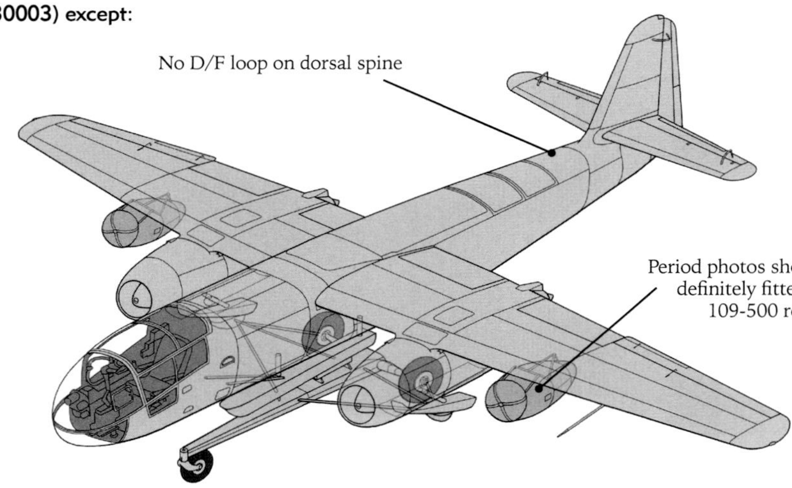

Note
This machine first flew on the 26th November 1943 and carried the code DP+AY. It was painted in a splinter pattern of RLM 70/71 over RLM 65 and again the demarcation was via a wavy soft line.

Ar 234 V5 (W/Nr.130005)

Same as the V4 (W/Nr.130004) except:

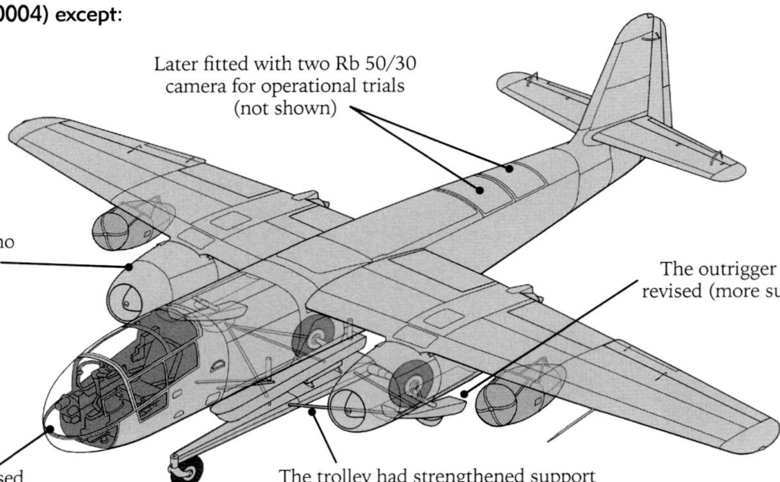

Note
This machine carried the code GK+IV and it was later allocated to 1./Versuchsverband OKL, where it was marked as T9+LH. Written off at Oranienburg on the 28th August 1944 after being damaged by German flak.

Ar 234 V6 (W/Nr.130006)

Same as the V1 (W/Nr.130001) except:

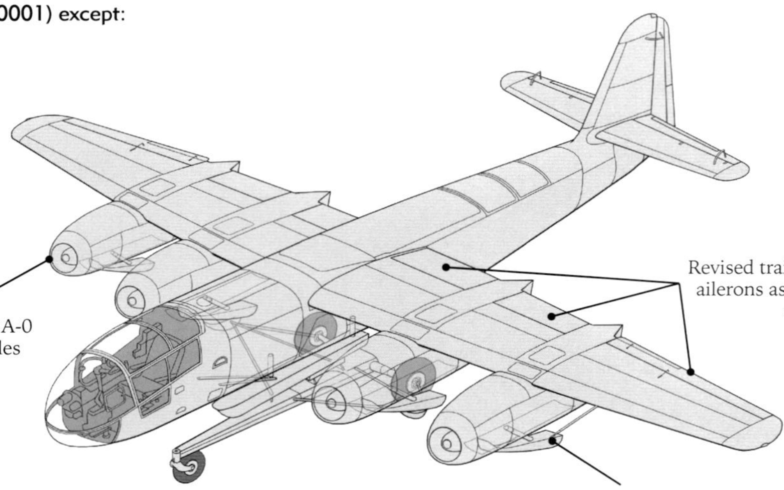

Note
This machine carried the code GK+IW. This machine was painted in a splinter pattern of RLM 70/71 over RLM 65 again with a soft wavy line demarcation.

Ar 234 V7 (W/Nr.130007)

Same as the V5 (W/Nr.130005) except:

Note
This machine carried the code GK+IX and was first flown on the 22nd June 1944. It was painted in a splinter pattern of RLM 70/71 over RLM 65 again with a soft wavy line demarcation. This machine was allocated to 1./Versuchsverband OKL in June 1944, where it was marked as T9+MH and it undertook the world's first reconnaissance mission by a jet on the 2nd August 1944. Retired from use on the 19th November 1944 and presumed scrapped or used as a ground test airframe.

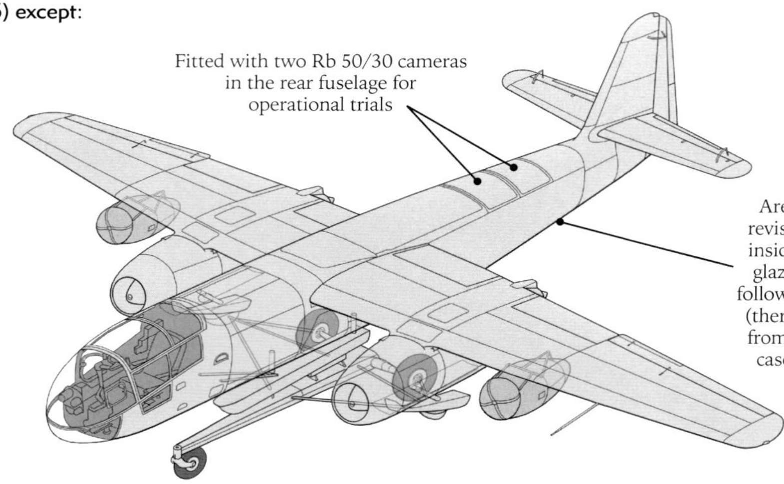

Ar 234 V8 (W/Nr.130008)

Same as the V6 (W/Nr.130006) except:

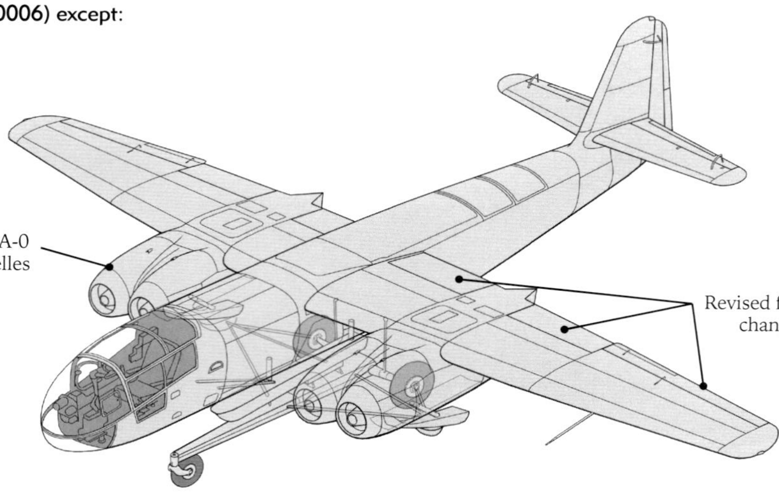

Note
This machine carried the code GK+IY and first flew on the 4th February 1944. This machine was painted in a splinter pattern of RLM 70/71 over RLM 65 again with a soft wavy line demarcation. This aircraft was withdrawn from the test programme on the 6th May 1944.

Ar 234 V9 (W/Nr.130009)

Same as V5 (W/Nr.130005) except:

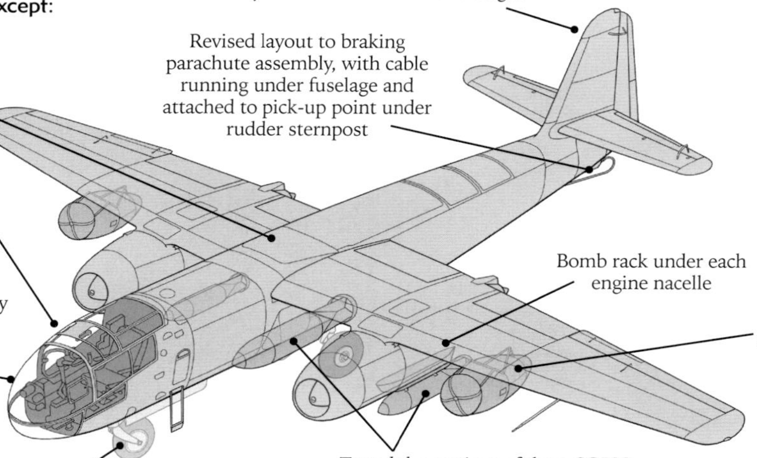

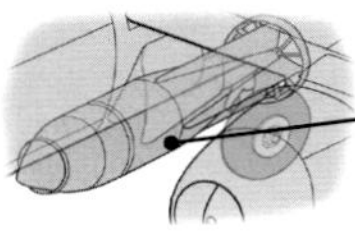

Note
This machine carried the code PH+SQ (some state GK+IW) and it first flew on the 12th March 1944. It was painted in a splinter pattern of RLM 70/71 over RLM 65 again with a soft wavy line demarcation.

Ar 234 V10 (W/Nr.130010)

Same as the V9 (W/Nr.130009) except:

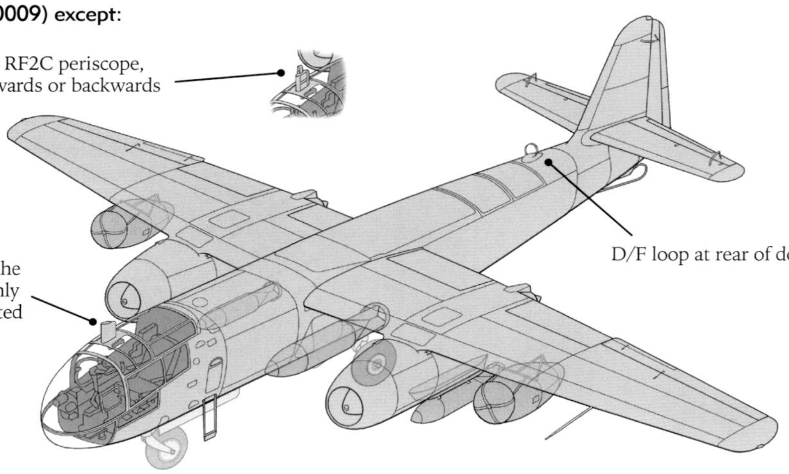

Note
This machine carried the code PH+SR and first flew on the 7th April 1944 and was lost on its 50th flight on the 27th July 1944, when its pilot Hans Richter (of the Patin company) bailed out.

Ar 234 V11 (W/Nr.130021)

Same as the V10 (W/Nr.130010) except:

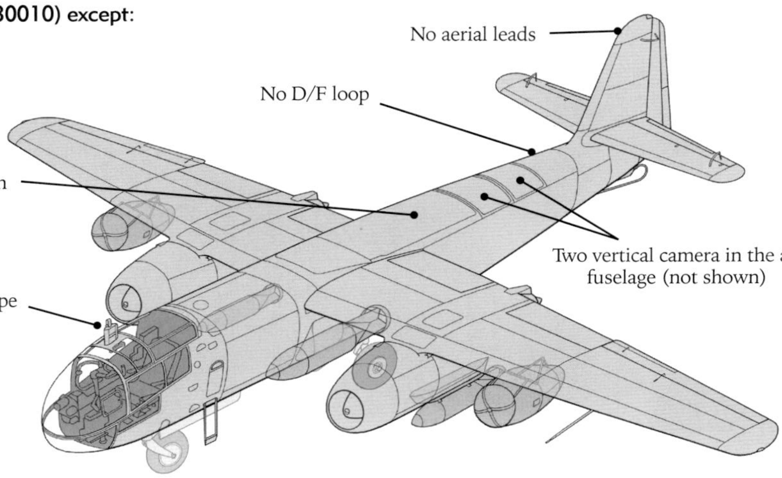

Note
This was the third prototype of the B-series, it carried the code PH+SS and first flew on the 10th May 1944. Only one photograph of this machine is known to exist, and only then with it partially in the background, so our comments about its physical nature are restricted by this partial port side view. Note that as a prototype for the B-1 series, this was to have had two fixed MG151 cannon in a gondola under the rear fuselage, facing aft, but it was never installed.

Ar 234 V12 (W/Nr.130022)

Same as the V10 (W/Nr.130010):

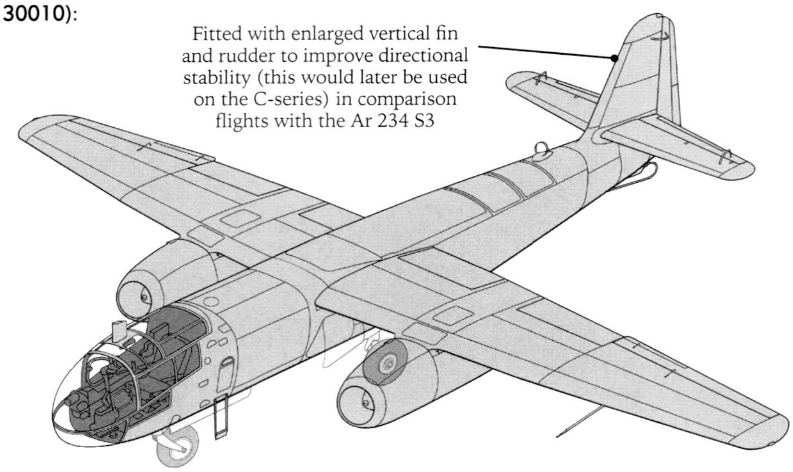

Note
This was the fourth and last prototype of the B-series, it carried the code PH+ST and first flew on the 15th September 1944. It was destroyed in an air raid at Wesendorf on the 4th April 1945.

Ar 234 V13 (W/Nr.130023)

Same as the V10 (W/Nr.130010):

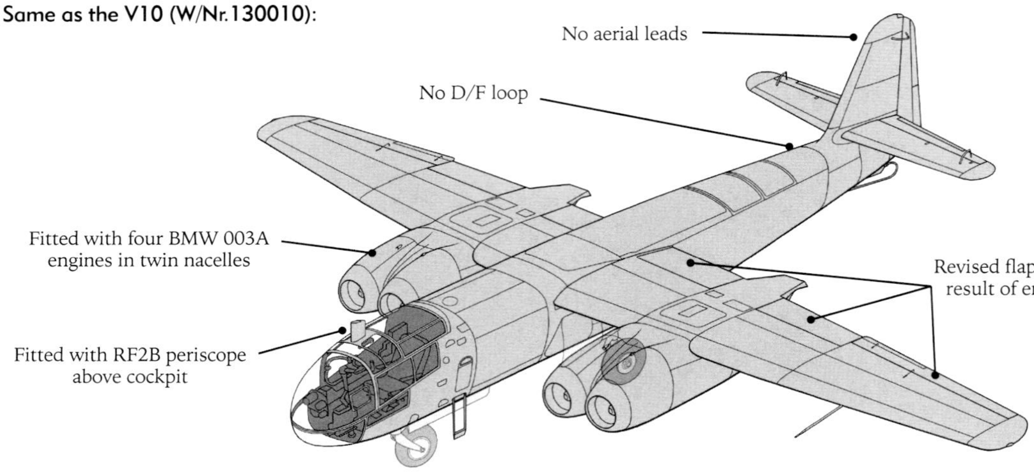

Note
This carried the code PH+SU and first flew on the 6th September 1944 but badly damaged due to a crash landing after the successive failure of three engines, so sent to the Technical School at Jüterbog on the 22nd September 1944.

Ar 234 V14 (W/Nr.130024)

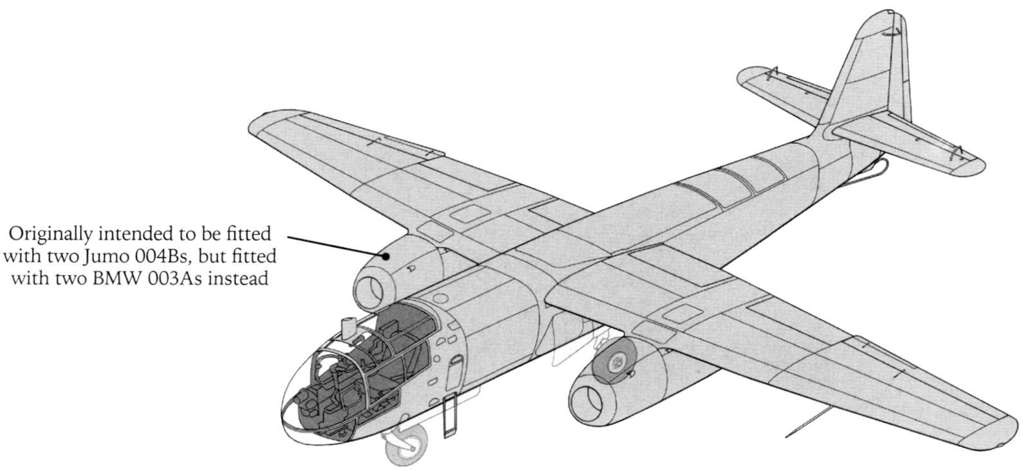

Note
This carried the code PH+SV and first flown in early December 1945. It was intentionally blown up to stop it falling into Allied hands in April 1945.

Ar 234 V15 (W/Nr.130025)

Same as the V13 (W/Nr.130023) – see Ar 234 V13 above

This carried the code PH+SW and first flew on the 20th July 1944. Later passed for operational tests by 3./Versuchsverband OKL as T9+HL and destroyed in April 1945.

Ar 234 V16 (W/Nr.130026) – Initial Form

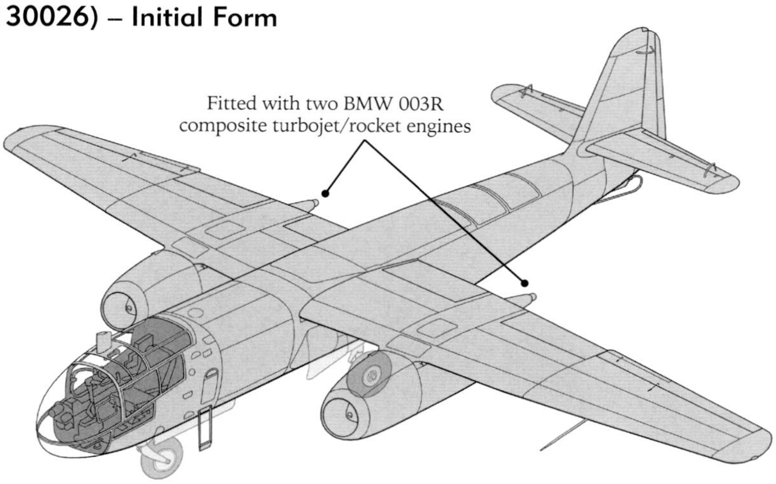

Note
This carried the code PH+SX and was never actually completed as it became the Versuchsflügel with the crescent wing (see below).

Ar 234 V16 (W/Nr.130026) – Revised Form (Versuchsflügel II)

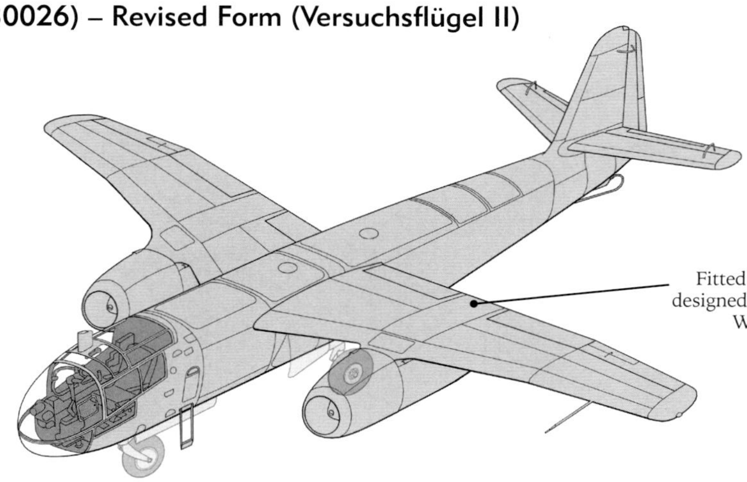

Note
It is not known which of the wing layouts (V1 to V5 with different sweep angles) was fitted before this machine was destroyed by advancing Allied troops in mid-April 1945.

Ar 234 V17 (W/Nr.130027)

Same as the V14 (W/Nr.130024) – see Ar 234 V14 opposite

This carried the code PH+SUY and first flew on the 25th September 1944. Later passed for operational tests by 3./Versuchsverband OKL as T9+LL and destroyed in April 1945.

Ar 234 V18 (W/Nr.130028)

Note
This machine was never completed before the war ended.

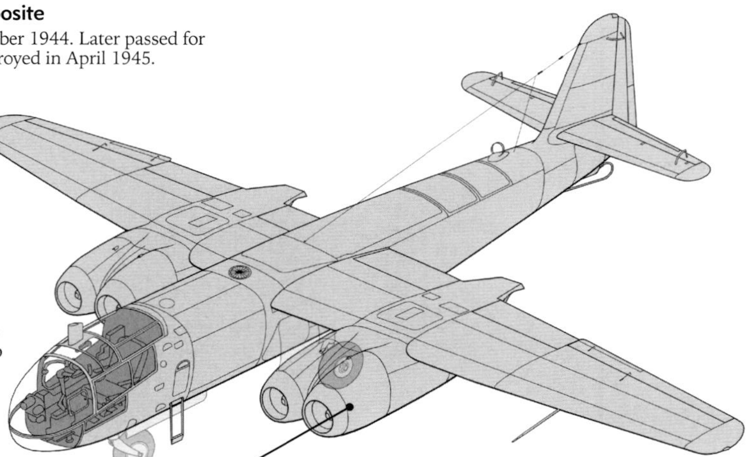

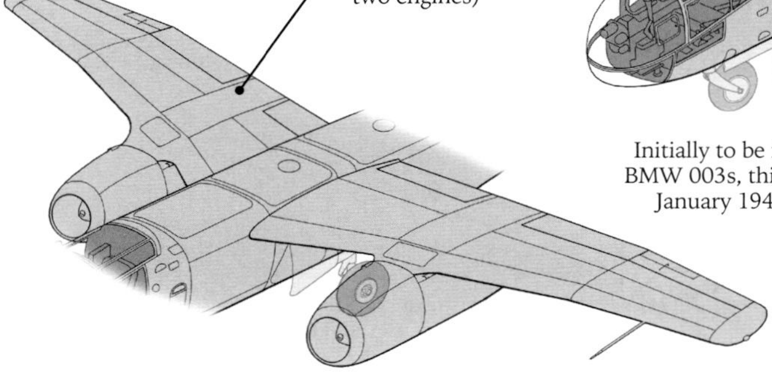

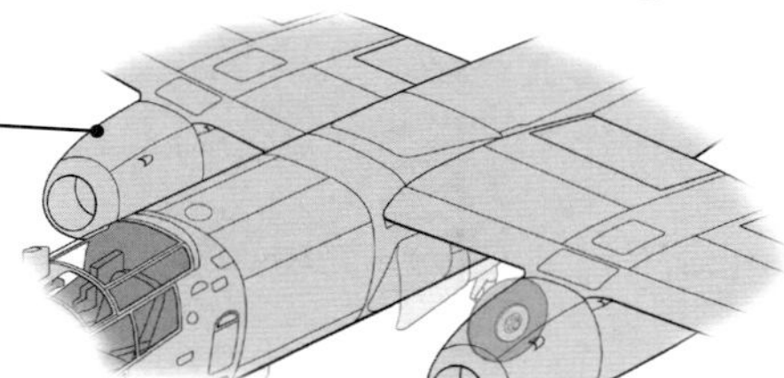

Ar 234 V19 (W/Nr.130029)

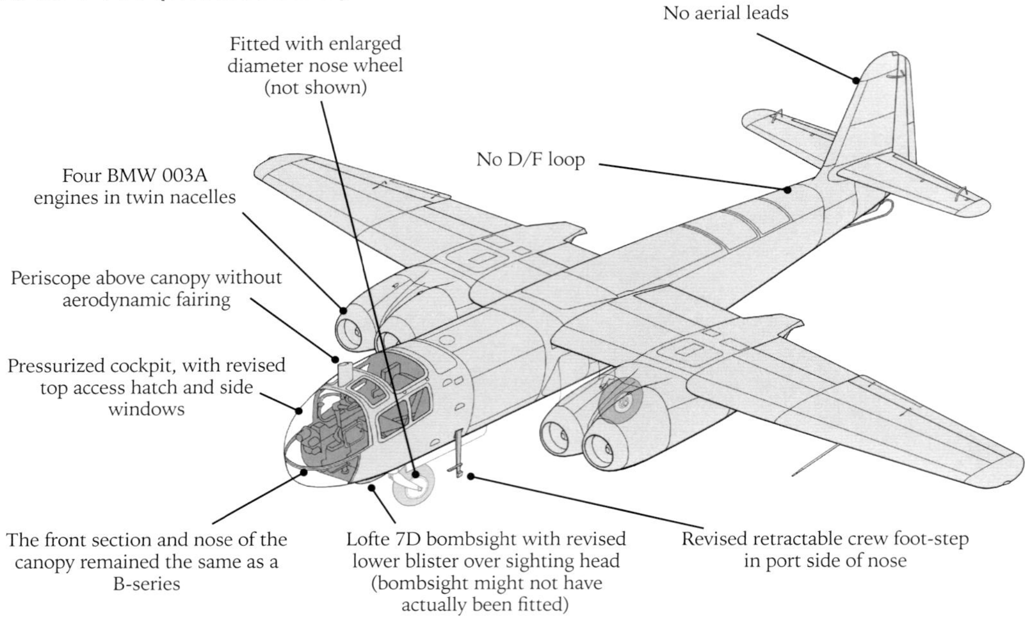

Note
Prototype of the C-3, this machine carried the code PI+WX, although it was not carried on the airframe. It first flew on the 16th October 1944. Transferred to the BMW test facility and eventually blown up to avoid capture by the Allied in the Hofoldinger Forest in April 1945. It should be noted that in documents from January 1945 it was intended to convert this airframe to the Versuchsflügel II (metal swept) wings by the end of March 1945, but this never happened. Many sources state this machine had air brakes, but no documents survive to confirm if they were airframe or wing-mounted.

Ar 234 V20 (W/Nr.130030)

Same as the Ar 234 V19 (W/Nr.130029) – see Ar 234 V19 above

2nd prototype of the C-3, this machine carried the code PI+WY, although it was not carried on the airframe. It first flew on the 5th November 1944, but was damaged when hit by a taxiing Fw 190 three days later. It was repaired and flew again, but it was badly damaged during an air raid on Wesendorf on the 4th April 1945.

Ar 234 V21 (W/Nr.130061)

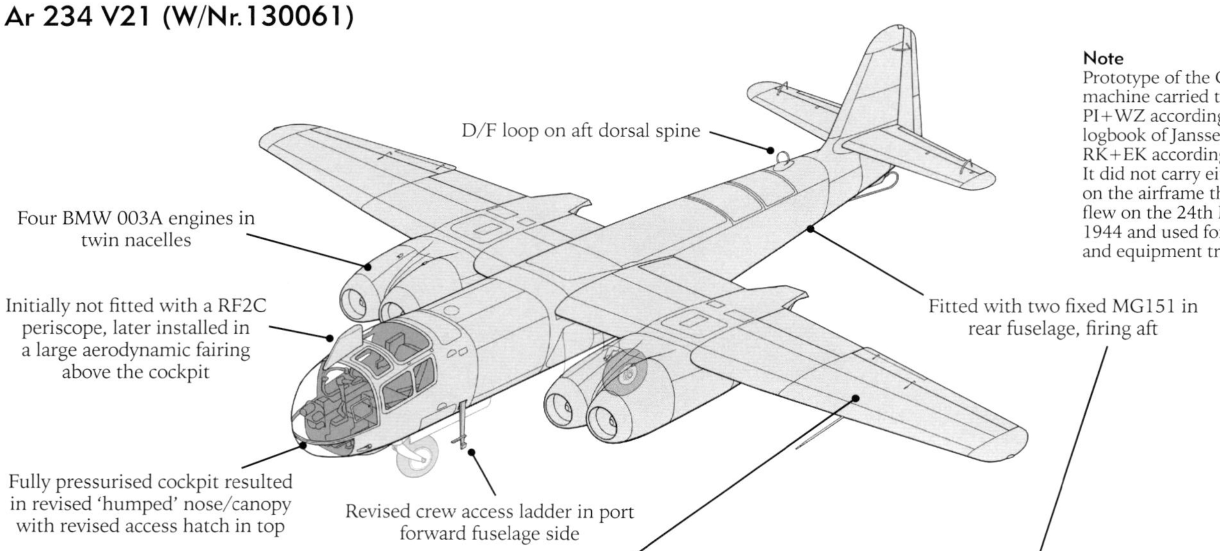

Note
Prototype of the C-3, this machine carried the code PI+WZ according to the logbook of Janssen, but RK+EK according to Eheim? It did not carry either code on the airframe though. First flew on the 24th November 1944 and used for weapons and equipment trials.

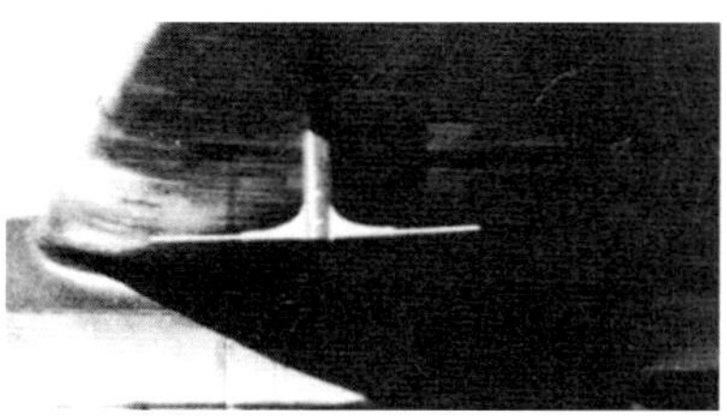

Late 'T' shape radio altimeter antenna under the port outer wing (there is no photographic evidence to prove it was also under the starboard wing)

Photos show a lack of braking parachute cable under the stern-post, although there is something there and this may just be the pick-up point without the cable yet having been installed

Ar 234 V21 – Rebuilt Form (Versuchsflügel)

Same as V21 except:

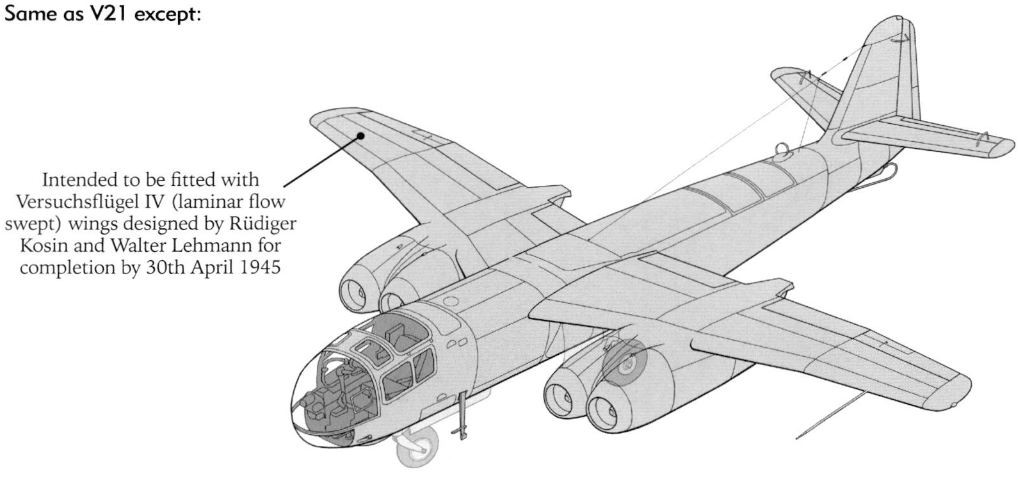

Note
It is not known which of the wing layouts (V1 to V5 with different sweep angles) was fitted (if at all) before this machine was destroyed by advancing Allied troops in mid-April 1945.

Ar 234 V22 (W/Nr.130062)

Same as V21 (W/Nr.130061) except:

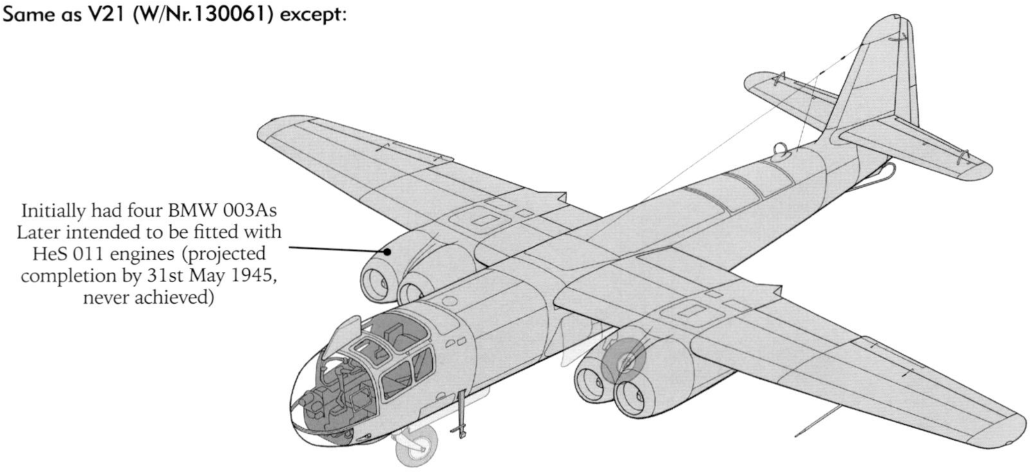

Note
Prototype of the C-3, this machine carried the code RK+EL and first flew on the 1st January 1945.

Ar 234 V23 (W/Nr.130063)

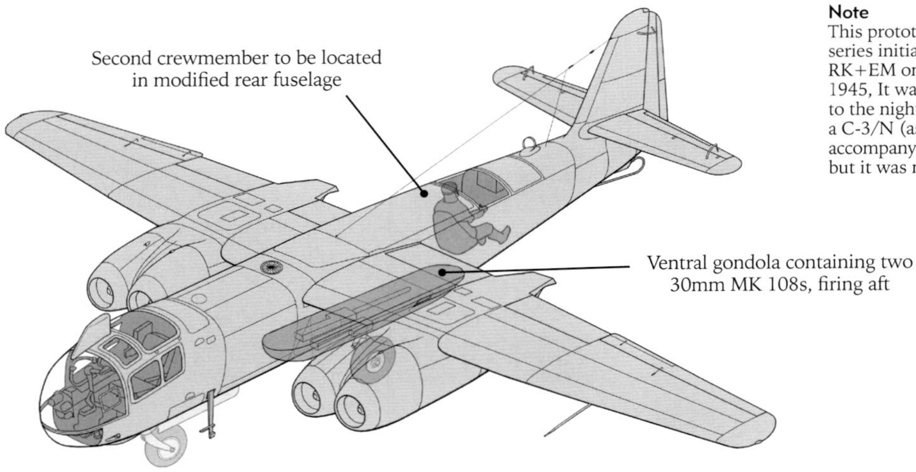

Note
This prototype of the C-3 series initially flew as RK+EM on the 14th January 1945, It was to be converted to the night fighter role as a C-3/N (as shown in our accompanying isometric), but it was never completed.

Ar 234 V24 (W/Nr.130064)

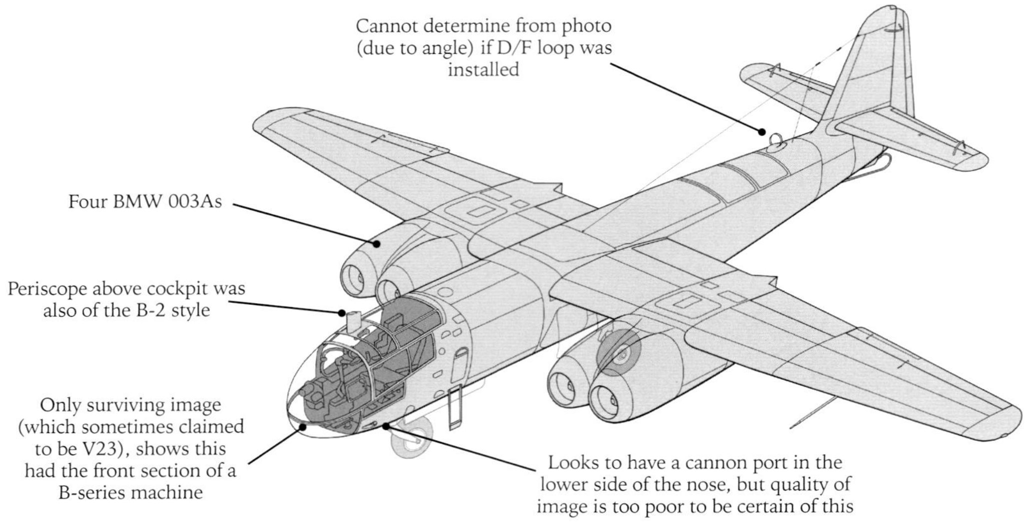

Note
This prototype of the C-3 series was coded RK+EN and first flew on the 12th January 1945. It was used for pressurised cockpit trials and was later intended to be converted to a ground-attack version with extra armour and BMW 003, Jumo 004 or HeS 011 engines, although this was never undertaken.

Ar 234 V25 (W/Nr.130065)

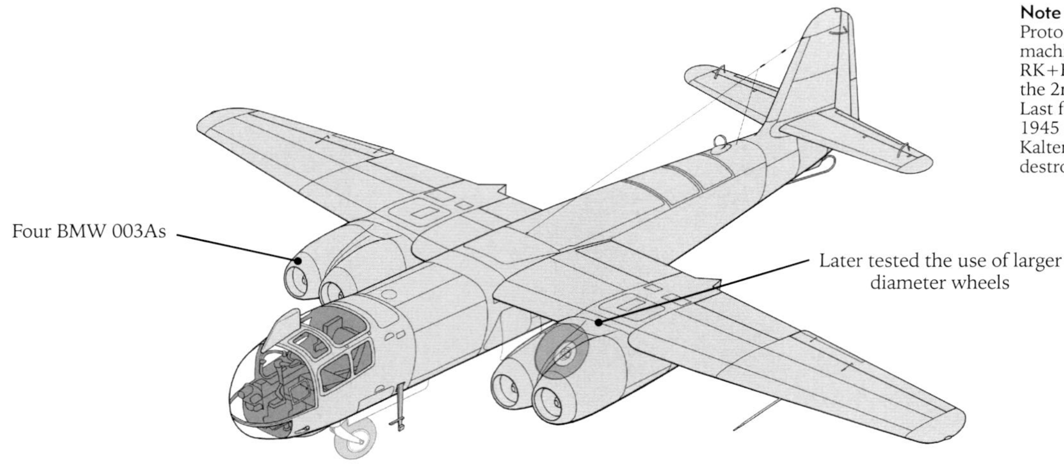

Note
Prototype of the C-3, this machine carried the code RK+EO and first flew on the 2nd February 1945. Last flown on the 1st May 1945 from Warnemünde to Kaltenkirchen, where it was destroyed.

Ar 234 V26 (W/Nr.130066)

1. Four BMW 003As
2. Intended to test the Versuchsflügel III (laminar flow) wings

Never completed.

Ar 234 V27 (W/Nr.130067)

1. Second crew member located in modified rear fuselage
2. Ventral gondola containing two 30mm MK108s, firing forward

This prototype of the C-3 series was to be converted to the night fighter role as a C-3/N, but it was never completed.

Ar 234 V28 (W/Nr.130068)

This was a prototype of the projected C-5 series, but it was never completed.

Ar 234 V29 (W/Nr.130069)

This was a prototype of the projected C-6 series, but it was never completed.

Ar 234 V30

It is claimed that this was a C-series airframe used for laminar flow wing development, however official documents from January 1945 state this airframe was to have four BMW 003 engines, normal wings, two-seat cockpit and larger wheels for flight characteristics and performance testing. The airframe was never completed though.

Ar 234 V31

This was the same specification as the V30, but it too was never completed.

Ar 234 V32

Two-man cockpit as C-5 prototype, never built.

Ar 234 V33

Two-man cockpit as C-5 prototype and later to have wings from another test airframe to become the Nachtigall night fighter Projekt I, never built.

Ar 234 V34

Completed as C-3 with wings taken from another test airframe, two-man cockpit and HeS 011 engines, never built.

Ar 234 V35

To test two sets of Versuchsflügel III wings, two-man cockpit and HeS 011 engines, never built.

Ar 234 V36

To test two sets of Versuchsflügel II wings and HeS 011 engines, never built.

Ar 234 V37

To test two sets of Versuchsflügel IV wings and HeS 011 engines, never built.

Ar 234 V38

To test two sets of Versuchsflügel IIIa wings (with rounded tips and no flaps) and HeS 011 engines, never built.

Ar 234 V39

To test two sets of Versuchsflügel IIIa wings and HeS 011 engines, never built.

Ar 234 V40

To test three sets of Versuchsflügel IIIa wings and HeS 011 engines, never built.

S-Series

All of these machines can be thought of as pre-production, but apart from the occasional difference, they were all identical to the production B-2 series. As a result, we will only offer isometrics here for those which photographs survive to prove what they looked like and when said photographs prove they had omissions or additions in relation to a production B-2. All others are simply listed here with notes about their markings and history.

Ar 234 S1 (W/Nr.140101)

First flew 8th June 1944, marked as GM+BA. Test flew at Rechlin, crashed at Lärz on the 25th July 1944, killing the pilot, Lt Herbert Lissau.

Ar 234 S2 (W/Nr.140102)

First flew 22nd June 1944 marked as GM+BB. To Rechlin from November 1944 marked as E7+10 to test the Lofte 7K bombsight and Patin PDS autopilot.

Ar 234 S3 (W/Nr.140103)

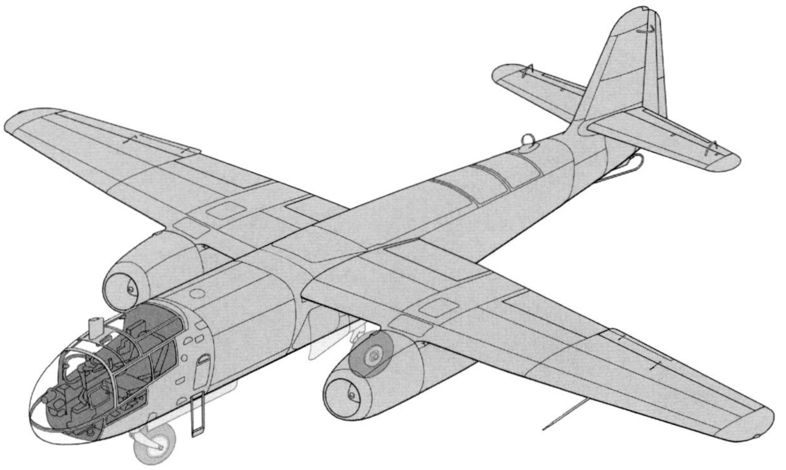

Note
First flew 10th July 1944 marked as GM+BC. Flown to Sagan for test including comparison flights with Fw 190 during 17th August to 17th September 1944 period. On the 19th September 1944 a fuselage extension (exact amount cannot be determined, as documents do no survive) fitted just aft of the cockpit. Without comparison to the S1 and S2, in identical port side views (which don't exist) it is impossible to tell if this extension was added to all machines from this point onwards, or in fact was also on the S1 and S2 as well.

Ar 234 S4 (W/Nr.140104)

First flight date unknown, marked as GM+BD and flown to Sagan for tests (heavy bomb loads) on the 8th August 1944. Later passed to KG 76 and lost on the 18th December 1944 during an attempt to land in bad weather.

Ar 234 S5 (W/Nr.140105)

First flew 18th July 1944, marked as GM+BE. Moved to Rechlin on 22nd July marked as E3+10. Used for general engine and fuel consumption tests.

Ar 234 S6 (W/Nr.140106)

First flew 29th July 1944 as GM+BF. To Rechlin as E7+15 and on the 21st August moved to Küpper for more tests. Returned to Rechlin during October 18th to December 17th 1944 period, where it was marked as E5+10.

Ar 234 S7 (W/Nr.140107)

First flew 28th July 1944 marked as GM+BG. Moved to Rechlin during the 28th October 1944 to 11th February 1945 period, where it was marked as E2+30. Captured by US forces at Rechlin at the end of the war.

Ar 234 S8 (W/Nr.140108)

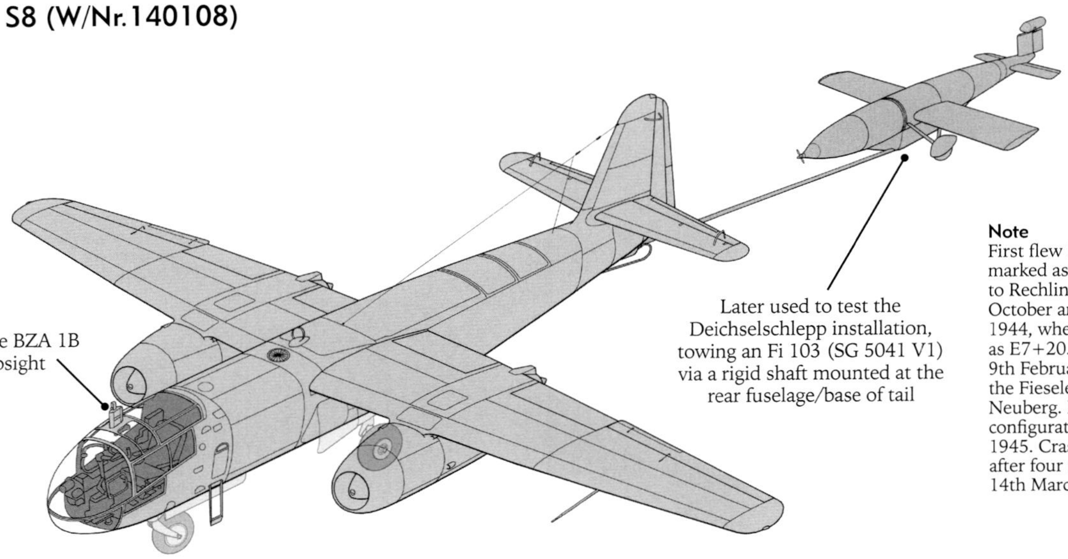

Note
First flew 3rd August 1944 marked as GM+BH. Moved to Rechlin between 28th October and 17th December 1944, where it was marked as E7+20. Modified from 9th February 1945 to test the Fieseler SG 5041 V1 at Neuberg. First flew in this configuration 25th February 1945. Crashed and destroyed after four test flight on the 14th March 1945.

Ar 234 S9 (W/Nr.140109)

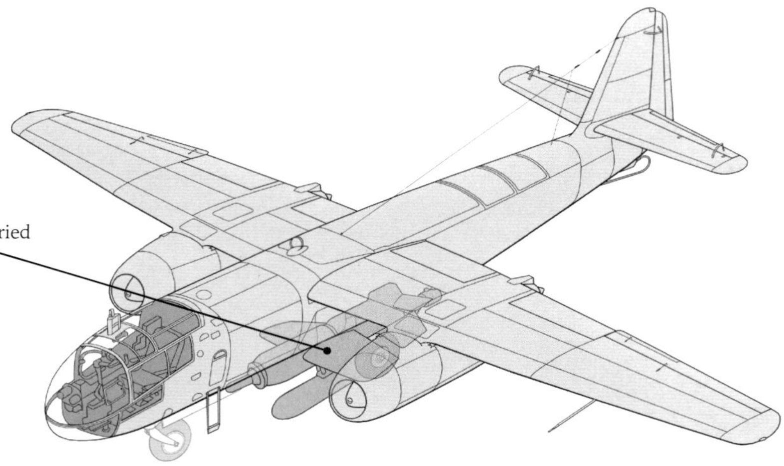

Note
First flew 10th August 1944 marked as GM+BI. To Rechlin 19th August 1944 and marked as E2+10. Undertook Hs 293 trails in September and October 1944. Damaged on landing 6th October 1944, repaired and back to Rechlin from 10th October to 17th December. Last flown on the 30th April 1945 by KG 76.

Ar 234 S10 (W/Nr.140110)

Same as the Ar 234 S9 (W/Nr.140109) – see Ar 234 S9 above

1. Tested Hs 293 missile, carried under the fuselage

Note
First flight date unknown, marked as GM+BJ. Second flight 10th August 1944. To Rechlin between 28th October and December 1944 marked as E2+20. From November 18th 1944 these trials included the Hs 293 and its FuG 203 control system.

Ar 234 S11 (W/Nr.140111)

First flew 15th August 1944 as GM+BK. To Rechlin on the 19th August 1944 and marked as E4+10. Used to test various radio equipment (e.g. FuG 102, 136 and 217) and antenna. Damaged in a crash landing on the 2nd September 1944.

Ar 234 S12 (W/Nr.140112)

First flight date unknown, marked as GM+BL. Converted to reconnaissance aircraft from 21st August 1944 and test flown alongside the V11 on 23rd August. Converted to full reconnaissance configuration with the fitment of two Rb 50/30 cameras in the rear fuselage. Passed to Kommando Sperling on the 22nd September 1944 and marked as T9+GH (flown by Oblt Hans Götz).

The S10 (E2+20) was also used by Rechlin and is seen here from the front with its bomb racks empty and a groundcrewman working in the cockpit

Ar 234 S13 (W/Nr.140113)

Same as a production Ar 234B-2 except:

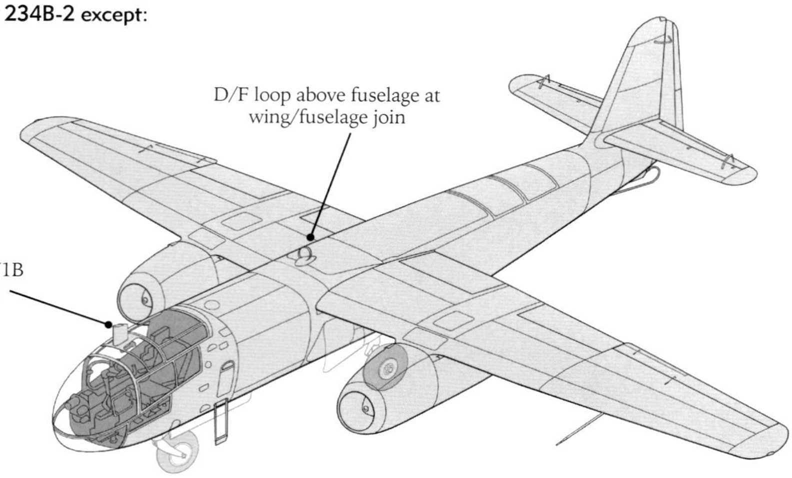

Note
Marked as GM+BM, damaged in air raid on 27th August 1944. Repaired and sent to Rechlin, where it was marked as E5+20. Damaged in crash landing on 2nd November 1944. Repaired and sent to KG 76 to replace W/Nr.140104. Marked as F1+AA and captured by the RAF at Schleswig. Later ferried to Farnborough where it became VH530, moved into storage at No.6 MU 7th September 1945 and SOC there 1st October 1948.

Ar 234 S14 (W/Nr.140114)

Same as a production Ar 234B-2 except:

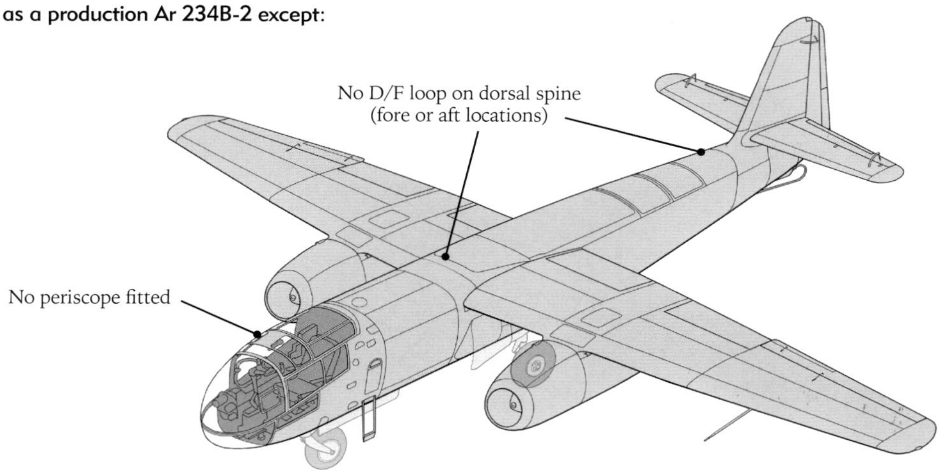

Note
First flight date unknown, marked as GM+BN. Delivered to III./KG 76 on the 26th August 1944. Moved to Rechlin on the 13th September. Crashed on 25th September and sustained 20% damage. Not repaired and wreck found in a hangar at Manching in April 1945.

Ar 234 S15 (W/Nr.140115)

First flight date unknown, marked as GM+BO. Delivered to III./KG 76 28th August 1944. Moved to Rechlin on the 3rd September 1944 and marked as E7+30. To Stab III./EKG 1 and marked as F1+AU. Destroyed on take-off on the 23rd January 1945, with the pilot Hptm. Karl Millahn being injured.

Ar 234 S16 (W/Nr.140116)

First flight date unknown, marked as GM+BP. To Rechlin for Lofte 7K bombsight and PDS autopilot trials. To 8./KG 76 on the 28th August 1944 and marked as F1+BS. Crashed on take-off on the 12th October 1944 in the Rechlin area, the pilot Lt Hans-Egon Arndt was injured and the aircraft was written-off (85% damage).

Ar 234 S17 (W/Nr.140117)

First flight date unknown, marked as GM+BQ. To 7./KG 76 10th September 1944 and marked as F1+DR. To Rechlin on the 11th October 1944 where it tested the Schmidding SG 34 solid-fuelled rocket motors; it is presumed it used a set of two (like those used on the Bachem Ba 349) under each wing, but it may have had them fitted to the rear (lower) fuselage sides (no photo survive of this installation, so we have not illustrated it here). Destroyed on the 7th December 1944.

Ar 234 S18 (W/Nr.140118)

First flight date unknown, marked as GM+BR. To KG 76 on the 31st August 1944. Later went to Rechlin to test bombsight and autopilot. To III./KG 76 at Burg in February 1945.

Ar 234 S19 (W/Nr.140119)

First flight date unknown, marked as GM+BS. Delivered to KG 76 on the 5th September 1944. Transferred to IV./KG 76 on the 7th December 1944.

Ar 234 S20 (W/Nr.140120)

First flight date unknown, marked as GM+BT. Delivered to KG 76 on the 14th September 1944. Damaged (6%) on the 2nd October 1944. Transferred to 8./KG 76 as F1+QS and lost during a training flight near Alt Lönnewitz on the 24th December 1944, Fw. Hans Wehrkamp was killed.

One of a series of shots of the S14 found by the Allies at Manching on the 29th April 1945. Note that this machine had no periscope or fairing installed *(©USAF)*

A very atmospheric shot of the S14 as found by the Allies at Manching in April 1945. The total devastation is evident, as are the three Ju 88 night fighters and the little Bü 181, all of which have been disabled by the retreating Nazi troops *(©USAF)*

Ar 234B-1

See the V11 (PH+SS), which has all the elements of this proposed production version. The B-1 series was cancelled before any were produced, with the B-2 being chosen in preference because it was dual-role (bomber and reconnaissance).

Ar 234B-2

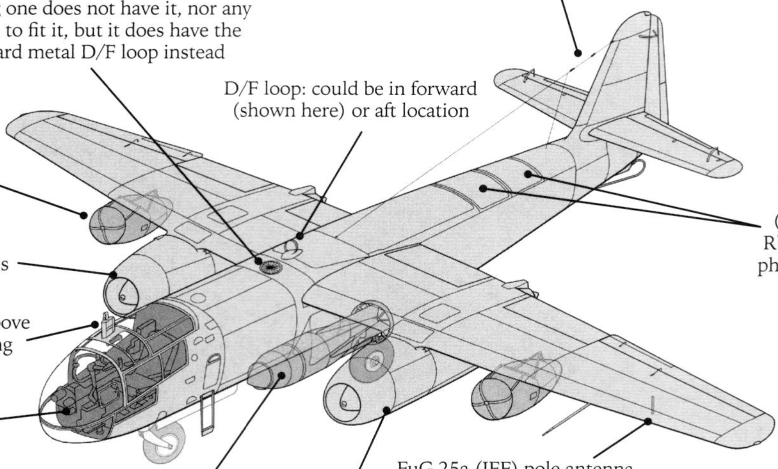

Note
Initial production W/Nrs.140141 to 140180 carrying the codes SM+FA to SM+FT (W/Nr.140160) and BM+LA to BM+LT. The second production batch was W/Nrs.140301 to 140360. The third production batch was W/Nrs.140451 to 140500.

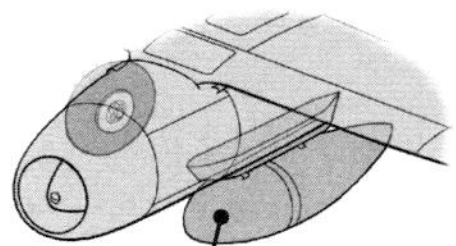

Ar 234B W/Nr.140153 as T9+HH outside its hardened shelter

Ar 234B-2/N Nachtigall (night fighter, conversions)

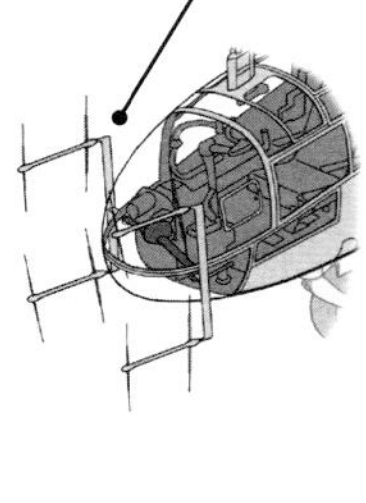

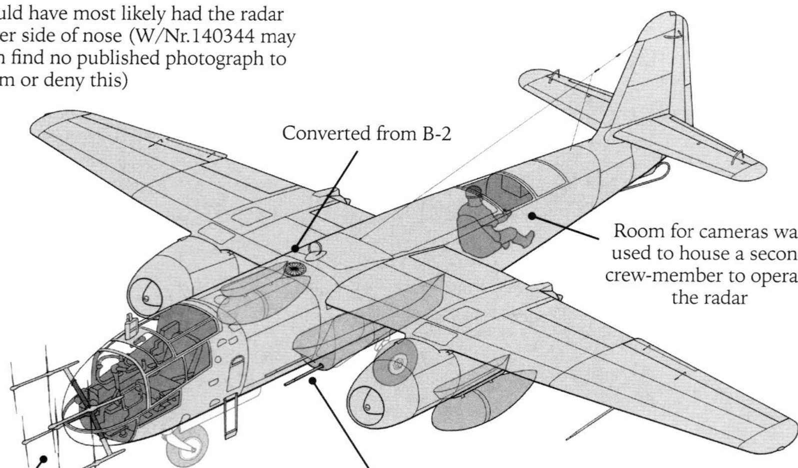

Note
The first conversion to the night fighter role, W/Nr.140145 was allocated the codes SM+FE. First flew in November 1944 but was damaged in a landing accident and not repaired until early December 1944. Crashed, killing both crew, on the 13th February 1945. The second B-2 converted to the night fighter role was W/Nr.140146 and the third was W/Nr.140344 from the third production batch. All three were operated by Kommando Bonow by the end of the war, although they never achieved any air-to-air victories.

Ar 234C-3 (W/Nr.250001 to 250019)

Same as Ar 234 V19 (W/Nr.130029) except:

Note
1,795 were ordered by the RLM, but only (possibly) 19 were ever completed. Images only exist to confirm W/Nrs.250001 to 250006 however.

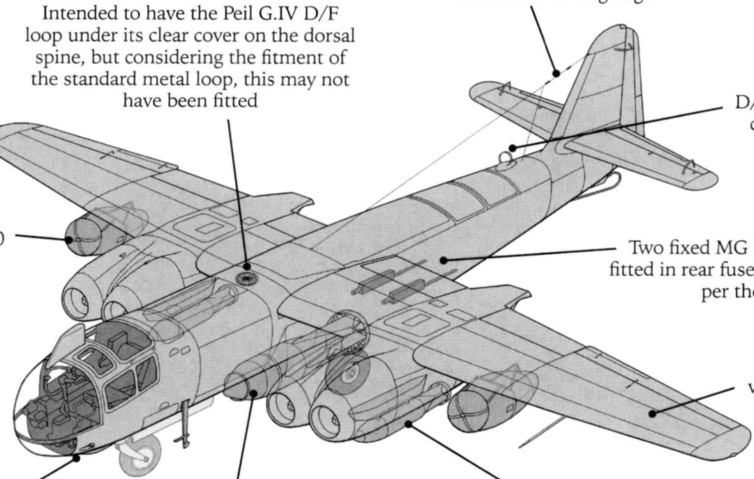

Ar 234C-4

Same as the Ar 234C-3 (W/Nr.250001 to 250019) except:

Note
330 were ordered by the RLM, but only a few (three?) were ever completed.

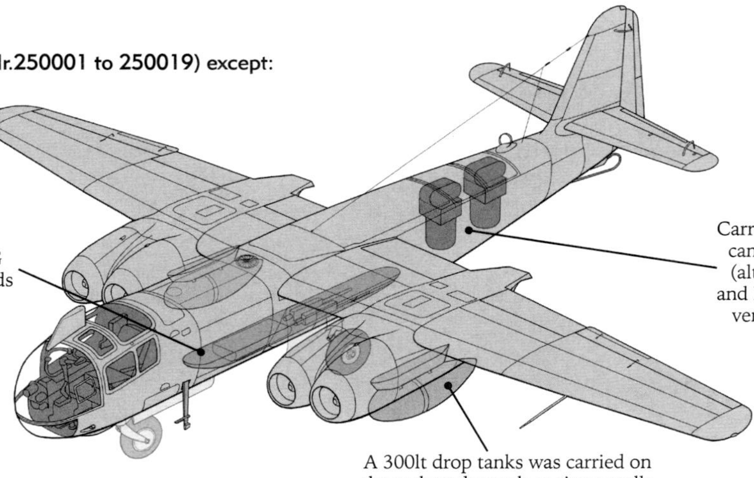

Few Ar 234C images survive, this one shows the prototype V21 (W/Nr.130061) from the front

US troops stand alongside captured Ar 234C-3 W/Nr.250006 at the end of war

The Ar 234 was to be built and developed into numerous forms, none of which were actually built and/or saw service and as such they are all outside the scope of this title.

Camouflage & Markings

This image shows the S7 when captured by the Allies and as you can see it carried the Rechlin codes E2+30 in black, with all the characters of the same size and style. The fuselage cross is B5, the swastika is the larger form of H4 and it has the S-series number applied in white below and ahead of the swastika ('07') and the Rechlin fleet number ('22') aft of the swastika. It is interesting to note that at this stage no braking parachute is installed and the aft section of the engine nacelle is not black, it has the demarcation of the camouflage scheme

Let us first start by saying that nothing is certain when trying to deduce colours from old black and white photographs. The best you can make is an educated, and with luck intelligent, guess using both photographic and documentary evidence.

Pre-production & Production

For details of the schemes applied to the various A, B and C-series prototype airframes, see the individual notes in Section 2.

There are two schemes for the Ar 234, the initial scheme applies to the B series pre-production and production B-2s in the W/Nr.140101 to 140120 range. This scheme was a typical scheme of RLM 70 *Schwarzgrün* and RLM 71 *Dunkelgrün* in a splinter pattern for the upper surfaces and for 3/4 of the fuselage sides and engine nacelles. The remainder, including all the undersides were in RLM 65 *Lichtblau*.

The second scheme applies to all production machines from W/Nr.140141 and it comprises RLM 81 *Braunviolett* and RLM 82 *Lichtgrün* in place of RLM 70/71 and RLM 76 *Lichgrau* replacing RLM 65. There is some confusion with the second colour in most accounts since WWII, as the colours RLM 82 and 83 were swapped in error in a well-respected title on Luftwaffe colours in the 1960s, that led to everyone since thinking that RLM 82 was *Dunkelgrün* and RLM 83 *Lichtgrün*, whereas in fact RLM 83 is the dark green (*Dunkelgrün*) and RLM 82 is light green (*Lichtgrün*).

Deviations to the overall scheme include many of the S-series pre-production machines operated by the Rechlin text facility and these machines had the lower section of the engine nacelles, which would be RLM 76, repainted in RLM 04 yellow (although I have to say that the contrast of this colour in black and white images is such that I wonder if it is a less 'intense' yellow and thus is RLM 27?).

During the winter of 1944/45 many aircraft had white distemper applied in a rough pattern to the upper surfaces. The desperate war situation in early 1945 meant that many of these machines retained this

As with many of the prototype V-series, many of the S-series had their number applied in white between the hand/foot holds on the port side of the nose. Here you can see this on the S3, which is marked as '03' in this region. This did not apply to all S-series machines, though

Here you can see W/Nr.140173 after capture and shipment to Farnborough in late 1944. The side of the fuselage has had the darker shade oversprayed with a loose misting of what is believed to be lightened RLM 76. Note that this has extended to the codes, with the 'M' partially obscured and the 'T' now just a ghost outline, the smaller 'F1' element aft of the cross may well be untouched within the darker region there. It is odd how the application is straight-lined from the front to the mid-section, but the back regions are all curved lines?

'temporary' paint right through until the war ended in April. You will also find some of the aircraft operating over Northern Italy in late 1944 also had a form of disruptive paint applied to the upper surfaces; this was to tone down the otherwise stark colours of the green and brown-violet, which over Italy would have been very obvious, so a lightened version of RLM 76 was loosely applied over the sides of the fuselage on the darker shade, but this was NOT extended up onto the upper surfaces, nor the wings. F1+MT, W/Nr.140173 is probably the best known for this, as it was captured and examined in detail in late 1944 and it had this scheme applied – see Libor's superb build of this machine in Section 4 of this title.

Many state that the night fighter B-2/Ns operated by Kommando Bonow were repainted, but going by recent research in Germany that is untrue, they all retained their daytime green/brown/blue scheme. Only the aircraft flown by Kurt Welter had the lower part of the cockpit glazing painted black, to remove the glare from lights during take-off and landing. All the profiles you therefore see showing the Ar 23B-2/N in RLM 76 with RLM 75 mottle over black have to be considered as pure works of fantasy, unless of course period photos turn up to prove otherwise?

National markings comprised B6 crosses (*Balkenkreuz*) of 1,000mm above the wings and B3 1,000mm crosses below the wings, whilst those on either side of the mid-fuselage were 1,000mm B6. An H4 swastika (*Hakenkreuz*) of 600mm was applied to each side of the vertical fin, positioned so that it did not overlap the rudder hinge line. Many of the later C-series airframes you will find had a smaller swastika, which was the same basic H4 style but only 350mm. The six-digit W/Nr. was

Nose art or art of any form is rare on Ar 234s and this machine, T9+KH with Kommando Sperling and flown by Walter Muffey, is believed to be the only machine with such artwork; as you can see it depicts a jet-propelled sparrow on the nose

This is W/Nr.140153 of Kommando Sperling and you can see that the 'T9' codes of this unit are applied in white aft of the fuselage cross. The Werke Nr. is applied in the usual manner, though, with the first three (140) half the size of the last three (153) at the top of the vertical fin

This is W/Nr.140116, the 16th production B-2 and it is seen here as F1+BS with 8./KG76. the interesting thing is the engine cowl, as the nose ring for 8./KG76 should be red, but there is no way it is, it looks more like yellow, which also means that the lower half of the engine cowling is also yellow as it is much too light in comparison with the lower section of the fuselage, which is RLM 76

applied above the swastika, at the top of the vertical fin, but this was applied in various styles and sizes. You will see photos where the first three ('140') are applied half the height of the remaining three and you will also see those that only have the last three on one side and all six on the other. The W/Nr. was usually applied in black characters and you will find images of both solid and stencil styles being used. The prototypes had their *Stammkenzeichen* (Primary identification) code letters applied either side of the fuselage with two characters ahead of and behind the cross. In service the aircraft carried a unit code that comprised a two-character code one side of the cross in small black characters, with the individual aircraft and *Staffel* code letters applied on the other side.

Units' codes for those operating the Ar 234 were as follows:

F1 – Kampfgeschwader 76
T5 – Aufklärungsgruppe (F)/100
T9 – Versuchsverband OKL (including Kommandos Sperling and Sommer)
4N – Aufklärungsgruppe (F)/22
4U – Aufklärungsgruppe (F)/123
8H – Aufklärungsgruppe (F)/33
9V – Aufklärungsgruppe (F)/5 (FAG 5)

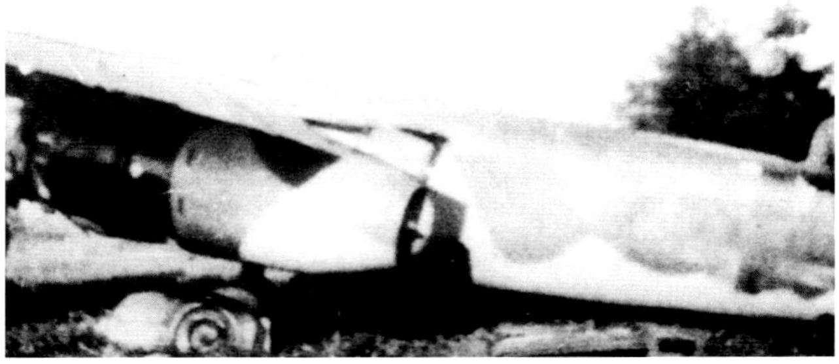

Just to prove there are always exceptions, this image is very poor, but it does show a derelict Ar 234B at Pocking. Bavaria in 1945 with a distinctly wavy demarcation on the rear fuselage?

The Staffel and Gruppe code letters were applied in a relevant colour as follows:

A – Geschwader Stab
B – I Gruppe Stab
C – II Gruppe Stab
D – III Gruppe Stab (Green)
E – IV Gruppe Stab
H – 1 Staffel
K – 2 Staffel
L – 3 Staffel
M – 4 Staffel
N – 5 Staffel
P – 6 Staffel (Blue)
R – 7 Staffel (White)
S – 8 Staffel (Red)
T – 9 Staffel (Yellow)
U – 10 Staffel
V – 11 Staffel
W – 12 Staffel

An example of why to be careful of images, this one is a nice clear shot of B-2s of III./KG 76 at Burg in the winter of 1944-45 and they are all in typical camouflage markings save for what looks like mottling to reduce the intensity of the swastikas on the tail

This poorer quality version of the image, however, proves that these machines had the standard big-size H4 swastikas on the tail, the previous image, although of better quality had been censored with an attempt to remove the swastikas!

Colours

- RLM 04 Gelb (Yellow)
- RLM 23 Rot (Red)
- RLM 27 Gelb (Yellow)
- RLM 65 Lichtblau (Light Blue)
- RLM 66 Schwarzgrau (Black-Grey)
- RLM 70 Schwarzgrün (Black Green)
- RLM 71 Dunkelgrün (Dark Green)
- RLM 76 Lichtgrau (Light Grey)
- RLM 81 Braunviolett (Brown-Violet)
- RLM 82 Lichtgrün (Light Green)
- RLM 83 Dunkelgrün (Dark Green)

Operational Markings

See the colour profiles on pages 22 to 25 for a selection of unit markings and insignia applied to the Ar 234.

Pictures of in-service C-series airframes are very rare indeed and usually of poor quality, as the case here with W/Nr.250006 captured by Allied forces at Munchen-Riem at the end of the war. The overall camouflage and colours are exactly the same as the B-series, as are the markings, with the '006' element of the Werke Nr twice the size of the first three on the top of the vertical fin

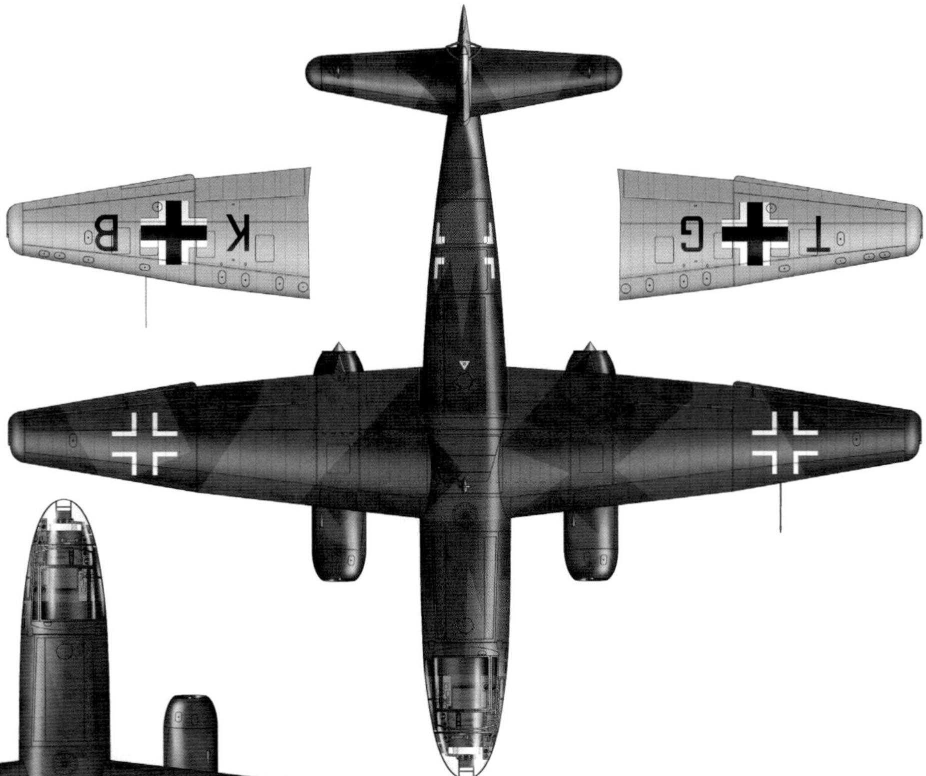

Arado Ar 234 top view showing the standard RLM 70/71 pattern on the upper surfaces. Scrap views show the under surfaces of the wings in RLM 65 and the style and position of markings particular to some prototypes and pre-series aircraft with the old style of national markings in black and white

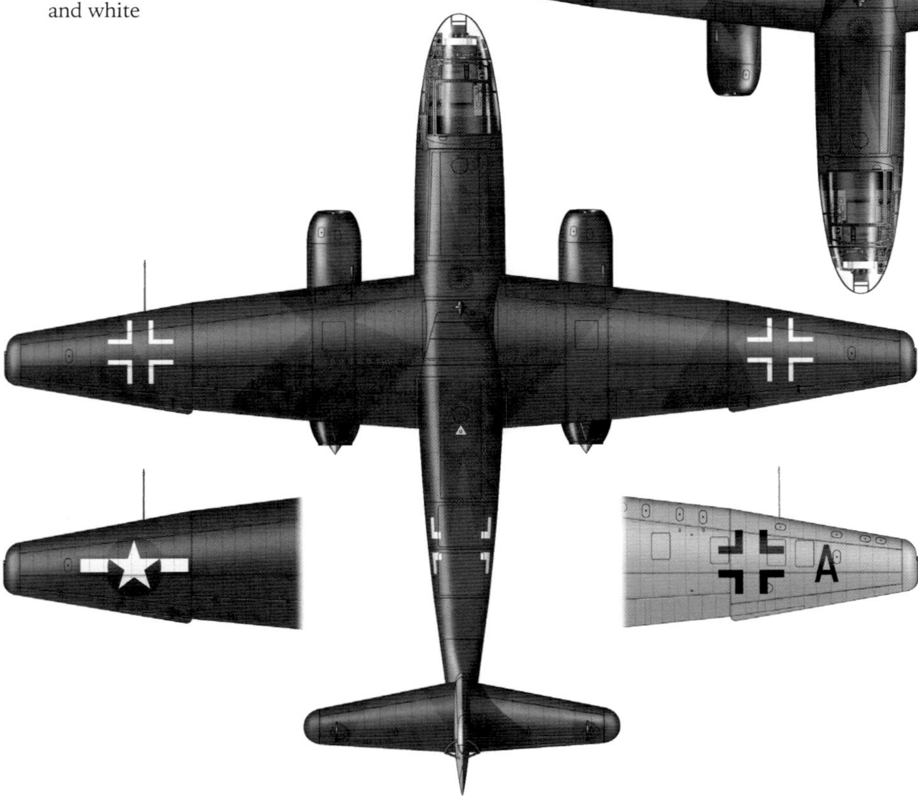

Arado Ar 234 top view showing the typical pattern of RLM 81/82 upper surfaces with plain white crosses. Scrap view on right shows the RLM 76 painted undersides and position of the plain black crosses; aircraft code letter often repeated, also in black, outboard of the crosses. Scrap view on the left shows the position of the US national markings above the port wing; they are repeated below the starboard wing

Not a huge number of kits of the Ar 234 have been produced over the years, but there are examples in all three of the major scales, so what follows are superb builds of what we consider the 'best' option in 1/72nd by Libor Jekl and 1/48th by Steve A. Evans.

Apologies for not doing a 1/32nd example, but we have limited space and the only kits are either limited-run plastic (Fly) or resin (MDC), both of which are expensive and complex.

Dragon 1/72nd

Ar 234B-2/ B-2b Blitz

built by Libor Jekl

Technical Specifications	
Scale: 1/72nd	Manufactuer: Dragon
Kit No.: 5003	Material: IM, PE
UK Price: OOP	

Being one of the 'wonder weapons' of the Third Reich and a pioneering design as a jet bomber, the Ar 234 could not remain unnoticed by model manufacturers and the first kit in 1/72nd scale was way back in 1966 by Lindberg. A much better effort was later introduced by Frog, who released an Ar 234 along with a V1 flying bomb, and this kit was reissued by the likes of Congost, Kikoler, Lodela, Revell and Matchbox. In the early 1990's the Dragon kit of the Ar 234B-2 arrived, shortly followed by the C-3/C-4 and 'Nachtigall' night fighter version. These kits were later accompanied by upgraded versions with the addition of a V1 flying bomb, E.381 Julia parasite fighter or as the P-series, all of which fall into the 'Luftwaffe 1946' category. The Ar 234B kit is one of the best aircraft kits released in their 'Golden Wings Series', because unlike other kits such as the P-61 and Ta 152, this kit has never been seen as being too complex and therefore challenging to build.

More than 100 parts are cleanly moulded in a light grey-coloured and rather soft plastic that feature fine recessed panel lines and petite surface details, although on the fuselage upper sides the lines become almost indistinct and this needs to be rectified. Careful placement of the ejector pins meant that these do not disturb any of the surface or interior detail and the sharply moulded small parts combined with the super thin edges (e.g. the undercarriage doors) and trailing edges show how good Dragon kits could be. Some thicker parts seem to suffer from some shrinkage marks, though, especially on the fuselage walls, but this can be easily overcome with drop of Mr Surfacer or cyanoacrylate. The cockpit is well detailed as are the auxiliary Walter RATO units and undercarriage parts. Also provided is a SC1000 bomb and racks together with 300lt drop tanks. The kit allows you to also build the photo-reconnaissance B-2b version thanks to the clear part with camera windows along with the cameras installed in the rear fuselage. The clear parts are perfectly thin and transparent, so I guess it was just bad luck that my example had a fine crack running along the

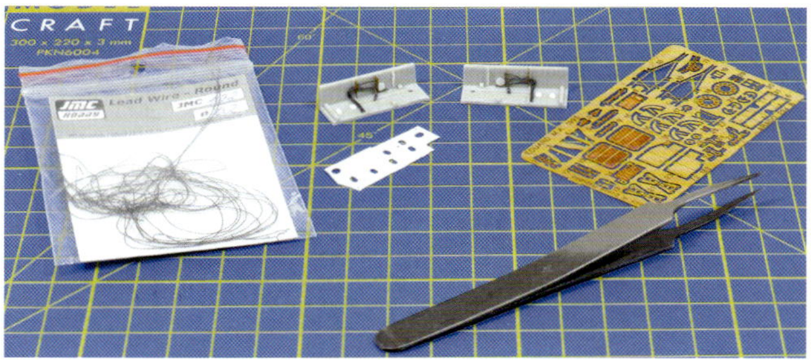

The wheel wells were detailed with 0.02mm round lead wire available from the JMC Hobby range

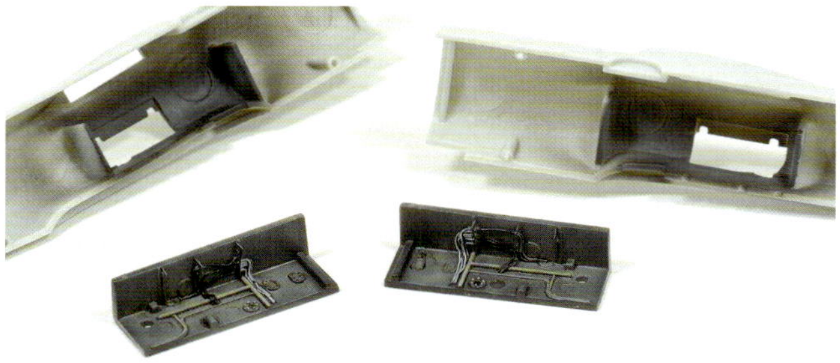
Tonal contrast in the wheel wells was achieved with the RLM 02 being applied over a base coat of black.

Lengths of plasticard were required along the edges of the lower rear fuselage clear insert to level everything out

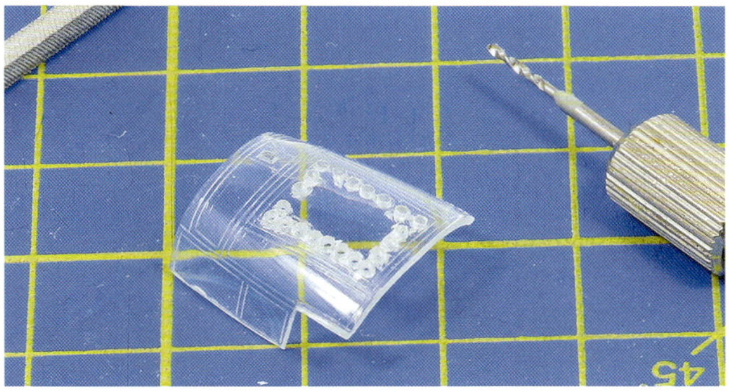
As I wanted the canopy hatch open, this was chain-drilled inboard of the edges, then cut and finally sanded to shape

nose and upper part (fortunately this is not that apparent on the assembled model). The kit also includes a small etched fret with tiny parts for the cockpit, DF loop and FuG 25a rod antenna. The airframe details obviously correspond to the world's only example (W/Nr.140312) as they differ from wartime machines, probably as a result of post-war testing and subsequent restoration work. For instance, the DF loop is placed in the middle of a circular cover under which should in fact be the Peilgerät 6 radio direction finder (which the preserved aircraft lacks) with the DF loop antenna moved further back. On the fuselage rear side the teardrop-shaped cover seems to be redundant and some deviations can also be found on the landing gear (for instance, the position of 'scissor' links on the main legs). The oval-shaped aperture in the underside lacks the bomb rack as does the museum example, so there is only a hole in the fuselage. Anyway, most importantly, the kit's basic dimensions and shapes correspond to the real thing very well.

The kit provides camouflage schemes for three machines: W/Nr.140312, F1+GS, ex-8./KG76 as displayed in 1990 at the National Air and Space Museum; W/Nr.140342, F1+AS, 8./KG 76 and an unidentified B-2b example coded T9+JH, which in fact was one of the Kommando Sperling machines. Unfortunately, the decal sheet suffered after years in the loft, being almost yellow and full of cracks, despite its bag being kept unopened. I would not have used it anyway as some markings seem to have the wrong proportions and colours (e.g. the Kommando Sperling 'Jet Bird' artwork is usually shown as two-coloured).

Construction

For my build I acquired the Eduard etched set (#72-182), canopy masks (CX074) and in my decal bank I discovered the Aeromaster decal sheet 'Arado 234 Blitz Bombers Part II' (#72-087), which I probably acquired earlier together with the kit (eventually I used it only partially, but more on this later). The construction commenced with the wheel wells, which were enhanced with etched ribs. Other structural details and hydraulic lines were added from plastic sheet and 0.2mm lead wires only in the rearmost, visible part of the well as the front parts covering the main wheels were closed whilst on the ground. The complete bays were primed with Mr Surfacer 1500 (black), then airbrushed RLM 02 (Gunze-Sangyo Mr Aqueous Color H70) and installed in the fuselage halves. Despite the instructions having you install the main legs before gluing the bays into the fuselage, it is possible to postpone this operation until the end of the construction, thus saving you some

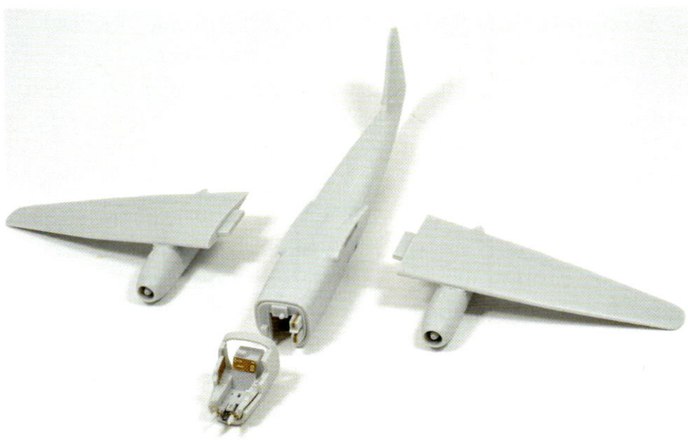
The overall airframe components prior to assembly, with the various etched brass detail parts added to the cockpit being quite visible

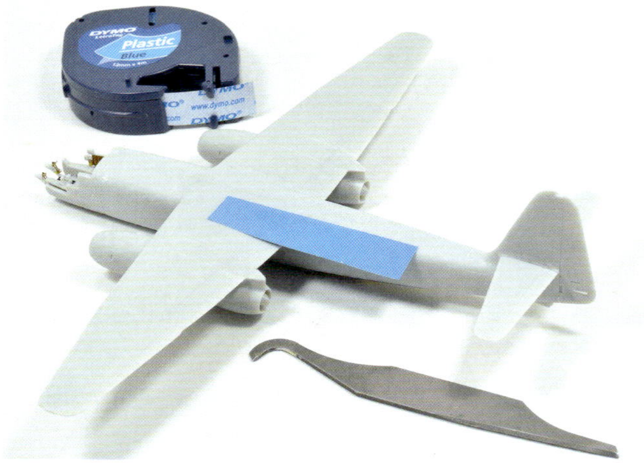

Any panel lines damaged by the gluing, filling and sanding processes were replaced with a UMM scriber with embossing tape used as a flexible ruler

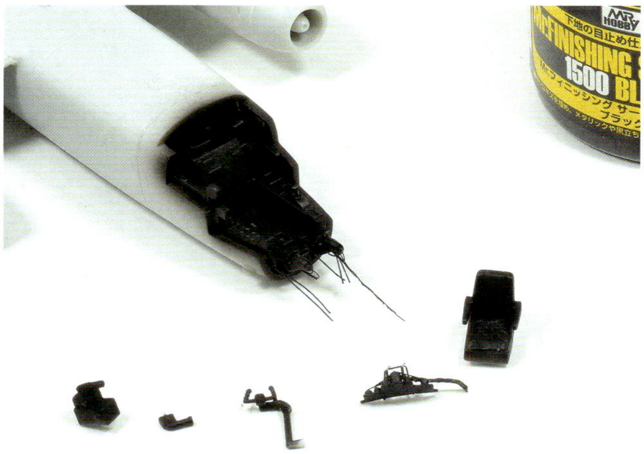

The cockpit area and all associated parts are first primed with Mr Finishing Surfacer 1500 Black

Details within the cockpit were all picked out in various colours from the Vallejo range

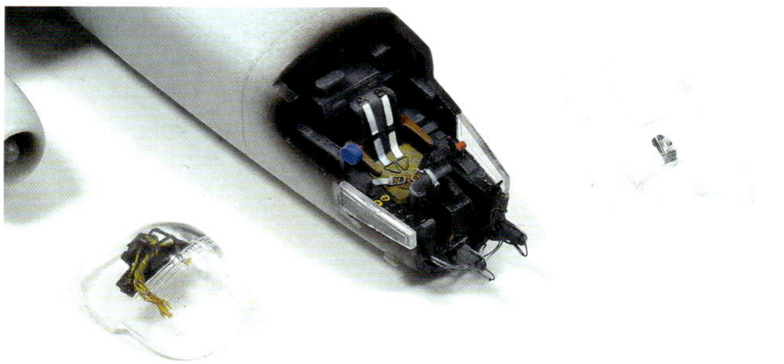

Take care attaching the instrument panel and periscope sight to the clear parts

The Eduard Express Masks make the whole task a lot easier

masking and making the handling of the model easier. After closing the fuselage I cemented the bottom clear part for the cameras, which highlighted the trouble with this area of the construction; it needed 1mm thick plastic strips to properly sit in the opening and the resulting seams were filled with cyanoacrylate. On the centreline I closed up the circular opening with the provided plug, and although it may be possible to scratchbuild the clear cover for the Peilgerät circular antennae, I relied on a decal item instead which is on the Aeromaster sheet. The DF loop teardrop-shaped base was removed and moved about 3mm back; of course you are saved this work if you decided to depict W/Nr.140312 as it is within NASM today.

I continued with the interior assembly, but most of the smaller details either from the etched set or scratch-built (e.g. cabling, levers etc.) were left out for the time being as they might be damaged during the airframe assembly. On the port side of the nose I cut out the opening for the footstep and backed it with a piece of plastic strip. The nose section was joined with the rear bulkhead and set aside for a while. In the meantime I worked on the wing and engine nacelles, which were quickly assembled thanks to their perfect fit. After some minor cleaning of the joints the wing halves with added nacelles were attached to the fuselage; again, this was quite straightforward and all I needed to take care with was obtaining the correct geometry against the fuselage (there is almost no dihedral). In front of the wheel bays I added about 10g of lead ballast, as there is not enough space in the nose, and then added the nose section itself. The joint needed some attention, though, and eventually was filled with cyanoacrylate and the damaged panel lines were restored. The same treatment was undertaken with various other panel lines using Dymo type and a UMM scribing tool, and apart from this I also added missing fuel caps and panel lines on the fuselage, wings and fin. The tip of the vertical stabiliser behind the position light was refined to the correct shape as well.

Now I returned to the final cockpit details where I scratchbuilt cabling on the back of the instrument panel plus various lines on the sidewalls and to the rudder pedals; on the seat I added a folded parachute shaped from two-part epoxy putty. All was carefully trial-fitted with the clear parts to avoid any interference and from the upper canopy glazing I removed the upper hatch using the chain drilling method followed by tidying up with superfine Vallorbe files. The cockpit was primed with Mr Surfacer 1500 (black) and sprayed with lightened RLM 66 (H417) for better contrast; the individual details were brush painted with Vallejo Model Color acrylics. In this case the cockpit forms the kit's natural focal point and therefore I chose to give more contrast to add depth and better detail definition because it would all be very visible under the glazing. The canopy is split into four parts that need careful assembly; at first I cemented the two smaller side panels, mated these with the nose and then attached the upper part. All of them matched up pretty well and any gaps that appeared were sealed with Gator Glue. The canopy was then masked off using the Eduard masks and I could then move on to the painting.

Paint

The model was first airbrushed with Mr Surfacer 1000 (grey), all imperfections were sorted using drops of the same and the surface then sanded over and polished with fine grades of Mr Grinding Cloth. On checking my references I came across photographs of a 9./KG 76 machine flown by Hptm. Josef Regler that in February 1945

The LF Model vinyl masks were used to do the camouflage pattern on the upper surfaces

The upper surface scheme comprises light green (RLM 82) and brown-violet (RLM 81), both from the Gunze-Sangyo range

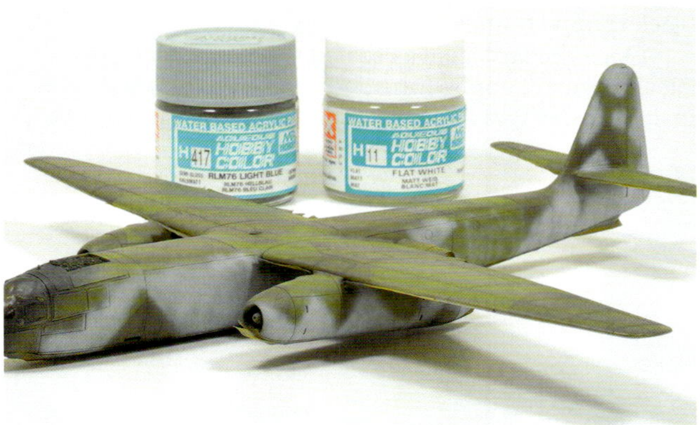

The mottling on the fuselage was applied with RLM 76 suitably lightened with white

Once the canopy was sprayed RLM 66, the whole airframe was primed with Mr Surfacer 1000

The first colour is the underside RLM 76, darkened with black along the panel lines

was shot down during an attack on Allied troops near Aachen by a P-47 from the 336th Fighter Group. After its emergency landing, the aircraft was recovered by Allies, the engines were removed and tested by the British authorities. As a result of being the first intact Ar 234 to fall into Allied hands, it was the subject of much military photographers and its camouflage and marking could therefore be pretty accurately reconstructed. The camouflage colours consisting of RLM 81 and RLM 82 were over-sprayed with white, or more probably RLM 76 in an irregular distemper on the fuselage sides partially overlapping onto the upper areas; the wings seem to have remained untouched. I first airbrushed the undersides in RLM 76 (H417) and for the upper side RLM 81/82 camouflage (H421/H422) I used LF Model's vinyl camouflage masks (M7226), although the resulting sharp paint transition was softened with a light overspray of the base colours. For the RLM 76 distemper I used a lighter variation mixed with white to give it a different hue compared to the undersides and the paint was airbrushed freehand in two phases. Initially I applied only the larger areas on the nose, tail and engines while the remaining portions around the markings were added after the decals had been applied, because these were partially over-sprayed as well. The paint was airbrushed with different contrast and intensity as can be seen in period photographs. At the end I masked off the nose and airbrushed on the black canopy frames.

Once the surface was sealed with Mr Color Super Clear varnish I applied the decals. While the national insignias and W/Nr. (140173) could be assembled out of the Aeromaster sheet, along with most of the code letters, the yellow letter 'M' came from my decal bank and for the smaller version on the fin I had paint masks made. The distinct rivets visible on the canopy framing are reproduced with the decals that are included on the Aeromaster sheet; initially I worried about the result, but once the individual strips were trimmed of any excessive carrier film and cut to shorter lengths, they did the job very well.

All the various sub-assembles were painted and weathered prior to final attachment to the model

The canopy edges were masked, and then the frames were sprayed black

Specially made vinyl masks allowed the small yellow 'M' to be applied at the top of the vertical fin

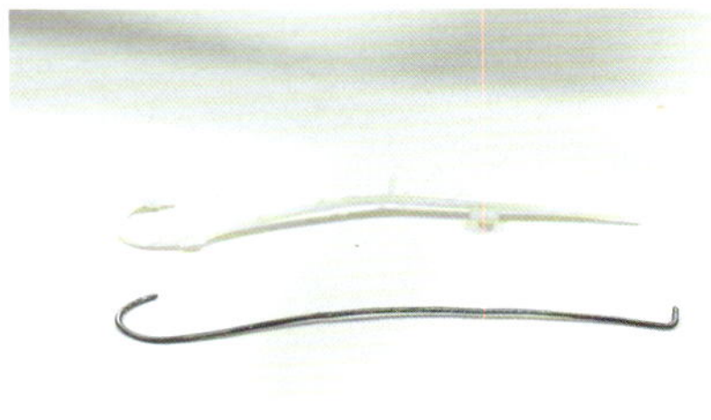

The parachute release cable (top) was replaced with wire (bottom), suitably brushed to look like the steel braided cable of the real thing

As a final touch I airbrushed the engine exhaust cones with a dilute black mixture and with a silver watercolour pencil I reproduced a few scratches around the footsteps. Otherwise the Ar 234 seemed to have been very well maintained and due to their limited operational use (compared to other Luftwaffe bombers) they looked almost untouched; I only added some dust in the tyres at the very end of the build.

Final Details

I focused my attention now on the landing gear that was assembled as per the instructions, however torsion 'scissor' links taken from the etched set were glued to the rear of each oleo leg and from a strip of self-adhesive silver tape I created the moving part of each oleo. The RATO units were airbrushed with Alclad II Duralumin, with the parachutes done in a weathered creamy colour using Tamiya XF-60 and Gunze-Sangyo H314. The parachute ripcords were cut from a piece of Uschi van den Rosten (Fine 0.03mm) rigging thread and secured on the wing in loopholes I sourced from an old etched set. Under the belly I cemented the 1,000kg bomb, which was painted light blue and fortunately, due to its size, the missing bomb rack is not apparent. The drag chute wire in the tail was replaced with aluminium wire as the plastic part looked too thick, but as the actual cable was made from steel I slightly sanded the wire and bent it to the required shape. Now I cut a new canopy hatch from 0.1mm clear plastic sheet, sprayed the frames black and scratchbuilt the handle and brace strut from fuse wire. The etched footstep was painted red/white and glued in situ as were the DF loop, periscope (which received a stencil from the spares box), part of the Lofte 7K bombsight that protrudes from the nose and the pitot, which was replaced with Albion Alloys brass tubing. At the end I added the antennae wires cut from Uschi van den Rosten (Superfine 0.01mm) rigging thread with insulators reproduced from white plastic micro tubing.

Verdict

Time proves the quality of any kit and the Dragon example in this regard passed the exam without fundamental loss. Despite its age it offers good value for money and I think some of the more recent kit manufacturers can only envy its great definition of small parts and fine surface detail. It is therefore the only buildable Ar 234 kit in 1/72nd scale, so my recommendation is obvious and without reservation. However, the kit is not without shortcomings and I'm convinced a modern and more accurate kit would find its place in the market, especially when you consider the limited availability and high price of Dragon kits.

Hasegawa 1/48th

Ar 234B-2 Blitz Bomber

by Steve A. Evans

Technical Specifications	
Scale: 1/48th	Manufactuer: Hasegawa
Kit No.: JT83	Material: IM
UK Price: £OOP	

**Note, at the time of writing this kit is out of production but there are subsequent reissues available with new decals and/or additional parts that still use the same basic tooling*

The Arado Ar 234 Blitz is a wonderful subject for a kit. It ticks so many of the boxes for many modellers, being Luftwaffe, end of war and one of Hitler's 'Wonder Weapons'. It also came in a number of actual and theoretical designs, giving plenty of scope for a little artistic licence. Hasegawa have made an excellent job of their versions in 1/48th scale, all of them being presented in gloriously decorated boxes and with some very nice looking plastic. This box is the original release (from 2002) so it represents the standard production B-2 version.

Inside the box are nine sprues of grey-coloured plastic and three of transparent parts. The plastic is all moulded very neatly indeed, with excellent interior detail work and smooth exterior skins with sharp, recessed panel lines. The clear parts, essential to this model, are also nicely done although there is a seam line to polish away on the front section (#P1). The instructions are the usual from Hasegawa, being a foldout, 8-page layout with two full pages of painting and marking guides and sixteen build stages. It is all beautifully drawn and printed with clear positioning of all the parts and paint references at every stage (all to Gunze-Sangyo paints, of course).

Construction

This starts with the interior and it's a cockpit made up of no less than twenty-seven parts, and seven decals if you don't fancy painting the excellent dials. It's a little tricky getting everything into place because a lot of it is quite delicate but it does slot together neatly enough in the end. That glasshouse nose means that you will have a very good view of this interior, which means that there are some necessary additions. First of all it needs some seat belts: Eduard's' finest in this case. The main instrument panel will need some wiring sprouting out of the

Some of the best art in the model world adorns the boxes of Hasegawa kits, and this one is no exception

back and the brake pedals need the hydraulic lines to be on prominent show. These last parts were all done with various gauges of wire, suitably posed and painted.

Back to the main build and the newly constructed cockpit pod slots onto the front of the fuselage, once that has been built of course. This fuselage is a long slim affair with the main gear bays centrally mounted. They are neatly moulded and fit perfectly, although because of the nature of the bays, the undercarriage legs need to be fitted now, which is a pain. There is a camera bay in the rear fuselage with two vertically mounted cameras in a framework. Once again, it's beautifully moulded and with clear sections for both the top and bottom of the fuselage, they could be on show in the finished item if you're going to do a reconnaissance version. Hasegawa also tell you to put about 20g of weight in the fuselage. I have to admit that I did just that and it is seriously over the top, I would suggest it only needs about 10g, especially if you leave out the extra weight of the camera gear. They also tell you to leave the cockpit off until much later in the build but I decided to fit it now to get it out of the way, but to be honest it's not going to matter at all which way you choose to do it.

The wings and tail are a simple fit, all very straightforward, as are the engine nacelles. Each of the Jumo 004 engines is built of seven parts, including the compressor and turbine discs and a neat little hollow cast intake on the side. The fit of the parts is good, considering the cowlings have caused a lot of model manufacturers difficulties in the past. They also fit onto the wings without too much fuss. It's not all a glowing report, though, because while the detail and general fit of the parts is good, some of the joints will need a little work to get them perfect. I used a considerable amount of filler along the centre line of the fuselage as well as around the clear inserts on the upper and lower sections where the camera bay is positioned. The exterior is also a little on the plain side, without much rivet detail at all. Now I know that in real life the rivets are all but invisible (as are the panel lines) but in miniature form it's sometimes nice to get a bit more detail on show. With that in mind I ran the riveting wheel over pretty much the whole surface to add a little more character.

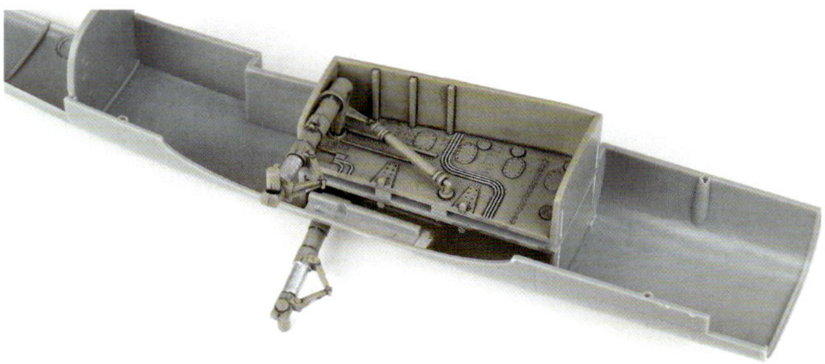

The main undercarriage bays are neat and cleverly designed but the legs are surprisingly delicate

Colour

The three versions on offer in the box are all typical of the B-2 variant: two are in full standard colours while the third is a little different with large areas of RLM 76 (or pale grey depending on who you believe). For the purposes of this article, however, the standard ones will be the choice and here it only comes down to which letters you like, as they are pretty much identical.

The way in which these aircraft were painted at the time means that you don't necessarily have to stick to the RLM 81/82/76 scheme, because the existing stocks of the older RLM colours (70/71/65) were to be used first. This means you can mix and match the shades to suit your own taste. I started with Humbrol 65 on the underside which is kind of like RLM 65, or 76, once again depending on who you want to listen too. Being Humbrol enamels, they spray well and the new upper colours of 251 (RLM 81) and 252 (RLM 82) also work well, although these last two are incredibly matt, not such a good thing when you need a glossy surface for the decals later. The splinter camouflage pattern is nicely represented in the instructions and is fairly easy to re-create with some masking tape. The base coat of RLM 82 is accentuated with some lighter centre sections of the panels but

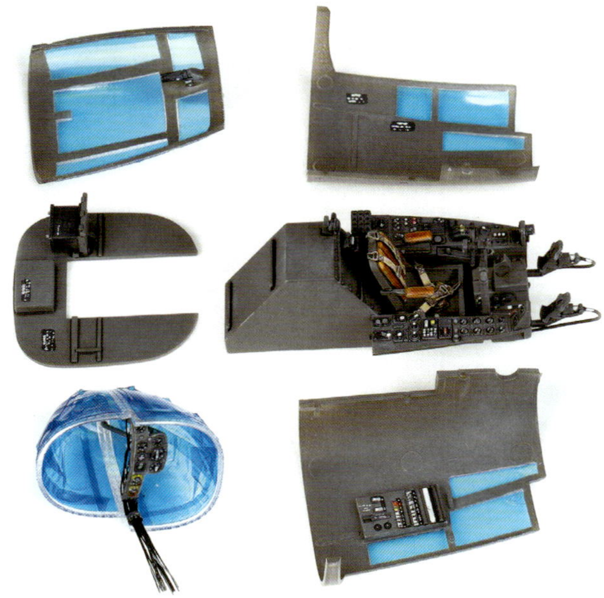

The cockpit is a little complicated with separate, wrap-around canopy sections and because you can see in there, it needs some additions

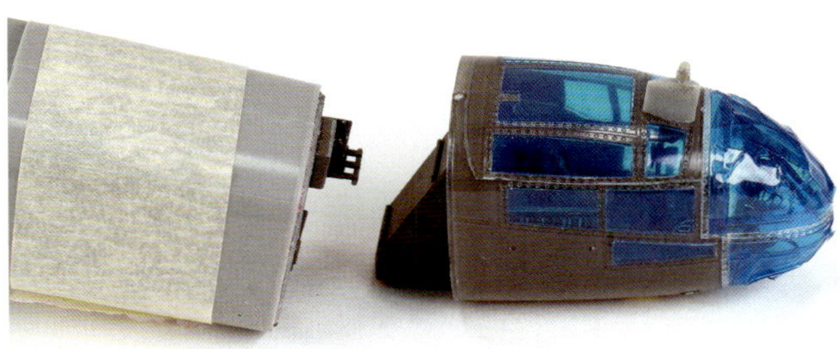

That cockpit 'pod' isn't the best fit in the world to the rest of the fuselage and because of the brittle nature of clear plastic you have to take a little more care

it's looking a little too pale for me, I think it should be a shade darker. Not to worry, the RLM 81 looks nice and with some weathering with pastels and lots of Tamiya X-19 Smoke, the contrast between the colours is easy to sort out. Other areas to note are the rear section of the nacelles. These can be black or any number of metallic shades. The instructions call for Burnt Iron, which is a good starting point. I opted for a number of the darker Alclad 2 lacquers around this area to make it look a bit burnt. There is also the frame around the cockpit glazing to mask and paint. The instructions say it should be black, which is exactly what I used but some of the period photographs look like it may have been RLM 66 on some aircraft? Last of the paintwork is the red nose section of each of the engine intakes. These were painted in the section colours of the aircraft, so if the ID letters are red then the intakes are red, yellow letters = yellow intakes and so on. RLM 23 is quoted for my version but just about any red will do. And with them masked and sprayed, it's time for the decals.

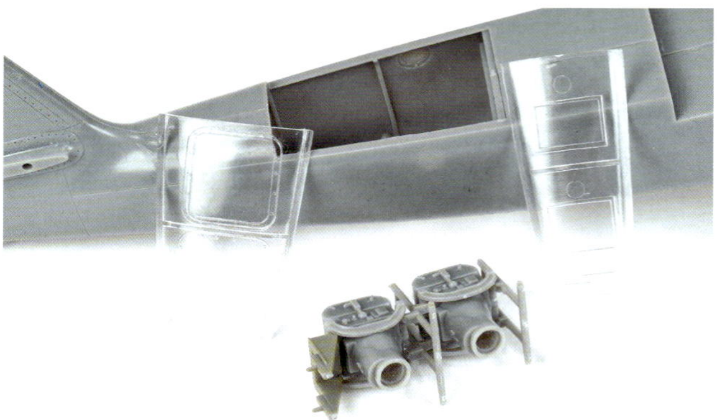

You get two very nicely moulded cameras for creating the reconnaissance version, although if you do, you'll need some new decals, as none of the options in the box are suitable

Decals

Luckily, there is still some Johnson's Klear in my paint box, to make the glossy surface with but just about any gloss acrylic varnish will do; both Tamiya and Airfix do very good ones. Whichever one you use, if you've also used the Humbrol matt paint then it will take several coats to get it anywhere near glossy enough for the decals. Dear Humbrol, please do your new RLM colours in satin, these matt ones are a pain to use! Anyway, the

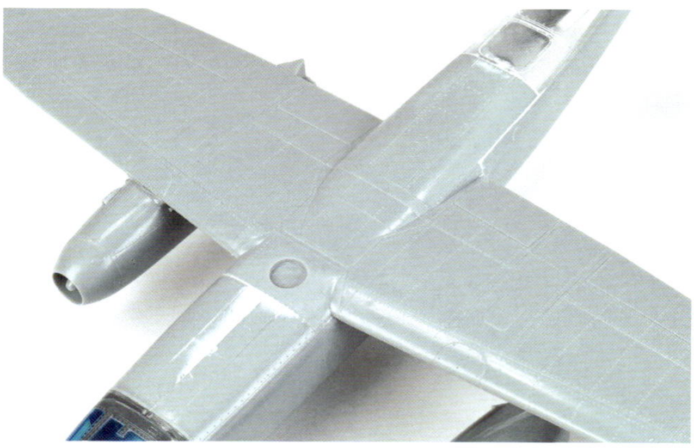

The upper wing section fits reasonably but I ended up using a surprising amount of filler to get everything blended in

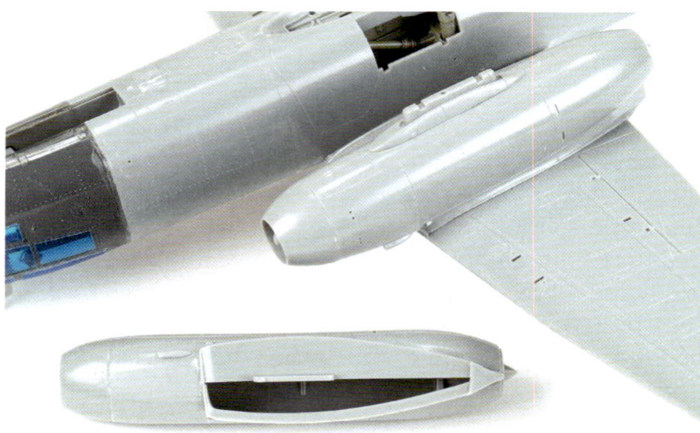

The engine nacelles are a seven-part sub-assembly with a good shape, and they fit well enough to the wing

Paint begins with the underside; in this case it's RLM 65 (Humbrol 65) for a transitional paint job

Top surface first colour RLM82, with lightened central areas of each panel and darker joints. The additional rivets I added have all but disappeared by this stage

Camouflage, as per the instructions. That's Tamiya tape for the sharp edges, filled in with cheap stuff from the local Lidl

The RLM81 is done and the contrast is much too high but not to worry, the additional layers of weathering will take care of that

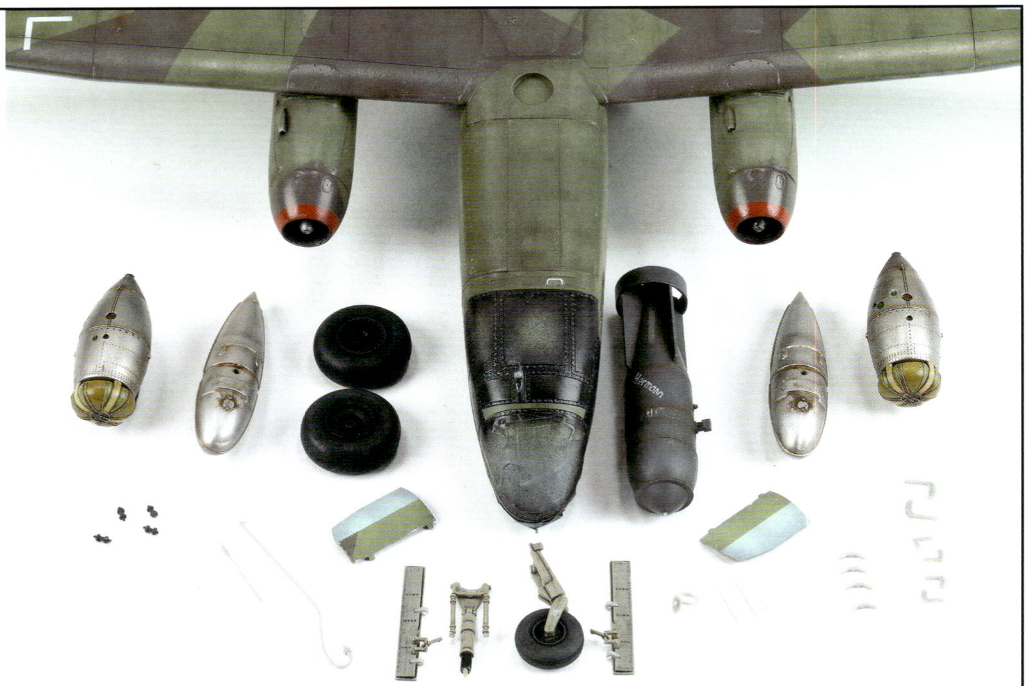

There are quite a few sticky out bits at the end, including the brake lines for the main undercarriage legs and the aerial wires, not shown here

Hasegawa decals come complete with the few stencils on show, as well as all the national and individual markings needed. They are beautifully printed and in great colours but they are a little thick and surprisingly for Hasegawa, resistant to the setting and softening solutions. This means a little bit of silvering here and there but it's not too bad, the glossier the surface, the better they are.

Decals on and dry it's time to sort the last of the weathering. The whole kit is given a thin coat of Klear to seal everything in and then a good old oil wash, black on top and Dark Dirt underneath. When dry this is wiped off with a soft cloth and cotton buds, to leave a little of the oil in all the recesses making it look a bit more lived in.

Now that is dirty! Don't worry, because about 90% of the oil wash will be removed with a soft cloth, leaving a suitably grubby residue

Finishing

The final stage for this kit is actually quite a big one as there are a lot of little bits left in the box yet to fit. The control horns for the tail, as well as various aerials and antenna, not to mention the nose undercarriage and the brake lines for the main units. The biggest and most noticeable bits are the drop tanks, the huge SC1000 bomb and the Walther rocket packs, complete with very nicely moulded parachute packs. The tanks and rockets were painted with Alclad 2 lacquers, while the bomb is simple RLM 66, although pale blue, grey or even green ones crop up in period photos. With this lot slung underneath, the sleek Arado is looking decidedly portly. The final bits are the overall finish of Xtracolor XDFF flat varnish and the aerial wires made from 1lb fishing line.

Verdict

The detail and the attention to it that Hasegawa put into their kits is glorious to see, but it does sometimes mean a more complicated build. All of that is true of this kit. It has some wonderful moulded pieces, like the cockpit interior, but the inserts and general fit of some of the parts aren't perfect. This means you have to take care with the build but there's nothing wrong with that, as long as you're ready for it. The finished article looks like an Arado and although these kits are quite expensive, there's in nothing in the market today that even comes close.

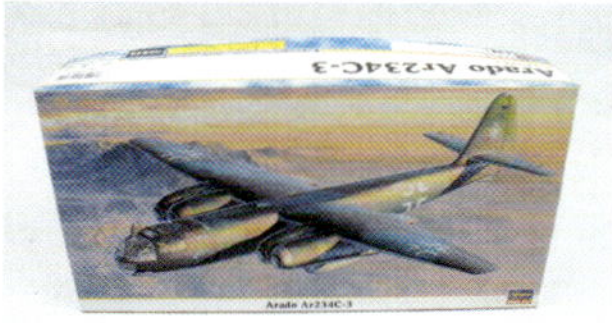

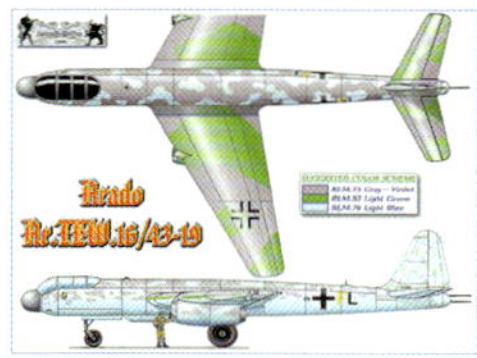

Below is a list of all static scale construction kits produced to date of the Ar 234 series. This list is as comprehensive as possible, but if there are amendments or additions, please contact the author via the Valiant Wings Publishing address shown at the front of this title.

1/87th Scale

- Artmaster [res] Arado 234 Blitz #80.142 (N/K) – *May be the same kit that CMK announced?*
- CMK [res] Arado 234B-1 #HOA005 (2003/4)

1/72nd Scale

- [Luis] Congost (ex-Frog) Arado Ar 234B/C with V1 rocket #162 (late 1970-80s)
- Dragon Arado Ar 234B-2/B-2b Blitz #5003 (1992) – Reissued, same item number, 2011
- Dragon Arado Ar 234C-3/C-4 Lightning #5004 (1992)
- Dragon Ar 234C-3 w/V-1 Huckepack #5011 (1993) – Reissued, same kit number, 2001
- Dragon Arado Ar 234B Nachtigall #5012 (1993)
- Dragon Ar 234C w/Ar E 381 Julia #9005 (1995) – *Orignally listed as the 'Ar 234C with He.1077 Julia'*
- Dragon Ar 234P #5026 (2006)
- Frog Ar 234C #F234 – *Planned 1968 but never made, resurrected as #F417 in 1976*
- Frog Ar 234 "Blitz" Jet Bomber #F.417 (1976)
- Lindberg Ar 234B #439-60 (1966-1975) – Also #472 (1975-1997) – Reissued as #70516 in the 'Air Power' series in 2013
- Matchbox (ex-Frog) Ar 234Blitz B-2/C-2/C-3 #40416 (1992)
- Mavi (Model Aviation) [vac] Arado Ar 234B-2/B-2b #7030 (1993->)
- Necomisa (ex-Lindberg) Arado Ar 234B #P-472 (1976->)
- Revell (ex-Frog) Arado Ar 234B-2/C-2/C-3 "Blitz" #H162 (1978) – *Also listed as #H-4162*
- Revell (ex-Frog) Arado Ar 234 Blitz B-2/C-2/C-3 #462 (1987)
- Revell (ex-Dragon) Ar 234B-2/C-2/C-3 #N/K
- Revell (ex-Dragon) Ar 234C-3 & E381 #04373 (1998)
- Unicraft Aer.TEW.16/43-19 #None
- Unicraft Aer.TEW.16/43-23 #None

1/48th Scale

- Airmodel [vac] 1/48th Ar 234B #AM-4811 (1980-2000)
- Airmodel [vac/res] 1/48th Ar 234C #AM-4812 (1980-2000)
- Chematic (ex-Hobbycraft) 1/48th Arado Ar 234 "Blitz" #010 (N/K) – *Often listed as 'Gomex'*
- Hasegawa 1/48th Ar 234B-2 #JT83 [also #09083] (2002)
- Hasegawa 1/48th Ar 234B-2/N Nachtigall #JT85 [also #09085] (2002)
- Hasegawa 1/48th Ar 234B-2 'Kommando Sperling' #09669 (2006) – *Limited edition*
- Hasegawa 1/48th Ar 234B-2/N Nachtigall 'with Naxos Radar' #09820 (2008) – *Limited edition*
- Hasegawa 1/48th Ar 234C-3 #09845 (2009) – *Limited edition*
- Hasegawa 1/48th Ar 234C-3 w/BT700 'Anti-shipping Attacker' #07332 (2013) – *Limited edition*
- Hobbycraft-Canada/War Eagle Incorporated 1/48th Arado Ar 234B #HC1671 (1990) – *later just marketed under the Hobbycraft label*
- Hobbycraft-Canada 1/48th Arado Ar 234C #HC1672 (1992)
- Hobbycraft 1/48th Ar 234B-2N #HC1673 (1995)
- Hobbycraft 1/48th Ar 234B 'Blitz Bomber' #HC1676 (2002)
- Hobbycraft 1/48th Ar 234B 'Elite series' #HC9671 (1991)
- Karo-AS Modellbau [vac/res] 1/48th Arado Ar 234C #AM48.12 (1989)
- Karo-AS Modellbau [vac/res] 1/48th Ar 234B Hecht #AM-48.11 (1989)
- Kitech, China [inj] 1/48th Arado Ar 234 #O8M-3309H (2003) – *Copy of the Hobbycraft kit*
- MHW Models Ltd (ex-Volks) [res] 1/48th Arado Ar 234B Blitz #N/K (1987)
- Monogram (ex-Revell/revised Dragon) 'Pro-Modeler' 1/48th Ar 234C-3/C-4 #85-5979 (2003)
- R&D Replicas (ex-Karo-AS) [vac] 1/48th Arado Ar 234B #48.12 (1994-1999)
- Revell 1/48th Ar 234C-3 Jet Bomber #04501 (2002)
- Revell (ex-Hasegawa) 1/48th Ar 234B-2/N "Nachtigall" #04505 (2007)
- Volks [res] 1/48th Arado Ar 234B Blitz #SD03 (1984-1994)

1/32nd Scale

- Combat Models (ex-Schmidt Vacu-modellbau) [vac] 1/32nd Ar 234B-2 #32-009
- Craftworks [res/pe/mtl/vac] 1/32nd Ar 234B Blitz #32202 – *Announced for Fall 1998, not released*
- Fly [inj/res/pe] 1/32nd Ar 234B-2 'German Reconnaissance Bomber' #32003 (2014)
- Fly [inj/res/pe] 1/32nd Ar 234B-2/B-2N 'German Reconnaissance Bomber & Night Fighter' #32008 (2014)
- ID Models [vac] 1/32nd Arado Ar 234 Blitz #3238 (1981-1999)
- Model Design Construction/RB Productions [res] 1/32nd Ar 234B #RB32002 (2008)
- Schmidt Vacu-Modellbau [vac] 1/32nd Arado Ar 234 Blitz #3224 (1984-2000)
- Scratchbuilders [res/mtl/pe] 1/32nd Arado Ar 234 Blitz #N/K – *Announced for 11/1994 ($111.95), release not confirmed, ceased all production in 2002*
- Tigger Models (ex-ID Models) [vac] 1/32nd Ar 234B #43 (2005->)

Notes
inj – Injection moulded plastic
ltd inj – Limited-run injection moulded plastic
pe – Photo-etched metal
res – Resin
vac – Vacuum-formed Plastic
(1999) – Denotes date the kit was released
(1994->) – Dates denote start/finish of firm's activities, the exact date of release of this kit is however unknown
ex- – Denotes the tooling originated with another firm, the original tool maker is noted after the '-'

Appendix II

Below is a list of all accessories for static scale construction kits produced to date for the type. This list is as comprehensive as possible, but if there are amendments or additions, please contact the author via the Valiant Wings Publishing address shown at the front of this title.

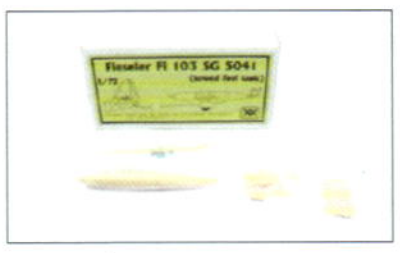

A and V AV127

Aires 4164

Antares Models ANT-06

Fusion FUS 4807

CMK 4122

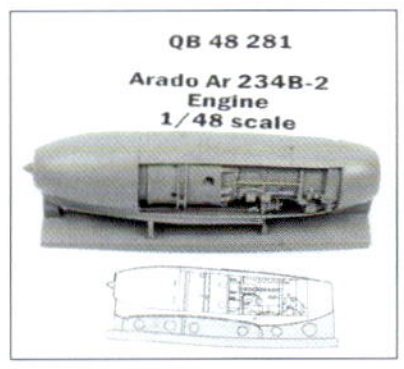

Quickboost QB48281

Scale Aircraft Conversions 48062

True Details 72042

1/72nd

- Airwaves [pe] Ar 234B-2/N detail set #AC7272 {Dragon}
- Airwaves [pe] Ar 234B detail set #AC7278 {Dragon}
- Antares Models [res/vac] Ar 234 V16 conversion #ANT-7212 {Dragon}
- A&V Models [res] Fieseler Fi 103 SG5041 towed fuel tank #AV127
- A&V Models [res] L.11 'Schneewittchen', German gliding torpedo (1944) #AV131
- Bird Models [res] Ar 234F-1 Wanderfalke conversion #72034 {Dragon}
- Cutting Edge [vma] Ar 234B wheel hub masks #CEBM72002 {Dragon}
- Cutting Edge [vma] Ar 234C wheel hub masks #CEBM72003 {Dragon}
- Eduard [pe] Ar 234B Blitz detail set #72-182 {Dragon}
- Eduard [pe] Ar 234C Blitz detail set #72-184 {Dragon}
- Eduard [vma] Ar 234B Blitz canopy and wheels #XS164 {Dragon}
- Eduard [ma] Ar 234B Blitz canopy and wheels #CX074 {Dragon}
- Equipage [res] Ar 234B wheel set #72063
- Equipage [res] Ar 234C wheel set #72064
- Falcon [vac] Luftwaffe Bombers WWII canopy set inc. Ar 234B Blitz #Set No.09 {Frog/Revell}
- Falcon [vac] Luftwaffe Part 6 canopy set incl. Ar 234B Blitz #Set No.29 {Dragon}
- Final Touch [res/vac] Ar 234 V16 conversion #FTC031 {Dragon}
- LF Models [ma] camouflage scheme paint masks for Ar 234B #MM7226 {Dragon/Revell}
- LF Models [ma] camouflage scheme paint masks for Ar 234C #MM7227 {Dragon/Revell}
- Master Models [br] FuG 218 'Neptun' radar #72089
- Reheat Models [pe] Ar 234B/N detail set #RH083 {Dragon}
- Reheat Models [pe] Ar 234C detail set #RH085 {Dragon}
- Toad Resin [res] 1/72nd Ar 234 V16 #N/K {Dragon kit}
- True Details [res] Ar 234B wheels, smooth tread #72042
- True Details [res] Ar 234C wheel set, smooth tread #72043
- Unicraft [res] Unicraft Ar 234E conversion #None {Dragon}
- Unicraft [res] Unicraft Ar 234P-5 AWACS #None {Dragon Ar 234C}
- Unicraft [res] Unicraft Ar 234 Jäger conversion #None {Dragon Ar 234B}
- Unicraft [res] Unicraft Ar 234R(b) Jäger conversion #None {Dragon Ar 234B}

1/48th

- Airwaves [pe] Ar 234B Blitz detail set #AC4806 {Hobbycraft}
- Airwaves [res/mtl] Ar 234 undercarriage #SC4802
- Aires [res/pe] Ar 234B-1 Blitz cockpit set #4151 {Hasegawa}
- Aires [res] Ar 234 Blitz main wheel bay #4153 {Hasegawa}
- Aires [res] Jumo 004B-1 exhaust nozzles for Me 262 and Ar 234 #4158
- Aires [res/pe] Ar 234B Blitz wheel bay and cockpit set #4164 {Hasegawa}
- Aires [res/ma] Ar 234 Blitz wheels and paint mask #4165 {Hasegawa, Hobbycraft, Karo & Revell}
- Aires [res] Ar 234B Blitz engine detail set #4205 {Hasegawa}
- Antares Models [res/vac] Ar 234 Jäger conversion #ANT-06 {Hobbycraft}
- Antares Models [res/vac] Ar 234 V16 conversion #ANT-31 {Hasegawa}
- CMK [res/pe] Ar 234B detail set #4122 {Hasegawa}
- CMK/Quick & Easy [res] Ar 234B Blitz fuel tanks #Q48016 {Hasegawa}
- Cutting Edge [res] Ar 234B flaps #CEC48051 {Hobbycraft}
- Cutting Edge [res] Ar 234B super detailed cockpit #CEC48406 {Hasegawa}
- Cutting Edge [res] Ar 234B flaps #CEC48407 {Hasegawa}
- Cutting Edge [vma] Ar 234B wheel hub masks #CEBM48012 {Hasegawa}
- Cutting Edge [vma] Ar 234C wheel hub masks #CEBM48013 {Hasegawa}
- Cutting Edge [vma] Ar 234 canopy & wheel hub masks #CEBM48380 {Hasegawa}
- Cutting Edge [vma] Ar 234B canopy & wheel hub masks #CEBM48524 {Hasegawa}
- Cutting Edge [vma] Ar 234B camouflage pattern masks #CEBM48525 {Hasegawa}
- Eduard [pe] Ar 234B Blitz detail set #48-399 {Hasegawa}
- Eduard [pe] Ar 234C Blitz detail set #48-442 {Hasegawa/Revell}
- Eduard [ma] Ar 234B Blitz canopy and wheel masks # EX085 {Hasegawa}
- Eduard [ma] Ar 234C Blitz canopy and wheel masks # EX121 {Hasegawa/Revell}
- Eduard [vma] Ar 234B Blitz canopy and wheel masks #XF184 {Hasegawa}
- Eduard [vma] Ar 234C camouflage scheme masks #XS555 {Hasegawa}
- Engines & Things [res] Ar 234 corrected engine inlets #48094
- Engines & Things [res] Jumo 004B-1 engine (Ar 234 & Me 262) #48095
- E-Z Masks [vma] Ar 234C-3/C-4 masks #239 {Hasegawa}
- FM Detail [res] Ar 234 Blitz cockpit set #480204 {Hasegawa}
- FM Detail [res] Ar 234 Blitz undercarriage set #480206 {Hasegawa}
- Fusion [res] Arado Ar 234C AWACS conversion #FUS4807 {Hasegawa/Revell}
- InSight Details [res] Pole-Tow fuel tank for Me 262 & Ar 234 #48001
- Falcon [vac] Luftwaffe WWII canopy set inc. Ar 234B Blitz #Set No.14 {Hobbycraft}
- Falcon [vac] Luftwaffe WWII Pt.2 canopy set inc. Ar 234C Blitz #Set No.16 {Hobbycraft}
- High Flight [res] Ar 234 flap set #HF-4830
- Kora [res] R4M Orkan with racks for Ar 234B #DS4805 {Hasegawa/Revell & Hobbycraft}
- LF Models [ma] camouflage scheme paint masks for Ar 234B #MM4824 {Hasegawa/Revell}
- LF Models [ma] camouflage scheme paint masks for Ar 234C #MM4825 {Hasegawa/Revell}
- Lumír Vesley [res] Fieseler Fi 103A1/Re2 #None {Hasegawa/Revell}
- Master Models [br] FuG 218 'Neptun' radar #48028
- Montex [vma] Ar 234B-2 canopy and decal option masks #MM48007 {Hasegawa}
- Montex [vma] Ar 234C 2 canopy and decal option masks #MM48087 {Hasegawa/Revell}
- Montex [vma] Ar 234B canopy masks #SM48007 {Hasegawa}
- Montex [vma] Ar 234C canopy masks #SM48087 {Hasegawa/Revell}
- Quickboost [res] Ar 234B-2 engine #QB48281 {Hasegawa}
- Scale Aircraft Conversions [mtl] Ar 234B landing gear #48062 {Hasegawa/Revell}
- Scale Aircraft Conversions [mtl] Ar 234C landing gear #48063 {Hasegawa/Revell}
- SBS Model [res/pe] Ar 234 wheel bays #48026 {Hasegawa/Revell}
- Squadron [vac] Ar 234 Blitz canopy #9518 {Hobbycraft}
- Squadron [vac] Ar 234C Blitz canopy #9543 {Hobbycraft}
- Squadron [vac] Ar 234B Blitz canopy #9644 {Hasegawa/Revell}
- Tauro Models [res] Radar operator's station cover for Ar 234B-2/N #L48001 {Hasegawa/ Revell}
- Tauro Models [res] FuG 350 Naxos radar with cover for Ar 234B-2/N #L48002 {Hasegawa/ Revell}
- Terry Dean (mtl) Ar 234B nose weight #None {Hobbycraft}
- True Details [res] Ar 234B wheel set, smooth tread #48070
- True Details [res] Ar 234C wheel set, smooth tread #48085
- True Details [res] Ar 234 cockpit set #48476 {Hasgawa}
- Verlinden Productions[res/pe] Ar 234B-2 Blitz detail set #1892 {Hasegawa}

1/32nd

- HGW [pe/pa] Ar 234B seat belts #132555 {Fly}
- HGW [pe/fb] Ar 234B/B-2N seat belts #132556 {Fly}
- Montex {vma} Ar 234B & Ar 234B-2N canopy & decal option masks #MM32156 {Fly}
- Montex [vma] Ar 234B & Ar 234B-2N canopy masks #SM32156 {Fly}
- New Ware [vma] Ar 234B-2/B-2N masks #AM001{Fly}
- Pmask [vma] Ar 234B-2 masks #PK32011{Fly}
- Scale Aircraft Conversions {mtl} Ar 234B-2/B-2N landing gear #32092 {Fly}
- Yahu Models [pe] Ar 234B-2 instrument panel #3201 {Fly}

Notes
br – Brass
fb – Fabric
ma – Die-cut Self-adhesive Paint Masks [tape]
pe – Photo-etched Brass
PP – Pre-painted (photo-etched)
res – Resin
SA – Self-adhesive
vac – Vacuum-formed Plastic
vma – Vinyl Self-adhesive Paint Masks
wm – White-metal (including Pewter)
{Academy} – Denotes the kit for which the set is intended

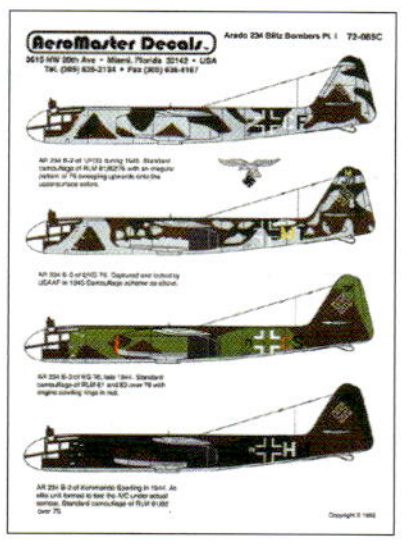
Aeromaster 72-085

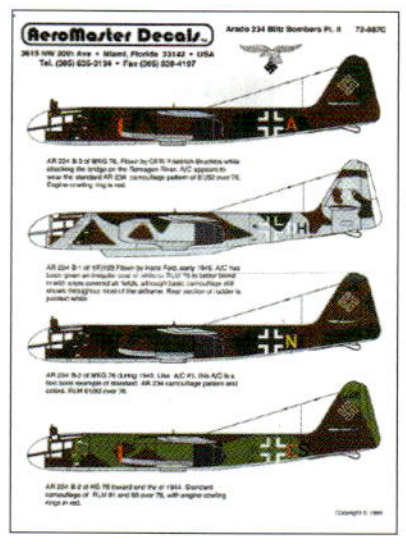
Aeromaster 72-087

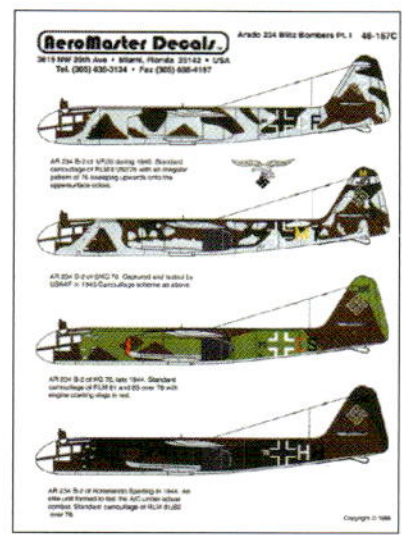
Aeromaster 48-157

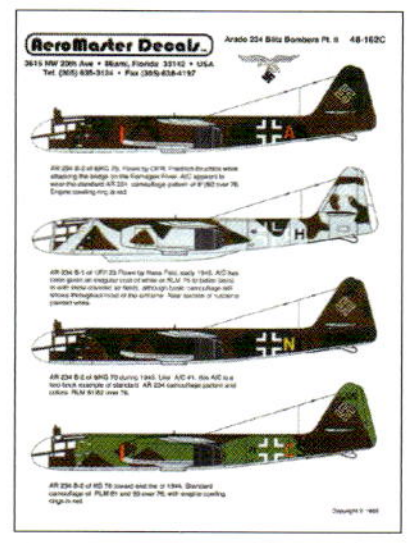
Aeromaster 48-162

Below is a list of all decals for static scale construction kits produced to date for the type. This list is as comprehensive as possible, but if there are amendments or additions, please contact the author via the Valiant Wings Publishing address shown at the front of this title.

1/72nd

Aeromaster

#72-085 Arado 234 Blitz Bombers – Part I
- Ar 234B-2, W/Nr.140301, 8H+CF, 1/F/33, 1945
- Ar 234B-2, W/Nr.140173, F1+MT, 9./KG76, captured and tested by USAAF in 1945
- Ar 234B-2, W/Nr.140325, F1+CS, KG76 in late 1944
- Ar 234B-2, W/Nr.140150, T9+HH, Kommando Sperling in 1944

#72-087 Arado 234 Blitz Bombers – Part II
- Ar 234B-2, W/Nr.140342, F1+AS, 8./KG76, flown by OFW Friedrich Bruchlos during the attack on the bridge over Remagen River
- Ar 234B-1, 4U+DH, 1/F/123, flown by Han Field, early 1945
- Ar 234B-2, W/Nr.140170, F1+NT, 9./KG76, 1945
- Ar 234B-2, W/Nr.140325, F1+CS, KG76, end of 1944

Peddinghaus Decals

#EP1316
- Ar 234B-2, F1+AD, flown by Maj. Georg Bätcher, II./KG76, 1945

#EP1317
- Ar 234 V1, TG+KB, flown by test pilot Selle, 1943

#EP1318
- Ar 234S-10, tested at Rechlin with FuG 203, 1944

#EP1320
- Ar 234B-2/R, Staffelkapitän Hans Feld, 1.(F)/123, 1945

Tally Ho!

#7109 Ar 234B-1
- F1+KH, Kommando Sperling, November 1944
- F1+EH, Kommando Sommer, April 1945
- F1+CS, 8./KG76, December 1944
- Ar 234B-2, W/Nr.140150, T9+HH, Kommando Sperling in 1944
- 1.(F)/33, May 1945
- 9./KG76, February 1944
- 8./KG76, March 1945
- 8./KG76, December 1944
- 1.(F)/123, May 1945

1/48th

Aeromaster

#48-157 Arado 234 Blitz Bombers – Part I
Same four options as on #72-085

#48-162 Arado 234 Blitz Bombers – Part II
Same four options as on #72-087

#48-245 Air War over Italy Part III
Inc.
- Ar 234B-2, W/Nr.140142, T9+DH, Kommando Sommer, which was shot down in April 1945

Cutting Edge

#CED48201 Ar 234B-2 Blitz Bombers Part 1
- W/Nr.140173, flown by Josef Regler, Staffelkapitän 9./KG 76, the first Ar 234 to be obtained by the Allies
- F1+AD, flown by Hans-Georg Bätcher, commander III./KG 76
- F1+AS, flown by Friedrich Bruchlos of 8./KG 76 during attack on Remagen bridge
- W/Nr.140311, 'USA 40', formerly II./KG 76, surrendered to RAF at Stavanger, Norway, May 1945
- W/Nr.140356, 'Air Ministry 226', formerly II./KG 76, surrendered to RAF at Stavanger on 10th May 1945

#CED48202 Ar 234B-2 Blitz Bombers Part 2
- W/Nr.140466, 'Air Ministry 24', formerly 8H+HH of AufklGr 33
- W/Nr.140312, F1+GS, KG 76 surrendered at Stavanger, Norway
- Ar 234 S2, W/Nr.140102, Rechlin Experimental Station
- #202, 'Jane I', ex-W/Nr.140489 or 140343 as BuAer No. 121445, tested at Patuxent River

#CED48230 Ar 234C-3 Blitz Bombers
- Ar 234C-3, W/Nr.250001, Prague-Rusin
- Ar 234C-3, W/Nr.250100, 9K+LR, KG51, 'What If?' option
- Ar 234C-3, W/Nr.250006, München-Riem
- Ar 234C-3, W/Nr.250120, 4D+MN, KG30, 'What If?' option
- Ar 234C-3, W/Nr.250012, Prague-Rusin
- Ar 234C-3, W/Nr.250150, 5K+DP, KG3, 'What If?' option
- Ar 234C-3, W/Nr.250101, T9+NH, Kommando Sperling, 'What If?' option

Eagle Strike

#48168 Arado 234 Blitz Bombers Part I
- Ar 234B-2, W/Nr.140301, 3H+CF, 1/F/33, 1945
- Ar 234B-2, W/Nr.140142, T9+DH, Kommando Sommer, shot down in April 1945
- Ar 234B-2, 4U+DH, 1/F/123, flown by Hans Feld, early 1945
- Ar 234B-2, W/Nr.140170, F1+NT, 9./KG76, 1945

#48169 Arado 234 Blitz Bombers Part II
- Ar 234B-2, W/Nr.140173, F1+MT, 9./KG76, captured and tested by USAAF in 1945
- Ar 234B-2, W/Nr.140150, T9+HH, Kommando Sperling in 1944
- Ar 234B-2, W/Nr.140342, F1+AS, 8./KG76, flown by OFW Friedrich Bruchlos during the attack on the bridge over Remagen River
- Ar 234B-2, W/Nr.140325, F1+CS, KG76, end of 1944

MikroMir

#D-48-003
- W/Nr.140145
- W/Nr.140146
- W/Nr.140151, F1+KH, KG76

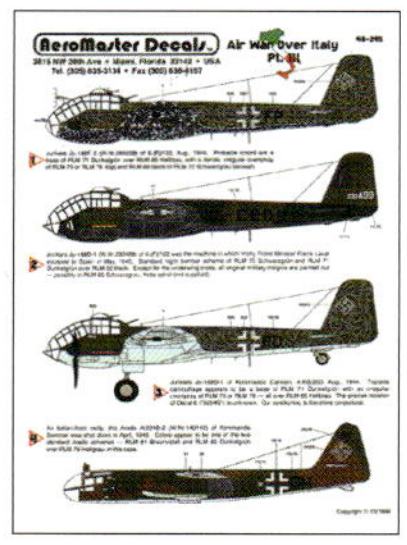
Aeromaster 48-245

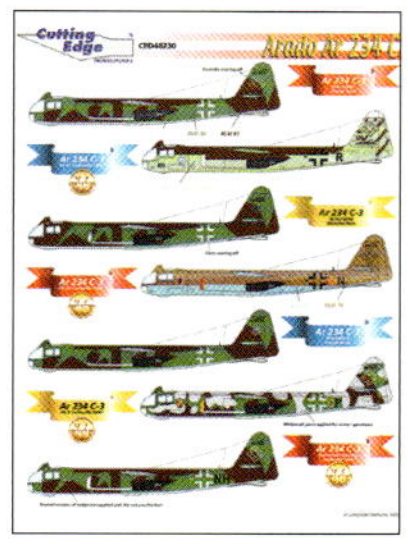
Cutting Edge CED48230

Peddinghaus Decals

#EP2614
- Ar 234B-2, F1+AD, flown by Maj. Georg Bätcher, II./KG76, 1945

Ventura

#V4866 American & British Captured Ar 234s
- Ar 234B-2, W/Nr.140466, captured and tested at Farnborough as VK877
- Ar 234B-2, ex-KG76 captured by American forces and tested by the US Navy as 'Jane 1'
- Ar 234B-2, ex-KG76 captured by American forces and tested by the US Navy as 'Snafu 1'

War Eagle

#N/K Arado Ar 234B
- W/Nr.140312, II./KG76
- W/Nr.140342, F1+AS, 8./KG76, flown by Ofw. Friedrich Bruchlos, during attacks on Remagen bridge in March 1945
- Ar 234 S2, W/Nr.140102, Rechlin Experimental Station

Xtradecal

#X008-48 Ar 234B KG 76, Kommado Sperling
- W/Nr.140173, F1+MT, 3./KG76, force-landed near Segelsdorf 24th February 1945, shipped to Farnborough for examination
- W/Nr.140113, F1+AA, KG76, flown by Obstlt Robert Kowalewski, captured at Schleswig, May 1945
- B-2br, W/Nr.140151, T9+KH, Kommando Sperling, flown by Oblt Werner Muffey
- W/Nr.140342, F1+AS, 8./KG76, flown by Ofw. Friedrich Bruchlos, during attacks on Remagen bridge in March 1945

Eagle Strike 48168

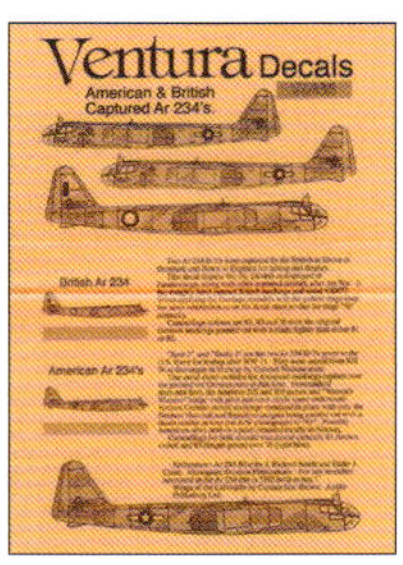

Ventura V4866

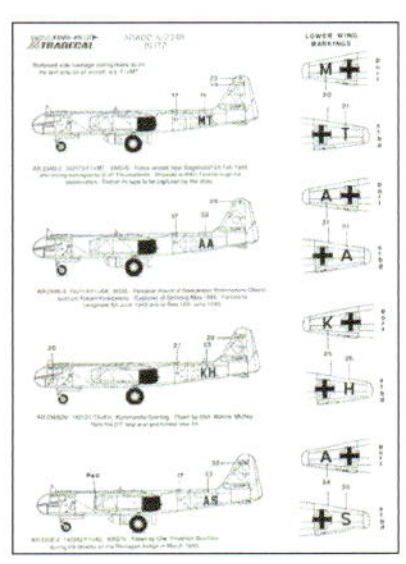
Xtradecal X008-48

War Eagle

The list of Ar 234 related publications below is as comprehensive as possible, but there are bound to be omissions so if you have amendments or additions, please contact the author via the Valiant Wings Publishing address shown at the front of this title.

Official Documents

- D(Luft)T2234 B-2, Flugzeug-Handbuch, 1944
- Werkschrift 2234 B-2/Fl, Bed., 1944
- JUMO 004 B-1 Triebwerk-Handbuch, Auszug D(Luft)T.g.3004 B-1, 1945
- JUMO 004 B-1 Ersatzteilliste, Mai 1944
- D(Luft)T7001, Lotfernrohr 7C, Beschreibung und Wirkungsweise 1941
- D(Luft)T5100/1, Reihenbildner 20 cm, 30 x 30, Fl 38 007., 1940
- D(Luft)T5100/3, Reihenbildner 75 cm, 30 x 30, Fl 38 016., 1940
- D(Luft)T4005/3, Bordfunkgerät FuG 16, Beschreibung, 1943
- Bordfunkgerät FuG 16 Z, ZS, ZE und ZY, 1944
- D(Luft)T 4010, Bordfunkgerät FuG 25A, Technische Merkmale, 1943
- D(Luft)T6151, MG 151 Waffen-Handbuch, 1942

Publications

- Aircraft Archive – Bombers of World War Two (Argus Books 1988 ISBN:0-85242-968-1)
- Aircraft of World War II by C. Chant (Dempsey Parr, 1999)
- Ar 234 Blitz by S. Fleischer & M. Rys, Aircraft Monograph No.10 (AJ Press 1998 ISBN: 83-86208-51-1)
- Ar 234 Blitz by S. Fleischer & M. Rys, Monografie Lotnicze No.35 (ISBN: 83-86208-52-X)
- Arado Ar 234 by M. Griehl, Flugzeug Profile No.33 (Unitec-Medienvertrieb 1997)
- Arado Ar 234 by M. Griehl, Luftwaffe Profile No.15 (Schiffer ISBN: 0-76433-1430-0)
- Arado Ar 234, Luftahrt document LD21 (Pawlas 1976)
- Arado Ar 234 Blitz, Profile No.234 (Profile Publications)
- Arado Ar 234 Blitz, Aero Detail No.16 (Dia Nippon Kaiga Co., Ltd 1996 ISBN: 4-499-22659-7)
- Arado Ar 234 Blitz, Aircraft Monograph No.32 (AJ-Press 1998)
- Arado Ar 234 Blitz by M.J. Murawski, Monograph No.33 (Kagero 2007 ISBN: 978-83-60445-66-2)
- Arado Ar 234 by J.R.Smith & E.J. Creek, Monogram Monarch No.1 (Monogram Aviation Publications 1992)
- Arado Ar 234B by J.R. Smith & E.J. Creek, Monogram Close-up No.23 (Monogram Aviation Publications, 1983 ISBN: 0-914144-23-5)
- Arado Ar 234 & Junkers Ju 287, The World's First Jet Bombers (Schiffer ISBN: 9780887402036)
- Arado Ar 234 & Junkers Ju 287 'Band 61' (Podzun-Pallas Verlag 1980)
- Arado Ar 234A by J.R. Smith & E.J. Creek, Military Aircraft In Detail No.1 (Midland Publishing 2005 ISBN: 1-85780-225-X)
- Arado Ar 234C: An Illustrated History by D. Myhra (Schiffer 2001 ISBN: 0-7643-1182-4)
- Arado Geschichte eines Flugzeugwerks (Aviatic Verlag 1995)
- Arado: History of an Aircraft Company by J.A. Kranzhoff (Schiffer ISBN: 0-7643-0293-0)
- Arado Jet Bombers – Reichdreams Dossier No.17 (Reichdreams Research 1998)
- Arado Ar 234 V6 und V8, Ar 234B-2 'Nachtigall', Luftfahrt History No.21 (Lautec Software und Medien GmbH 2014)

- Aufklärer: Luftwaffe Reconnaissance Aircraft & Units 1935-1945 by D. Wadman, J. Bradley & B. Ketley (Hikoki Publications1997 ISBN: 0-9519899-8-7)
- Bodenplatte: The Luftwaffe's Last Hope by J. Manrho & R. Pütz (Hikoki Publications 2004 ISBN: 1-902109-40-6)
- Bomber Units of the Luftwaffe 1933-1945 Vol.2 by H.L. de Zeng IV & D.G. Stankey (Classic Publications 2008 ISBN: 978-1-903223-87-1)
- Camouflage & Markings Luftwaffe 1939-1945 by M. Reynolds (Argus Books 1992 ISBN: 1-85486-066-6)
- Cockpits Deutscher Flugzeug (Aviatic Verlag 2000)
- Cockpit Profile No.4 – Deutsche Flugzeugcockpits und Instrumentenbretter by P.W. Cohausz (Flugzeug Publikations GmbH)
- Colours of the Luftwaffe by S.W. Parry & F.L. Martshall (Clifford Frost Ltd 1987 ISBN: 1-8700666-03-0)
- Eagles of the Third Reich: Hitler's Luftwaffe by S.W. Mitcham (Airlife Publishing Ltd 1988/Guild Publishing Ltd 1989)
- German Aircraft of the Second World War by J.R.Smith & A.L. Kay (Putnam, 1972)
- German Air Projects 1935-1945 Vol.1 – Fighters by M. Rys, red Series No.5105 (Mushroom Model Publications 2003 ISBN: 83-916327-5-X)
- German Air Projects 1935-1945 Vol.3 – Bombers by M. Rys, Red Series No.5110 (Mushroom Model Publications 2007 ISBN: 978-83-89450-30-2)
- German Jets in WWII, Model Art Special No.348 (Model Art Co., Ltd 1990)
- German Jets of World War II, Planes & Pilots No.17 by D. Breffort & A. Jouineau (Historie & Collections 2013 ISBN: 978-23-52502-24-1)
- German Jet Aces of World War 2 by H. Morgan & J. Weal, Osprey Aircraft of the Aces No.17 (Osprey Publishing Ltd 1998 ISBN: 1-85532-634-5)
- German Jets in Combat by J. Ethell & A Price (Jane's Publishing Co., Ltd 1979 ISBN: 0-354-01252-5)
- German Jets of World War Two by M. Griehl, Warbirds Illustrated No.52 (Arms & Armour Press 1988 ISBN: 1-85368-884-2)
- German Night Fighters in World War II by M. Griehl (Schiffer 1990 0-88740-200-3)
- Hitler's Spyplane over Normandy 1944: The world's first jet by P. Baudin (Pen & Sword Books 2014 ISBN: 978-1-473823-29-0)
- Jet Planes of the Third Reich (Monogram Aviation Publications 1982)
- Kampfflieger – Bombers of the Luftwaffe Summer 1943 – May 1945 by N. Beale (Classic Publications 2005 ISBN: 1-903223-50-4)
- Luftwaffe Advanced Aircraft Projects to 1945, Vol.1 Fighters & Ground-Attack Aircraft; Arado to Junkers by Ingolf Meyer (Midland Publishing Ltd 2006 (ISBN: 1-85780-240-3)
- Luftwaffe Colours 1935-1945 by M. Ullmann (Hikoki Publications Ltd 2002/Crécy Publishing Ltd 2008 ISBN: 9-781902-109077)
- Luftwaffe Im Focus, Edition No.8 (Start 2005 ISBN: 3-9808468-8-1)
- Luftwaffe in World War II, Aero Pictorials 1 (Aero Publishers Inc. 1968)
- Lufwaffe Warbirds Photo Album Vol.2, 3, 4, 5 & 6 Tank Magazine Special Issue (Delta Publishing 1992-1994)
- Reichdreams Dossier No.16, Arado Jet Fighters by J. Miranda & P. Mercado (Reichdreams Research Services)
- Reichdreams Dossier No.17, Arado Jet Bombers by J. Miranda & P. Mercado (Reichdreams Research Services)
- Restoring Museum Aircraft by R. Mikesh (Airlife 1997)
- Secret German Aircraft Projects of 1945 (Toros Publications 1997) – *First published as 'Paper Planes of the Third Reich' by them in 1996*
- Strahlflugzeug Arado Ar 234 'Blitz'; Technik und Einsatz 1944/45 by Manfred Griehl (Motorbuch Verlag 2003, ISBN: 3-613-02287-7)
- The German Jets in Combat (Janes 1979)
- The Warplanes of the Third Reich by William Green (Macdonald & Co Ltd, 1970)
- The World's First Jet Bombers – Arado Ar 234 & Junkers Ju 287 by F. Kobel (Schiffer 1990 ISBN: 0-88740-203-8)
- Unknown! No.5 by J. Miranda & P. Mercado (Reichdreams Research Services 2007)
- War Prizes: The Album by P. Butler (Midland Publishing 2006 ISBN: 1-85780-244-6)
- Wings of the Black Cross No.2 by J. Crandall (Eagle Editions Ltd 2006 ISBN:0-9721-060-9-X)
- Wings of the Luftwaffe by Capt. Eric Brown (Airlife Publishing Ltd 1987, 1993, 1996 & 2000 ISBN: 1-85310-413-2)
- World War II Fighting Jets by J. Ethell & A. Price (Airlife Publishing Ltd 1994 ISBN: 1-85310-406-X)

Periodicals & Part-works

- Aerei nella Storia No.72, 2010
- Aeromodeller, March 1972
- Aeroplane Monthly, May 2004, Vol.32 Iss.373
- Air Enthusiast, February 1973
- Air Forces International, May 1990
- Airplane Issue 133
- Aviation News Vol.13 No.20 (22nd February – 7th March 1985), Vol.14 No.1 (21st May – 13 June 1985) & Vol.21 No.6 (31st July – 15th August 1992)
- Avions & Pilotes No.79
- Flight Journal Vol.11 No.2
- Flug Revue International, October 1967
- Flugzeug 6/87 & 3/93 (Fluzgeug Publications 1987 & 1993)
- Flugzeug Classic No.9, September 2012
- Jet & Prop 3/95, 6/95 & 3/01
- Mach 1, No.69 (1978)
- Model Aircraft Monthly Vol.1 No.9
- Model Airplane International Vol.4 Iss.38 (September 2008)
- Replic No.10 (May 1992) & 135 (November 2002)
- Scale Aircraft Modeler, Summer 1975
- Scale Aircraft Modelling Vol.13 No.11 August 1991 & Vol.18 No.4 June 1996
- Scale Aviation Modeller International Vol.8 Iss.9 September 2002
- Take Off No.79
- Tamiya Model Magazine, Winter 1989
- Wings Vol.19 No.3